Our Family Outing:

A Memoir of Coming Out and Coming Through

By

Leigh Anne Taylor

and

Joe Cobb

www.TotalPublishingAndMedia.com

ISBN: 978-1-937829-15-5

Leigh Anne Taylor
leighanne@ourfamilyouting.com

Joe Cobb
joe@ourfamilyouting.com

To our first loves and the four who carry on our story—

Emma, Taylor, Ginny and JJ

In memory of Thomas Graham Jefferson, Jr., 1953-1973

Gratitudes

To speak and act in loving ways requires, at the deepest level of all, a spirit of gratitude. Our story is easier to share because of the countless sages who have journeyed with us, sharing a bit of their lives as they listened and lived along with us. To all of you who bless our lives with your sharing, thank you.

Telling our story has led us into a season of vulnerability, knowing that by telling the truth of our lives, we are foremost interested in honoring the truth of our interactions with the many who have walked with us. For those who have given us permission to use their names in this story, we are grateful. For those who preferred a different name to honor confidentiality, we have honored this request and are grateful. For all of the congregations we have had the honor of serving or being served by, we have changed some names, and left others with their actual name (based on permission) to honor the integrity of each. We are grateful for your presence in our lives.

Gratitudes (Leigh Anne)

As I read again the story that fills these pages, I am struck by the abundant love and support I have been surrounded with all my life, from so many sources. I am grateful for my husband Hugh, my parents, my guides Maureen Morrison and Susan Marney and all of my colleagues, past and present. I am especially grateful for Joe and the precious gifts of Emma and Taylor that our marriage gave to us and to the world. Through our relationship, I have learned my life's greatest lessons. I am blessed to have learned these lessons in the context of our extraordinary extended family.

Gratitudes (Joe)

I am grateful for James Matthews, Tom Stephenson, Larry Provo, Mark Smith, Andy Hagler, Chris Glaser, Christian de la Huerta, Chris Garrison-Archer, Natalie Goldberg, all of my writing friends from the Mabel Dodge Luhan House retreats, Metropolitan Community Church of Winston-Salem and Metropolitan Community Church of the Blue Ridge, and all of my colleagues, past and present. I am especially grateful for the continuing presence of Leigh Anne in my life, the gifts of our marriage, and now, the gifts of our deeper intimacy as sacred friends. Emma, Taylor, Ginny and JJ—you are my greatest spiritual directors. Thank you.

The space we write in needs to inspire creativity, so I am grateful for CUPS Coffee and Tea in Roanoke, and its proprietor, Michelle Bennett, for creative space, consistent encouragement in the writing process, and endless cups of fabulous coffee. I also want to thank the former Mojo Café as the place where this project began taking written form.

Together, we are grateful for all who read our earliest book proposal, and a variety of drafts of the manuscript along the way. Special thanks to Cara Ellen Modisett for her extraordinary work as our editor; Julie Pfeiffer, Cathy Hankla, John Anderson, Sharon Rapoport, Stephanie Koehler, Bruce Bryan, Jeanine Stewart, Nick and Mary Lee Warner, Jeanine Hathaway, Miriam Hall, Saundra Goldman, and Boyd Lemon for reading our earliest book proposal and differing versions of our manuscript; and to the many who have helped guide our first venture into publishing.

Table of Contents

Preface

The pass-off (Leigh Anne)
June 2008

"I'm going to write our story," I told several trusted friends after listening to a stirring sermon that challenged us to have the courage to do what God was calling us to do. As soon as the words were out of my mouth, waves of doubt and fear came over me. "It's too personal, we'll be too vulnerable, it's too hard," I told myself over and over again, trying to talk myself out of it.

A week later, I was reunited with some longtime friends at a conference in North Carolina. One friend told me of the heartbreak of learning her husband was gay. He seemed trapped in silence and sadness. I listened and shared some of our story. She was encouraged to know that she was not alone and relieved to find someone who understood the private agony she was going through. This was the affirmation that I needed to overcome my doubt. If telling the story of how we had come through our trials could help someone, I could take the risk of being vulnerable. I decided to tell Joe the first time I saw him.

The pass-off (Joe)

Late on a hot, June afternoon, I pulled off of Interstate 40 near Charlotte and into the parking lot of a convenience store. Steering past the gas pumps, I parked next to a white SUV.

The car's license tag was a familiar sight, as Leigh Anne, Emma, Taylor and Hugh climbed out of the car and onto the hot pavement. The kids gave quick hugs, asked for money, then disappeared into the store. Hugh paced the perimeter of the parking lot, finishing up a business call. Leigh Anne and I talked by the car.

Leigh Anne, smiling, said, "I'm ready to write." "Me too!" I said. "It's time," we said in near unison. One by one, Hugh hung up the phone, Emma and Taylor emerged from the store, and each of them joined our conversation. We shared our readiness to tell our family's story and asked for their support. Each, in their way, said, "Go for it."

Of all the pass-offs we had made with the children through the years, from early meetings at a hotel in Illinois after a twelve-hour drive, to our usual weekly meeting at Dixie Caverns between Blacksburg and Roanoke after a thirty-minute drive, this pass-off marked our passage into a new season of life—a season of story telling, truth telling, and moving forward.

Now we have passed into the season of sharing. Here is our story.

COME OUT, COME OUT

Queen Anne (Joe)

I am sitting in a Queen Anne chair, talking to my therapist. This is my reality. I am 36 years old. I have a wife and two children whom I love very much and don't want to hurt. Leigh Anne and I have been married for thirteen years. I am one of four pastors at a large, downtown United Methodist church. My wife is the director of music. The worship services are broadcast live every Sunday morning on a major network. I've been a pastor for more than seventeen years. This is what God called me to, what I trained for, what I have been ordained to. My grandma, parents and brother's family are all members of the church. According to my mom, I am the perfect child.

The therapist asks me if there is something I'd like to share. I nestle into Queen Anne. "I'm struggling with homosexuality." Brace yourself, queen, here it comes.

"I'm honored that you shared your struggle with me."

So it begins.

There. I said it. Homosexuality. I spoke it out loud then. Now I'm saying it in print. All of those awkward moments in church bible studies, at annual meetings debating scriptural authority and whether or not homosexuals should be ordained, thinking that everything I was feeling inside would just, gradually, go away. Better to keep the closet door closed.

I thought a long time about whether or not to open the door. I was more hesitant than Dorothy before she walked out of her black and white house and into a technicolor world. Open the door and everything changes. Open the door and lose myself. Open the door and control flies out. Once I opened the closet door, I could never close it.

Safety *in the closet* breeds captivity. And captivity, when lived in long enough, becomes normal. Glimpses of freedom are as fleeting as light flickering through the cracks in the door. Each glimpse becomes a life and death struggle for freedom to open the door. The first steps into freedom lead from fear into joy, but the joy is often short-lived because I find myself in a wilderness that has no safe places. Everything is laid open, raw, dangerous, scary as hell, and nowhere near over the rainbow.

When I spoke the words that opened the door to set me free, I braced for the worst. Here it comes, I thought. You can't be homosexual. This isn't a struggle. It's a sin. An abomination. An abnormality. A phase. Once we identify your issues, we can heal you.

"I'm honored that you shared your struggle with me," is all she said. Of everything I could have hoped for in sharing my deepest, best-kept secret, my therapist delivered. What she gave me that day was a rare and precious gift: gratitude for my honesty and an invitation to grow in my authenticity and integrity. She created a safe space where the stranger I had kept hidden deep in my soul could emerge and speak truth. It was the first sprinkling of grace.

As I spoke my truth, I knew it was an inconvenient one. Truth, centered in and spoken in love, is always inconvenient because it leads to a place beyond where we are. Once I spoke the truth, I knew I had to keep speaking it. And, frankly, this was the scariest part of all. This truth would impact everything and change every relationship.

I knew I couldn't stay where I was. I was spent. The questions, fantasies, and longings I kept locked away were clamoring to be released and my body could no longer contain their dis-ease. As a dear friend told me weeks later, "I can't believe you've kept this inside for eighteen years and have never been able to talk about it. It's a wonder you're still here."

In the nest of Queen Anne, grace prepared a place for me to rest in the truth of who I was created to be, to speak it, and to receive grace in return.

Confession (Joe)

My therapist and I talked about a variety of issues, all, in retrospect, a gentle dance around the obvious.

I was experiencing overexposure in my life. As a natural caregiver and pastor, I was a magnet for people in need. I didn't know how to set boundaries. The greater the need, the more I gave of myself, without taking into account the damage this was doing to my own body. At times this seemed like an addictive high, to be needed by others, even in their insecurities and dramas.

Therapy was a first step in being gentle with myself.

Sharing brought relief and a deep sigh of acknowledgement. I spoke the words and named my feelings. Yet I knew that telling my therapist was only a first step. The next, much more difficult, would be telling Leigh Anne.

That night, after putting the kids to bed, Leigh Anne and I went downstairs and sat on the couch to talk. I told her about my meeting with the therapist. I told her about my struggle. I told her about my encounter with a man in St. Louis. I told her I didn't know if I was gay or straight.

She was quiet. Then she punched me in the arm. "Don't you ever do that to me again."

We both sat in silence. I slept in the basement. Leigh Anne slept upstairs in our bedroom.

3

The next day, numb, I stumbled around in my own self-pity and loathing, trying to make some sense of why I hurt like hell and why I would say and do something that would make Leigh Anne hurt like hell. Leigh Anne took the kids to school and went to work. I stayed home. I sat in a recliner trying to pray. I couldn't relax. I got up and started pacing. My mind was racing. I called my therapist and she helped me focus. Leigh Anne needed time to let everything sink in. I should do something other than sit.

I baked pies. I cleaned house. I wrote in a small wire-bound journal I had begun keeping to get the mess out of my head and onto paper. I wrote:

Well, Lord,
I feel like shit.
I've hurt Leigh Anne.
And I ache inside.
I know telling her was the right thing to do.
But I've hurt her.
I called my therapist.
She told me that Leigh Anne needs space.
I don't even think she wants to look at me.
I feel dirty, disgusting, filthy.
I know you love me.
I feel crappy because I'm here and she's working.
I was in crisis and now I've put her in crisis.
I've pushed her away.
I've pushed you away.

I have sinned.
Against you.
Against Leigh Anne.
I've broken my vows.

I want to run away from everyone and everything.
I need to accept what I've done.
I need to live with the shit I've heaped on Leigh Anne.
I need to be broken.
I can't go on living like this.
I need to think about others.
I need to do whatever I can to help around here.
I've neglected Leigh Anne, Emma and Taylor.
I've neglected my family.

I don't want to hurt Leigh Anne again.
My therapist said my honesty was important.
That it will help in the future.
If I really believe in you,
in Leigh Anne, Emma and Taylor,
I need to confess,
and repent,
and know forgiveness.

I want to be healed.

Lord, forgive me.
Create in me a clean heart.
Put a new and right spirit within me.
Bring healing to Leigh Anne.
Bathe her in your love and light.

All I wanted to do was fix everything and make it better.

I tried to write a letter to Leigh Anne, each draft a desperate attempt to make everything better, to bring instantaneous healing to a traumatic situation.

After several drafts, I came up with this:

Dear Leigh Anne,
I've hurt you and I'm sorry.
I do love you and I don't want to hurt you again.
I want your life, my life, and our lives
to be whole.
God forgive me, please.
Joe

I don't remember if I gave the note to her.

Monday night (Leigh Anne)

Joe and I were sitting on the couch in the basement, in front of the television. Joe had been to the therapist that day and I was hoping he would talk about his session with her, about his depression and workaholism. I was completely unprepared for what he was about to say to me.

He started by reminding me about the trip he had taken eighteen months earlier to a national singles ministry event in Missouri instead of coming to the beach with my extended family in North Carolina. He explained that he had met a man there, that they had been intimate. "I've been with a man. I don't know if I'm gay or straight."

I simply did not register the meaning of the words. My immediate response was to punch him playfully in the shoulder and say to him, "Don't you ever do that to me again." We did not say much more to each other that night, but simply followed our usual evening routine and went to bed.

I have no idea how I slept that night. I slept all night long, without waking. On Tuesday morning, I remember getting up and getting dressed in a full denim skirt and navy blue cotton sweater with big, pastel flowers embroidered on it. As I was blow-drying my hair, I looked into my own reflection and understood clearly for the first time what Joe had said to me the night before. The reality of his words felt like a knife. I doubled over with physical pain, feeling as if I had been sliced from my breastbone to my belly. It hurt so intensely that I was sure there must be blood on my clothing. In retrospect, I believe I went into shock at this point. I numbly went through the motions of the morning ritual and drove myself to work. Joe did not go to work.

When I got to work, I realized it was Tuesday, staff meeting day. I didn't want to be with people but I went because I didn't know what else to do.

I walked down the long hallway toward our meeting room and met up with our administrative assistant whose friendly "Good morning, how are you?" were the first words I heard that day. "Linda, I don't want to be here. All I know is I can't be at home and I don't know what else to do. Just don't be surprised if I leave." Once we gathered for our staff meeting, I said something along those same lines to the rest of my colleagues.

I don't remember if I was able to sit through the meeting at all. I don't remember anything about the day except making up my mind that I was going to the mall to buy myself an outfit that felt like a hug from head to toe. I had no idea what it would look like but I knew what I wanted and needed it to feel like.

Early in the afternoon, I drove myself to the mall and parked far away from any other cars in the lot. I sat for a long time, unable to get out. Finally, I felt as if an emotional dam burst in my body and everything I had been holding back came roaring out of my mouth. I screamed. I cried. I wailed. I lamented like I had never done before in my life and have never done since. The searing physical pain in my solar plexus burned hot again and I lifted my sweater to make sure I was not bleeding.

As the intensity of the lament waned, a strange and quiet awareness came over me. "This is what it feels like to be alive," I thought. "This pain is proof that I am alive, not proof that I am dying." With that, I was able to dry my face and go inside. I bought a pair of black velour slacks and two long chenille sweaters with long sleeves and cowl necks in blue and purple. Black, blue, purple, the color of bruises, soft and warm. After I purchased the garments, I did not go back to work but went home to be with the children and Joe. I took off the denim skirt and flowered sweater and never put them on again. I threw them in the trash.

I was able to see our therapist on Wednesday that week. I deliberately chose to wear the comfort clothes I had bought for myself the day before, along with some flat, black boots that laced up. When I arrived, I took my usual place across the room from her in the comfortable Queen Anne chair. "How are you, Leigh Anne?" she asked. Before I answered, I bent over to untie my boots so I could tuck my feet in under myself. I could not sit up. I collapsed forward, sobbing. She was beside me in an instant and held me in her arms until my crying ceased. This was the first moment of my new, real life, the first moment on the other side of denial.

The wound of truth (Leigh Anne)

Secrets are toxic in relationships.

Joe's secret had become a toxic poison in our marriage, a toxin that we both bore in our bodies. Even though hearing the truth was like a knife slashing through all the denial in our relationship, the open wound allowed the toxins that had been festering to pour out. I began to feel better. The first rush of relief came the moment I understood that I was not the cause of Joe's emotional distance or of our lack of sexual intimacy as a couple. Sex was not working, but that was not because anything was inherently wrong with me. Joe was not attracted to me because he was attracted to men and I simply could not compete with that.

Now what? (Leigh Anne)

After the initial shock of hearing Joe say, "I don't know if I'm gay or straight and I've been with a man," I had an important decision to make for our future. I knew that Joe was so ashamed of himself for being unfaithful to our marriage vows that I could say "get out" and he would go. But did I really want him to leave? If there was a possibility that he was straight, and his words seemed to leave that possibility open, did I want to throw away our love, our marriage, our hopes and dreams for our future because of one illicit encounter? I didn't think so. The only thing I could do was to say, "I will stay with you as long as you are in therapy to determine if you are gay or straight. We'll decide if we stay together or divorce after you are sure of yourself."

I have always appreciated the fact that Joe never wavered in his search for his true identity. He worked with an individual therapist, he went with me to a marriage therapist, he wrote in his journal, he prayed, he sought guidance. He remained, to my knowledge, faithful to our marriage vow as long as we lived in the house together.

What if? (Leigh Anne)

During the year that Joe and I were both in therapy, I tried to prepare myself for what was coming next. I imagined several scenarios: what would life be like if, after therapy, Joe said he was straight? I was prepared to accept this, but there was some deep healing work that needed to happen for our marriage to continue. I was afraid to think about this too much because I did not want to continue in denial and cause myself to be blind to the obvious.

What would life would be like if, after therapy, Joe said he was gay? As I prepared myself to accept this, I had an almost unbearable sense of sadness as I mourned the death of dreams, of our future, of how I thought our life would be. I also had an unbearable sense of loneliness, since I had no one but my therapist to talk to about it. I had a sense that I was in the closet with Joe. He had shared his secret with me and now I was in the terrible loneliness of the closet.

Outside of the therapist, the only other people I could trust with the truth were our clergy colleagues. One of our colleagues, Nancy, invited both Joe and me to her home individually to talk with her the week that Joe told me his truth. She was offering her pastoral support to us but also needed to know, as a colleague, what was going on with two of her fellow staff members.

"You seemed to be in shock at staff meeting this week. You reminded me of someone who just found out that a family member had died."

An apt description, I thought. I wondered if the man I was married to had died and been replaced by a stranger. I felt incredibly vulnerable telling her what Joe had said to me, knowing that this could set in motion some sort of supervisory response, which no doubt would have an effect on me and the children. But I was desperate to talk with someone and I felt I could trust Nancy.

Worst-case scenario (Leigh Anne)

"This is not the worst-case scenario," I would say to myself as I soothed myself by rocking in my rocking chair in the bedroom. "The worst-case scenario would be if my husband had sex with a man and contracted AIDS and infected me, leaving our children orphans. *That* would be the worst possible thing that could happen." Then I started to wonder, "Could that worst-case scenario be possible? Did this man have AIDS? How could Joe be so cavalier with my health? What about the children? How could he engage in such risky behavior and put our children at risk? What would happen if both of us contracted AIDS? Would our children become orphans?"

Fear and rage welled up in me because I felt that Joe had played Russian roulette with my life, my health, our children's lives, and our future. When I confronted Joe with my fear, he reassured me that there was no way that he could have been infected, even if the other man had been ill, and that there was no risk to me. I believed him but that did not stop me from having HIV tests for several years after that just to reassure myself that I was not infected.

No more smiles (Leigh Anne)

Long before Joe told me that he had broken our marriage vows, his expression gave him away. I just didn't know how to read what I saw on his face. After Joe returned from the national singles conference and cried in our bed, "I don't want to hurt you," he stopped smiling at me. For a full year and a half, my husband did not smile at me. Joe, who had always been my favorite companion, who I loved to talk with, who I loved to spend time with, stopped smiling at me. He traded his smile for a tight-lipped expression that curved upward slightly at the corners, but stopped before it reached his eyes. The expression that he substituted for smiling looked more like pity than pleasure and gave the impression that he was physically forcing his lips to close tightly. If I had known how to read what I was seeing, I would have been able to pinpoint the time of Joe's indiscretion just by the expression on his face.

COMING TOGETHER

I heard her voice before I met her (Joe)

September 1984

I had just arrived back in my room at Perkins Dorm to begin my second year in the Master of Divinity program at Perkins School of Theology. I was hanging up clothes and reconnecting with my roommate. My head was in the closet when I heard her voice, talking to someone down the hall. "Hi, I'm Leigh Anne Taylor. I don't believe I know you!" She's very happy, I thought. I wonder who she is? My roommate had met her and told me that she was living in the room next door. I turned back to the closet and put more clothes away.

In a few moments, Leigh Anne came around the corner, saw our door open, and peeked in. Our rooms were in a small cul-de-sac at the end of the hall, around the corner from a small kitchen and dining area and near the exterior door. She introduced herself and we shook hands. I didn't know what to make of her, but a few things were clear. She was outgoing, charming, and pretty. And she was a sacred music student. The light in her began to kindle the light in me.

In addition to being next-door neighbors, and seeing each other in our waking glory (the community bathrooms and showers were down the hall), we soon discovered our mutual love for coffee and for singing. We both sang with the Seminary Singers (a choir comprised of seminary students). We began walking together to rehearsals and getting acquainted. The more we talked, the more we connected. The unlikely paths of a Kansas boy and a Virginia girl were converging.

She was a soprano. I was a tenor. She played the piano and was studying choral conducting. I was following my calling to be a pastor. She was an exceptional student. I was a moderately exceptional student. She had a great southern accent that grew stronger each time she called home. I gained energy when I was around her.

From the moment she woke up until nightfall, Leigh Anne lived each moment with a passion I'd never seen. Her life was a spark that kindled little fires wherever she went.

I wanted to ask her out but felt awkward. I sought regular advice from my best friend, Tom. We would often pass notes in "The Interpretation of the Christian Message," a theological title for the class in which we were writing our credos (statements of belief).

I had met Tom on our first day in seminary. All of the first-year seminary students were gathered in a large parlor at Perkins, awaiting a walk up to the main SMU campus for orientation. Tom introduced himself and we became fast friends. Following orientation, we went to dinner and I met his fiancé, Wendy.

Tom was born and bred in Texas and knew his way around. And even if he didn't, I trusted him to find it. In my own, subtle ways I began to ask his advice on dating: where to go, what to do, when to ask. Some of my awkwardness was my introverted nature. Some was my uncertainty about my sexual orientation. I had dated girls in high school, but all of my sexual experiences had been with men. While I enjoyed the company of women, I hadn't always felt a physical connection or sexual connection. I loved everything about Leigh Anne and wanted to have a relationship with her. Yet, my love for her couldn't overcome my fear of being completely honest with her about my sexual history and I didn't feel comfortable talking with Tom about it. So I stayed mum.

But, mostly, I was just plain nervous.

Leigh Anne was fun to be with and I wanted to be with her whenever I could. I finally mustered the courage to ask her out. She said yes, much to my relief, and we picked a night. I offered to drive in my 1970 pale green Toyota Corolla, and off we went to the west end in downtown Dallas for dinner at the Spaghetti Warehouse. We enjoyed wine and pasta and relaxed into a long conversation. Following dinner, we went back to campus and sat in the car and talked some more. We talked about our childhoods, our families, our education, the paths that led us to Dallas. We decided to go to a late movie, and when it was time to leave for the movie, I tried to start my car. The battery was dead.

In her silver diesel VW Rabbit, we drove to the theater to see "Places in the Heart." I soon discovered that watching a movie with Leigh Anne was a multi-sensory experience. She got so involved in the movie that she talked to the characters on the screen. I was embarrassed and was probably thinking of some way to quiet her. I didn't want to squelch her spirit, but tried to figure something out. I remember asking her if I could hold her hand and squeeze it when she was talking too much. I'm lucky she wanted to go out with me again.

We started going out more frequently. We arrived at a weekend when we had made no plans and I was headed out to the church where I was a youth minister. I often stayed in the old parsonage there, along with the choir director, for the weekend, saving on gas. As I prepared to leave and we said our goodbyes, I remember saying what was truly one of the most insensitive things I ever said: "Well, whatever you do this weekend, I hope you have a good time."

She was mad. Mad at my insensitivity and mad that she cared. I cared and didn't know what to do next. We talked, made amends, and continued to date. I was so enamored with her that I began telling my family about her. I was thinking about her all the time.

By the winter, we were inseparable. She went home to Virginia and I went home to Kansas. We talked nearly every night. We were both giddy, anticipating a future together. In January, I began talking with Tom about where to buy an engagement ring. What should I look for, where should I go, how much should I spend, how can you tell a good diamond, how will I get her ring size? Tom patiently guided me through the process. He went with me to look at rings and even helped me pick one out.

I made a plan. I worked out an arrangement with Karen, one of Leigh Anne's good friends, to keep her busy on the evening of February 13, so that she would return to her room just at the eve of February 14, Valentine's Day. Karen called to let me know they were back and I went to her room. I hid the ring box behind the pillow on her bed, and when she arrived, we sat on the bed in her room, talking, embracing. Shortly after midnight, I pulled the ring out from behind the pillow, opened the box, and asked her to marry me.

I had known the odds were in my favor. Following her trip home at Christmas, she had told her parents she was certain I was going to ask her to marry me and she was going to say yes. Though I had not met her parents, I felt their blessing through her.

Leigh Anne said yes and kissed me. She may have screamed too. I'm not sure. We slid the ring onto her finger and there it remained.

The next few months were a whirlwind. We set a wedding date: August 10. We decided on a place: Wesley United

Methodist Church in Shawsville, Virginia, her home church. We began considering bridesmaids and groomsmen. I asked my brother to be my best man. Leigh Anne asked her childhood best friend, Linda, to be her maid of honor. I filled out my line-up of groomsmen with her brothers and my friend, Tom. I asked one of my college friends, Todd, but he declined, saying he had to work. (Years later he told me that he really declined because he was concerned I wasn't addressing my sexual orientation.) Leigh Anne included her cousin, her sister-in-law, and my sisters.

We planned a trip to Virginia in May so I could meet her parents and brothers. Everyone we told was thrilled.

Leigh Anne had told me many things about her family. "They will love you," she said, over and over. I was still anxious about meeting them. I loved Leigh Anne and wanted to make them happy. I was happy that she was happy and happy that we were happy.

In April, we boarded the plane in Dallas and landed at the small airport in Roanoke, Virginia. I had never been to the Blue Ridge mountains. As the plane circled the cascading blue-green mountains, I marveled at their beauty. We landed, walked down the plane steps onto the tarmac and made our way to the terminal. As soon as we walked in, her parents saw us, raised their hands, smiled, and let out a big "hey." My anxiety disappeared into their hugs.

I wasn't accustomed to hugging. My parents were affectionate through their love and care, but we weren't a hugging family. Leigh Anne brought hugging into our family and I immersed myself in it. Over the next few days, there was a whole lot of it! Each day I fell in love with her family's warmth, hospitality, and welcome.

Each day I met more of her family and extended family.

First, I met her three brothers, Mike, Butch and John. We all shared dinner at the nearby Huckleberry Inn, talking and laughing through the night. Then I began meeting their neighbors: a doctor's family who shared a practice with Leigh Anne's dad in their small town, friends who attended their local United Methodist church, acquaintances who had known the Taylors for the more than forty years they'd lived in the area. Each and every one welcomed me. I felt at home with them.

Leigh Anne's parents lived in her childhood home, a brick ranch, poised atop a knoll in a beautiful rolling valley, nestled in the Blue Ridge mountains. Next to the house was a large, blooming magnolia tree, and beautifully kept lawn and garden. Near the driveway was a bed of rose bushes and a grape arbor.

Experiencing the beauty and peaceful spirit of her home, I began to realize what a salve home was for Leigh Anne. She went home to fill up, to renew her inner light. She always shone more brightly after time in the mountains. We went on long walks on back roads and she took me to a favorite spot, Camp Mountain Top (owned by the United Methodist Church and located about five miles from her home), where she camped as a youth and served as a camp counselor as a young adult. We hiked up to the waterfalls on High Creek at Camp Mountain Top, immersing ourselves in the sun and the cool water.

My next visit to Virginia would be for our wedding.

You can be whatever you want to be (Leigh Anne)

"You can be whatever you want to be. If you want to be a ditch digger, just be the best ditch digger you can be. There will be people who are better than you and there will be people that are not as good as you. Don't bother comparing. Just do the best job you can at whatever you choose to do."

This was one of my dad's oft-repeated sayings as we were growing up. When it came to selecting a career, my parents never pressured us to pursue any particular career. Both of my parents were medical professionals—my dad was a family practitioner and my mom a registered nurse who also taught nursing—but none of the four children decided to follow in their footsteps. That never seemed to bother either one of them.

They were supportive of all my musical interests growing up, giving me the benefit of years of piano and dance lessons and coming to countless band and choir concerts and piano and dance recitals. My parents could not count the number of boxes of grapefruit they sold and delivered on behalf of my high school band boosters. When I chose to study music in college, they were not surprised and supported my decision, providing me with a college education and driving the two and a half hours to attend my concerts and recitals at James Madison University.

When I went to graduate school in Texas to study church music, I was able to support myself financially, but they still made the long journey halfway across the continent to attend my senior recital. I was, and still am, happiest when they are in the audience to enjoy the music I am making.

Joe felt like home (Leigh Anne)

The summer I moved to Texas for graduate school, I had just ended a three-year, long-distance relationship with Greg, a man I had met working at a summer church camp. Dating him had been so frustrating and ending the relationship so painful, that by the time I got to Dallas, I was ready to take a break from dating men. They were fine as friends but not worth spending my precious emotional energy on. I had my education and my future to focus on.

When I imagined my future, two distinct images came to mind. The exciting new image, which was only just beginning to come into focus, was becoming a professional church musician. I began to think about "going wherever the four winds blow" after graduate school to pursue my career. I began to dream about where I would eventually like to live and work.

The other image was becoming a wife and mother, a desire I'd had since I was a child playing with baby dolls in my room. I had a strong maternal instinct and hoped that motherhood was in my future, sometime in the next decade of my life, provided I met the right man. I figured that I would get my education, find a job and somewhere along the way I would meet someone, fall in love, get married and start a family.

When I arrived at graduate school, I was not looking for a mate. I was totally focused on being an A student and getting the most out of my education. As an extrovert, I was thrilled with meeting new people. I collected new friends every day. It was amazing to be surrounded by so many like-minded people. I loved all the church musicians and future clergy I was meeting. My cup was overflowing with friends and I couldn't have been happier.

I was particularly happy to meet my neighbor Joe the first week I arrived. He greeted me shyly from behind his door the first time I met him. The second time I saw him was at our first community lunch, a weekly gathering of seminary students and families. He was inviting all the new seminary students to be a part of the Seminary Singers. The boy could sing! He was funny, confident, clean-cut, and handsome. I wanted to go to Seminary Singers just to get to know him better. I wanted to add him to my overflowing cup of new friends.

We started going to Seminary Singers rehearsals the first week of classes and, soon after, we were sharing a morning cup of coffee before rehearsal. The more I knew him, the more I liked him. I could tell he liked me too.

Initially, I was irritated at myself for liking him at all. I was finished being frustrated by men. I was irritated that I cared about what he was doing when I wasn't around. I was irritated with myself for being interested in a man when my main focus was my education. But the more time we spent together, the more being with him felt like home. I felt happy, comfortable, loved, cared for, and desired.

I had a real comfort level with Joe. In my family, I was the only girl, with three brothers. I was the smallest member of the family and had always been outnumbered. I felt intimidated by the size, the volume, and the intensity of the feelings, particularly anger, of my many male relatives. My older brothers at times patronized me (I remember being patted on the head) and my younger brother tormented me. Joe was a welcome respite from all of that testosterone-charged maleness. He was even-tempered. He didn't patronize or torment me. He was a good man.

I imagined Joe as a potential husband and father. I began to imagine how my dreams for my career and his dreams for his career could fit together. The more I imagined it, the more comfortable it felt. The more I knew him, the more I loved him.

When I went home for Christmas in December of 1984, I told my parents all about Joe. I also told them, even though Joe and I had not talked about it at all, that Joe was going to ask me to marry him and I was going to say yes. I was sure they would love him as much as I did and I couldn't wait for them to meet their future son-in-law.

We married on August 10, 1985 in the little church I had grown up in. We had a fantastic celebration, surrounded by family and friends from all over the country. One of our professors, the late Rev. Roger Deschner, and the director of the Seminary Singers, came to Virginia to officiate.

I cannot say that there was any time in our courtship or early marriage that I wondered or worried that Joe might be gay or even bisexual. I was a young, happily married, graduate student with the handsomest groom any girl could want. I was living my dream.

Interlude: A reading from our wedding
August 10, 1985

As God's chosen ones, holy and beloved, clothe yourselves with compassion, kindness, humility, meekness, and patience. Bear with one another and, if anyone has a complaint against another, forgive each other; just as the Lord has forgiven you, so you also must forgive. Above all, clothe yourselves with love, which binds everything together in perfect harmony. And let the peace of Christ rule in your hearts, to which indeed you were called in the one body. And be thankful. Let the word of Christ dwell in you richly; teach and admonish one another in all wisdom; and with gratitude in your hearts sing psalms, hymns, and spiritual songs to God. And whatever you do, in word or deed, do everything in the name of the Lord Jesus, giving thanks to God the Father through him.—Colossians 3:12-17

The worst week in my life (Leigh Anne)

Joe and I had mutual love for each other, for music, for God, for the church, for people.

We were compatible emotionally and spiritually, and as far as I could tell, as a virgin with very little experience, we seemed sexually compatible. At least we turned each other on. We saved intercourse for our wedding night and while it was not a comfortable or enjoyable experience for me, I was hopeful that with some practice we would get there. I chalked our first uncomfortable encounter up to inexperience and exhaustion.

Things did not improve during our honeymoon. Unfortunately, I contracted my first case of "honeymoon cystitis," which made sex increasingly uncomfortable for me. I finally called my dad, the family doctor, on the last day of our trip when I could no longer tolerate the symptoms. He ordered a prescription for me that was ready as soon as we returned.

When we arrived at my parents' home, my mother greeted me at the door with a big hug, "How are you, sweetheart?" I whispered in her ear, "It was the worst week in my life." My symptoms cleared up in a few days but my mother's worries for me did not. She told me years later that my comment created a shadow of concern for our marriage that she carried from that day forward.

COMING TO
When did you know?

Grammy's death (Joe)

1971

I remember the moment I became an adult. I was nine years old. I was sitting in my fourth-grade classroom, working on a project at my desk. My teacher, Mrs. Mason, with her beautifully coiffed blonde hair, called out my name. I looked up and saw my grandmother Clara standing next to her.

Grandmother lived in Lyons, Kansas. What was she doing here? I lifted the lid of my desk, put away my papers and pencil, and gathered my things. I walked to the front, gave my grandmother a hug, and we walked into the hallway. She came to tell me that my great-grandmother, whom we called Grammy, had died that morning. My parents had gone to Larned, Kansas, to help my grandma make funeral arrangements. Grandmother was here to take care of us and drive us to Larned.

I knew that when someone died they didn't move anymore. The body stops. There is no breathing. They can't talk to you. They can't hear you. The body gets cold.

Standing in the hallway, I thought of my grandma and how sad she was feeling about her mother dying. I thought of my mom and dad and how sad they were feeling. I thought of my sisters and brother and how sad they would be feeling. I

23

decided to be grown up. I decided to take care of everyone and help them feel better.

On the day of the funeral, I wasn't sure what to expect. I knew that Grammy was dead. Mom and Dad asked me if I wanted to see her. I said sure. We walked into the chapel of an old church owned by the funeral home, Beckwith Mortuary. I remember walking up the steps to a side door and entering the chapel from the front. I turned to my right and saw the casket. Grammy was lying in it.

She looked really old. Just like she looked when she was alive. I kept waiting for her to move, to raise her arm, to open her eyes. But she didn't move. "Do you want to touch her?" my mom asked. I reached in and touched Grammy's hands. They were crossed, resting on her stomach. They were cold.

I stood there awhile, then Mom and Dad led me to a room behind the casket where we could see the preacher and the casket, but no one could see us.

I sat upright in my suit and listened to every word. I looked over at my grandma and listened as she cried. I listened as other people cried. I don't remember if I cried. I felt sad. I wanted to help everyone feel happy again.

Learning to love (Leigh Anne)

If it is true that our earliest influences are the ones that make the deepest impressions on our character, then I am grateful for the early impression my maternal grandmother Ora made on me.

Among my favorite memories of childhood are the visits we made as a family to my mother's home in North Carolina to visit Grandmamma and Granddaddy Flanagan. In his later years, Granddaddy continued to tend, as he had done all his life, a beautiful, big vegetable garden.

When our family of six visited, Grandmamma showered her love on our family by hosting family dinners that included two sets of aunts and uncles and cousins plus our family and a great aunt and uncle too. There were so many young cousins that we had to sit at the children's table in the kitchen while the grownups sat at the dining room table, lovingly set with the good linen, china, silver and crystal. We filled our plates at the buffet laid out on every available space in the kitchen.

Grandmamma always cooked three meats: roast pork with North Carolina barbecue sauce, fried chicken and beef. She prepared creamed corn, sliced tomatoes, cucumbers and onions in vinegar with a touch of sugar, coleslaw made with cream, mashed potatoes, sweet potato casserole, and green beans cooked all day with fatback and onions, all from Granddaddy's garden. To accompany this, there was a generous supply of golden brown, homemade biscuits dripping with butter and clover honey or locally made molasses.

My grandmother's sister, Aunt Carrie, always brought dessert for these happy family gatherings. Everyone hooted with delight when she came in the back door bearing her homemade specialties, German chocolate cake and rum cake, made with pecans right out of the back yard. Our family shared love in the form of food and in the sweetness of celebrating together. The love, like the food, was delicious, abundant, generously given and gratefully received.

I felt especially loved by my grandparents but I was not singled out; they loved us all. It gave me a sense of security as a child to see how happy my dad was when he was with my grandparents. He worked hard and I seldom saw him as relaxed as he was when we were in my grandparents' home. Grandmamma said to Dad many times during these family gatherings, with a good-natured chuckle in her voice, "Clarence, I love you in spite of your idiosyncrasies!" As a child, I had no idea what "idiosyncrasies" meant and I was too young to understand what habits or qualities she would have named as such, but I understood the essential meaning of the phrase. I knew that Grandmamma could be counted on for love, no matter what. She taught me well and early what love looks like and I have always wanted to grow up and love like her.

Beautiful feet (Joe)

1972

When I was ten years old, our family went on a long trip in our green Gran Torino station wagon to Dallas, Texas. We followed Grandma and Grandpa. Grandma drove the lead car, because she liked to drive fast. I enjoyed watching them from behind, because Grandma filled the driver's seat in a commanding, get-the-hell-out-of-my-way style. Grandpa's head barely showed above the passenger seat.

We went to Dallas to see my uncle in the play *There's A Girl in my Soup*. We were all very excited. When we arrived at his temporary apartment, we met his roommate and fellow actor, Rob.

Rob had curly brown hair, and deep brown eyes and a sweet, sweet smile. He was wearing a light blue denim shirt, sleeves rolled up to just below his elbows, showing strong wrists and hands. His shirttails hung down over his jeans. At the end of his long legs were beautiful, brown feet.

Rob sat on the couch. My sisters fell instantly in love with him and sat close to him; one on his left and one on his right.

I wanted to sit there too. I really liked his beautiful feet.

I recalled this moment about a year after I came out to myself, and my family. While I was driving, my mind muddled in the chaos that coming out brings, I experienced an epiphany of solitude. I knew there was something about the memory that awakened me to a new understanding of my identity.

I was ten years old when I met Rob. And I saw a beauty in him that I couldn't speak then. It was enough to look and take in his presence, which helped me, years later to see my own, beautiful presence.

Recently, while looking through a set of photo albums Grandma made for me, I discovered photos of our trip to Dallas.

I was there, again. And there, standing tall, just as memory described him, was Rob. As I scanned the photos, I found one with him sitting on the couch. My sisters sat on his left knee and right. And, as a gift my memory had forgotten, I was sitting as close as I could on his right, hands folded, one knee over the other, smiling.

Rouge on my cheeks (Joe)

1974

In another photo, found in my Grandma's photo albums, I am young, twelve or thirteen. I'm standing in a hallway, leaning forward as if walking. I'm wearing a shoulder-length wig, brunette, with light rosy rouge on my cheeks. I don't remember if I wore lipstick. A purse is slung over my arm. My mother is standing behind me, smiling.

When I was old enough to understand that human beings are both feminine and masculine, I sensed that my feminine self was more fully developed, or perhaps more natural. I wanted to be more masculine—to have muscles and hair on my body, to be able to grow a mustache or beard and feel more like a man. I wasn't athletic, and wasn't interested in weight-lifting or working out. I steered away from contact sports.

I rarely wore jeans. As a small boy, photographs often show me in a bow tie, looking quite dapper. I asked Mom recently if this was how she dressed me, or how I wanted to be dressed. She said, "You liked to dress up."

In elementary school, and on up the educational ladder, I wore pants, slacks, and nice shirts. I don't know that I had any fashion sense. The clothes I wore were not flashy, just a little unusual for a boy.

Beach Boys (Joe)

1977

at the still point/there the dance is—T.S. Eliot[1]

Dancing has always been awkward for me. When I learned to step-touch in junior high, I thought I'd broken new ground. If I could step-touch, imagine what was next!

I was surrounded by buff, acrobatic boys who could leap, do back flips, and be beautiful all at the same time. I admired their grace.

During a rehearsal for Coleman Capers, our annual variety show, we were practicing a Beach Boys medley. I felt an urge begin to rise up, giving me an inner confidence, that I, who had never even attempted a flip—in any direction—could do it that day.

I began my sprint on the wooden stage, thrust my hands out and toward the ground, threw my head toward my hands, and then heaved my legs and feet into the air. My imagination saw a gazelle-style leap, beautifully completed, winning the adoration of the other boys.

Instead, I landed with a thud, my arms crumbling beneath me, my head hitting the floor. Tears streamed down my cheeks from the pain. I lay there wondering if I could move. I was hurt and embarrassed and fed up with my body. In the rest of my life, nothing felt right, except my singing. I could sing a blue streak around anyone. But, in that moment, the singing didn't matter. I lay sprawled on the floor, sobbing in front of boys, overwhelmed by failure. Discouraged, I began to disconnect from my body and spirit.

Polaroid (Joe)

1979

I am seventeen. I am naked, stretched out on a mattress on the floor of his garage. The mattress is rigged to pulleys, lowered from the ceiling to the floor for sex. He has a Polaroid camera.

"Can I take your picture?" he asks. "You have a beautiful body."

I lie there, wondering who he is talking about. My mind says, sure, go ahead. But I don't have a beautiful body. Why do you want to take a picture of me?

Click. The image appears from the camera. We hold the picture and watch it develop. An image of a naked boy emerges. I look closely and wonder who it is.

Lovers' quarrel (Joe)

1981

During my sophomore year in college, I was having great struggles with one of my roommates. We met during our freshman year, sang in choir, and spent a lot of time together. He was outgoing, confident, and had a great sense of humor. He helped me develop a new sense of confidence and I felt stronger when I was around him. We talked about everything, including our own questions about sex.

Midway through our freshman year we moved into a new dorm together, sharing a two-room suite with two other roommates. One room served as a living room with two study desks, and the second served as a bedroom, with two sets of bunk beds and two more desks. We became very close, and our friendship shifted from conversation to experimental sexual touch. As our sexual involvement increased, I began to feel very uncomfortable with the situation and tried to find ways to have some privacy in a small room on a small campus.

I called Rev. George Gardner, a pastor in town and someone I could trust. My roommate and I went to meet with him in his office. He asked us to describe what was going on. We each expressed our feelings, frustrations, and struggles. He listened for a while, and then said, "This sounds like a lovers' quarrel."

I was stunned. Lovers? I felt some of the same angst I had felt when my previous male sexual partner whispered in my ear, "I love you." I didn't know what it meant then either.

This isn't a lovers' relationship, I thought. I'm not a lover. How can I be having a lovers' quarrel? I was still very unclear about my own sexual identity and confused about how to live with the tension.

Partial truth (Joe)

Fall 1985

As a high school student, I developed a sexual relationship with a man twelve years my senior. I was introduced to him by a neighbor and was drawn to his sexual energy. On Saturday nights, when I was working a part-time job at the Moose Lodge in Wichita, I would call him when I was finishing up my shift, usually around 11:00 pm, and ask if he was home and wanted to get together. I would drive from work, park at the end of the quiet street near his house, and sneak back to his garage apartment. This became part of my secret world. The allure of sex was powerful and he was a patient and passionate teacher. I kept going back for more.

We eventually developed code names for each other so that when we called, on the off chance that someone else would answer the phone in our homes, they would assume it was a wrong number. Our sexual relationship continued through high school, and occasionally my college years, when I was home for break.

The last time I saw him, shortly after finishing college, I said nothing about my future. I found the opportunity of moving away a time to move on.

Shortly after Leigh Anne and I were married, I received a letter from him. I was now living in Texas, with my new wife, and a bright future as a United Methodist pastor. I was home alone that day, and sat down on the couch and opened the envelope. Inside was a single sheet of notebook paper. The pressure of the pen had left ridges in the paper. The tone of the letter was seething and angry, like that of a spurned lover. He'd heard I was married and he threatened to write the bishop and district superintendent and tell my wife. I was shaking and didn't know what to do. I folded up the letter, put it back in the envelope, and put it in a secret place. Ignore the problem and it will go away.

About a month later, I received a second envelope, this one with a hand-drawn satanic symbol on the sealed flap. I opened it. More anger, more threats. I didn't understand why he was so angry. We had had sex. We hadn't been in a relationship. During sex he once whispered in my ear, "I love you," and I hadn't known what that meant.

I wrote him back. I wrote several drafts and finally sent a letter, apologizing and asking forgiveness for anything I'd done to hurt him. I prayed he would forgive me and leave me alone.

One evening, some weeks later, Leigh Anne and I were getting ready for bed. The phone rang. It was my brother, Alan, calling from home in Wichita.

"Hey Joe, are you okay?"

"Yes," I answered, "what's going on?"

"Someone just called the house and said, 'Joe's dead.' Then he hung up."

I nearly dropped the phone. I sat down, stunned. I knew who had called. I felt my world collapsing. My body was tense, my heart racing, and Leigh Anne was in the next room unaware of what was happening. I knew I had to tell her, though I was afraid of the consequences.

I stepped through my fear and told her about the call, about him, about having some sexual experiences in high school and college.

Leigh Anne listened and held me as I told her and cried. The telling was liberating. I was ready to move on, to leave this chapter behind. I wanted to bury all of it.

We decided to move forward together.

The truth I told Leigh Anne that night was partial. I wasn't able to talk about the deeper truth, that all my previous sexual experiences were with men, that I had dated women but nothing ever clicked, that I saw in her a savior of sorts—one who could rescue me from myself. I didn't have the maturity or wisdom to tell the whole truth. So I kept going, the best I could, trying to be the best husband I could be.

Not all right (Leigh Anne)

1985

I had never seen Joe as upset as he was after the phone call from his brother. "Joe is dead," a stranger's voice had announced before hanging up. Alan had called Joe to make sure he was all right. He was alive, but he was not all right.

He told me that night that he had been involved in a sexual relationship with another male in high school, and about the friend who had introduced them. He didn't give me too many details and I did not probe for more. He seemed afraid, weak and ashamed.

My first thought was this: I wish Joe had told me this before we were married. I had been utterly candid with Joe about my sexual experience (or lack thereof) before marriage. He had not been as candid. I could see that embarrassment might have prevented him from revealing this to me but I was still disappointed and angry. Mostly I felt sorry for Joe because he was obviously hurting so deeply. I wanted to protect him from feeling any worse, so I comforted him, reassured him of my love for him and let it go.

For the first time in my life, I considered the question: How much same-gender sexual experimentation is within the bounds of normal? How much could be considered non-threatening? I was willing, based on my experience with Joe so far, to believe that this sexual experimentation with a man had been a one-time thing, that it was in the past and would not disturb our present or future. If I had understood the extent of that relationship, I would have thought differently, but based on what Joe told me at the time, I let it go. My only fear was that Joe seemed to have an old acquaintance with psychotic tendencies and I hoped that he could distance himself from this man.

The pastor before me (Joe)

Fall 1987

When Leigh Anne and I arrived in Plymouth, England for a year-long pastoral residency, we quickly connected with the four churches in our care. I was one of several students from Perkins School of Theology serving in Methodist churches that currently had pastoral vacancies. Both the students and the churches were eager to participate in this cultural and spiritual exchange.

Our manse was located about a mile from the Edgehill Methodist Church, the largest of the four. The manse sat on a corner lot, and seemed like a mansion to us. It was surrounded by a tall rock wall; and inside the wall was a path of slate stones, lined by large flowering hydrangeas. The main floor had two large sitting rooms, a small office, a large bedroom, bathroom, and kitchen. The upper floor had two additional bedrooms. The back garden was small and peaceful, and there was an exterior office converted from an old garage.

We eagerly began meeting people, and hearing stories about their church.

The senior steward, Marion, (who became a close friend and confidant, long after the year we served there) gave us a brief history of the church, including the circumstances surrounding the previous pastor's leaving.

She told us that Raymond and his family had been there for five years. He was bright, engaging, clearly called to pastoral ministry, and gay. After leaving Edgehill, he separated from his wife and devoted himself to his partner, their life together, and a secular counseling job. After years of struggling with his sexual orientation, he had made the decision to honor it, despite the impact it would have on his marriage and his calling.

I don't remember if the church as a whole knew about his sexual orientation, but he had entrusted his story to Marion, and she gently shared it with us. I remember receiving this news quietly, adding it to my own inner struggle, which at that time was deeply buried.

Dancing with Tina (Joe)

Summer 1993

When we lived outside of Lyons, Kansas, we grew accustomed to the openness and silence of the wide-open space. One of our churches, Wildwood, was located on the corner of a rural intersection. Just behind the church was the small parsonage. Adjacent to the church and the house was the cemetery. Surrounding everything were fields in various states of being.

In our small house, the bedroom was located at one end of the house and the shower at the other. In between was a long living room, with a large picture window. The only traffic that passed by the country parsonage was an occasional truck from one of the hog farms a few miles away.

I was used to undressing in the bedroom and dashing to the shower, then dashing back to the bedroom to get dressed—picture window and all.

When Leigh Anne, Emma (our one-year-old) and I moved into the parsonage in Medicine Lodge, Kansas, we began adjusting to a parsonage four times the size of our home at Wildwood.

One of our first mornings in the new house, Leigh Anne and Emma were out visiting some new friends and I was in the process of getting ready for the day. I was standing in the den, across from a large sliding glass door leading onto the patio behind the house. The curtains were open. I turned to the stereo and cued up Tina Turner's "I Don't Wanna Fight Anymore." I was wearing only a T-shirt.

When Tina started to sing, I started to dance. I lost myself in the music. As I turned to dance toward the sliding glass door, I saw a woman from the church reaching for the doorbell with a plate of cookies in her hand.

I froze. She was looking at the doorbell. I was looking at myself, mostly naked, embarrassed, and at her, wondering, what am I going to do? It was a Garden of Eden moment.

I could dash around the corner and run to the bedroom, but I was pretty sure she'd see me. I could hide behind the glider rocker that stood between us. (O God, I heard you walking on the patio and I was naked and hid.)

So I ducked and hid. She rang the doorbell again. I froze. I peered around the corner of the rocker and noticed the plate of cookies on the stoop outside the door. She was gone.

Tina was still singing in the background. Proud Mary. I got up, went to the bedroom and got dressed. Like Mary, mother of Jesus, I pondered this moment in my heart. And I wondered if the woman who brought cookies had done the same.

The glance (Joe)

August 1996

I glanced and he smiled. I had just arrived at the hotel lobby with my two female traveling companions. I glanced again. I found him attractive and was torn in two. This conference was work-related, a singles leadership conference. I was here on the weekend of my wedding anniversary and my wife and children were traveling with a friend. Had work become so engrossing and consuming that my family was lost? Or was my life so distorted that I was lost?

The glance was an invitation—the eye dance among men who find each other attractive. He was a little shorter than I, ivory skin, black hair, muscular. His smile was gentle, his eyes tender. I wanted to be near him and knew I shouldn't. We talked at dinner and sat together during sessions. Throughout the weekend, I felt my attraction growing, and my guilt gnawing. They fed on each other.

I wondered about how to be close to him. I asked if I could get his notes from a workshop I wasn't able to attend. I went to his room after dinner. We sat on the edge of the bed, and pulled up the notes on his computer. Our knees touched as we talked. I wanted to pull away, but didn't. His fingers lightly touched my right leg.

"What am I doing?" I thought with a loud, silent voice. My body was at war. I don't remember if I asked him to stop me, but it went through my mind. Please stop me from doing this, this thing I want so badly.

We continued to touch. He held me. I had missed the feeling of being held by another man. He gave me a massage. We kissed. My body rose with his touch and then relaxed. Sweet release mingled with soured guilt.

What have I done? The tender moment turned to inner terror. I got up, dressed and went to my room. I couldn't sleep. The next morning, I didn't know how to be. I showered, but felt dirty. I tried to carry on conversations, but felt as if my guilt were visible to everyone. I spent the morning rationalizing my actions, and the ride home trying to make sense of something that made no sense. Leigh Anne and the kids weren't due home for another day, so I had some time to rest and think and decide what to do.

I'll confess, I decided. When Leigh Anne gets home, I'll confess. Get it over with.

No, I'll bury my secret. I didn't do anything unsafe, and it will be my secret. Just put it away, and all will be well.

I decided to keep the secret, and went shopping. I wanted to pick out something for Leigh Anne and the kids to welcome them home. That would make me feel better. I don't remember what I bought for the kids; probably a book or a stuffed animal. I went to Victoria's Secret to find something sexy for Leigh Anne, some special lingerie. I didn't find anything there, so I went to Frederick's of Hollywood. I bought a lacy top and panties and had them gift-wrapped.

When Leigh Anne and the kids arrived home, I welcomed them, but didn't know how to be with them. I couldn't relax. My mind was a wreck. My body was a wreck. We got the kids to bed and I gave Leigh Anne the package. She opened it. I don't remember how she reacted. I remember her putting the lingerie on. I wanted to hold her, but had forgotten how. I remember kneeling before her and telling her, through tears, "I don't want to hurt you anymore." It was all I could say.

Everything changed. The secret I carried didn't hide, but burrowed into every fiber. It was always with me, gnawing at my insides, crying out for attention. I threw myself more deeply into work at the church, hoping my increased activity would distract me. Within a couple of weeks, still trying to restore my bearings at work, I attended a two-day mandatory training on clergy sexual misconduct. I sat and listened, thinking several times that I should stand up, confess, and be a poster child of what not to do.

I kept quiet.

Later that fall, I attended another single adult ministry conference. I shared a room with the man I'd met that summer. He slept in a bed on one end of the room and I slept on a bed at the other end of the room. One night, thinking it would be better to move and avoid the temptation of being in the same room with him, I stayed in another room, with another man. He came on to me. I closed my eyes tight and pretended to be asleep.

With any resolve I had left, I used it to guard my secret and stop acting out. My secret burrowed deeper. I lost motivation. I couldn't stay focused. I tried to be cheery and upbeat on the exterior and felt like shit on the interior. Later the next year, two senior single men (participants in our singles ministry) filed complaints in the church against me for creating a new leadership structure for the church's singles ministry and for making an (admittedly) bad joke with sexual innuendo. Both complaints were worth a conversation, but not the full-scale investigation and resolution process that followed.

My life was spiraling rapidly out of control. I didn't know how to stop the spinning. The shame corroded every bit of energy I had left. Something had to give.

Poured out: A journal entry (Joe)

August 1996

I am sitting alone today.
The darkness is hovering like a brooding cloud.
I look over to the corner table in my office to examine
my carefully placed chalices.

One is missing.
How odd.
I stand up, walk over to the table,
and look behind.

A jagged stem lies sprawled
on the floor,
broken pieces lying around it.
Still.

I stand still for a moment, looking,
then turn and go back to my desk.
This becomes my daily ritual.

Come in.
Look behind the table.
See if the brokenness is still there.
Yes.

One day, I look and the pieces are gone.
Someone moved my brokenness!
The darkness that once hovered on the outside
has taken residence inside.
I don't know who I am.
I can't seem to make sense of what has
happened these days.

I'm listless. I'm sinking into a deep depression.
I don't know where to turn. I keep going, throwing myself
into work. Ministry is no longer my passion. It is my
burden.

One day, late in the afternoon,
the sun breaks through the west windows and the light
is blinding.

I go to the curtains, reaching behind to
pull the strings and darken the room, and there
is my chalice: the pieces picked up
and placed in the cradle of the jagged stem.
My brokenness is still here!
Someone has picked up my brokenness.
I can keep it safe and hidden.
No one needs to know.

Then my courage makes a brief
appearance and I move the
chalice from behind the curtain,
out onto the counter and into the light.

I can see the chalice again,
and watch the dust collect on its
broken edges.

Later that day, my friend Nancy stops by,
crosses the threshold of
my office and says,
"Joe, that's beautiful!"
"What?"
"Your chalice...the way the light is touching it.
There is beauty in the brokenness."

What?
I wake up.
I don't have to remain in grief.
There is something striking,
light stirring courage
and friends walking along with us,
shining light in dark places.
I carry the chalice into worship
on Sunday and
set the broken chalice on the altar,
and, introducing the community prayer of confession
and forgiveness, speak of light in broken
places.

It feels good to speak the pain out loud.

Three days later a package arrives.
I go to the business office counter and look at
the return address:
Hamilton County Drug Store, Syracuse, Kansas.

I didn't order any drugs.

*I ask for some scissors and carefully cut through
the packing tape.
I open the lid, and reach inside, through
styrofoam peanuts to something bound in
bubble wrap.
I carefully unwrap the object,
and hold an old silver chalice,
worn with years
and wear
and many hands.*

*With the chalice is a note.
The handwriting is beautiful.*

*Dear Friend via TV—
Last Sunday you remarked about collecting
chalices in sharing the story of your broken
chalice.*

*We have one we'd like for you to add to your
collection.*

*It was last used for communion in 1919 in the
Episcopal Church in Dodge City, Kansas. It was given
to me by an elderly lady I cared for until she died.
Because our only child, a son, was taken from us in
a convenience store robbery and murder, we
now have no one to pass things on to.
Your friends,
Betty and Lonnie*

I stand, trembling. I go and find my friend, Nancy,
to share the chalice and note.

On the next Sunday, I carry both the broken chalice
and the worn silver chalice into worship and share
the story.

We are celebrating holy communion, and
when it comes time to consecrate the elements of bread
and juice, Nancy takes the pitcher of juice in her left
hand and the silver chalice in her right hand, and pours
the juice inside.

Poured out then, in 1919, in Dodge City.
Poured out now, in 1996, in Wichita.

Joe coming out, Leigh Anne going in (Leigh Anne)

Joe opted to go a national singles ministry meeting rather than vacation with the extended Taylor family at the beach in North Carolina, so my dear friend Mandi, who had just graduated from college, took the road trip with me. She was the kids' nanny while I drove the miles and miles from Kansas to the Atlantic Ocean. We had a great time, stopping along the way at restaurants with playgrounds, enjoying time with each other and with family. The children, at ages two and a half and four, loved playing at the beach with the cousins, and I loved sharing a house and meals together with everyone in my family. It was a happy time, a wonderful vacation.

When we returned from our trip, Joe had gifts for each of us, clothes wrapped in the store. He had never given any of us gifts like that before. It felt strange. It felt even stranger when I opened my package: a lace teddy and underpants from Frederick's of Hollywood. I never shopped in that store; the styles were too trashy for my taste, and the lace teddy's style did not suit my figure. I wore them that night but I never wore them again.

Joe's message was clear. You do not turn me on. If I dress you in slutty undergarments, maybe that will make you sexually attractive to me. I felt diminished, sad, unattractive, lacking, unable to do whatever I was supposed to do make our sex life work. In my mind, it was all my fault. There must be something wrong with me.

That night, Joe sat in bed with the covers pulled up under his chin, crying. He said to me, "I'm tired of hurting you." I could not imagine what he meant. I said to him, "You're not hurting me, Joe," and I meant it. It did not occur to me to ask him what he meant by his comment, or how he thought he was hurting me. I simply felt deep compassion for my husband, who, like a child, was crying in bed. It seems like I held him while he cried. If we were intimate, I don't remember.

In retrospect, I realized that this was Joe's attempt to tell me something, that he had lost courage mid-stream. We continued our self-deception and mutual denial.

In the year before Joe finally came out to me, I steadily sank into depression. We lived in a gray house. It was gray on the outside, and gray on the inside, gray walls and gray carpet all through the house. I hated how that house made me feel. I felt as gray as the house, inside and out.

My days were rote repetitions of this frenzied routine: get up early, get dressed, get the kids up, dress the kids, feed the kids, pile the kids into the car, drop the kids off at preschool, work frantically to get everything done, pick up kids at preschool, run kids to child care over lunch, dash back to work for the afternoon, pick up kids at child care, hurry home, fix dinner, feed hungry kids, bathe kids, read stories (truly the best time of day), fall into bed, dream disturbing dreams, and start all over again.

For Joe and me, bedtime was no longer together time. Joe slept with his back to me. There was a wall between us. I was exhausted all of the time and had no sex drive. I did not feel desire, nor did I feel desirable. I felt cut off from Joe. From my perspective, he was totally focused on work. I was totally focused on taking care of children and trying to balance work with mothering. I enjoyed my job immensely, and enjoyed my time with the children, but there was no enjoyment in our relationship as a couple. I have very little memory of Joe helping out with the children or the daily tasks of housekeeping, grocery shopping or meal preparation during this time. I have no memory of asking for Joe's help during this time either. I behaved like a quietly suffering martyr. I did not ask for what I needed because I did not know what I needed and I did not know how to figure it out. I thought I was doing all the right things: taking care of our children, our house, my job, and being a faithful wife.

I realized later that what I could not work out consciously was working itself out subconsciously in the form of a recurring dream. Night after night I dreamed that I was searching for *my* house. I was in a house, the one in which I lived in my dream, and all I could do was wander, searching for *my* house, sure that it was there somewhere, sensing that it had shrunk to the size of a doll house, thinking it was hidden away in the attic, and sure that if I kept looking for it, I would find it.

In retrospect I realized the image of the house was a metaphor for my heart, my self. Home is where the heart is. My home, my heart, my self was lost, shrunken, hidden, stashed away somewhere, if I could just find it. Night after night, my subconscious self knew the truth and tried to gently bring it to my attention.

I was crying every day, several times a day, many times not even sure why. I remember sitting at a stoplight, driving the kids to preschool one morning, tears streaming down my face. That weekend I asked a friend of mine about the therapist I knew she loved. I went home with a name and phone number.

The following week, my sobs woke me up in the night. I was crying in my sleep. It did not awaken Joe. I sat up in bed, shaken awake and shaken into the realization that this was not normal behavior. This was a clear sign of depression, and I needed to get help. I resolved I would call my friend's therapist first thing in the morning.

I called and was able to see the therapist quite soon. I had never been to a therapist before and was reluctant, scared, hopeful, and desperate. I drove to the therapist's house. At the time, it was terribly frightening and took an enormous amount of courage.

I remember coming home exhausted after work, and sitting in the rocking chair after the evening meal was done, sobbing, again. Joe came and knelt before me and said, gently, almost pastorally, "What can I do to help you?" My answer shocked even me. "You can go to the therapist too," I said through clenched teeth. I don't remember what he said at the moment, but I do remember him taking total care of the bath and bedtime ritual with the children that night.

He called the therapist the next day.

COMING OUT

Shards (Joe)

October 1997

I was sitting in my room at the Spirit United Methodist Center in southern Kansas. It was Sunday morning, the last morning of a retreat I was leading for single adults from the church I served. Our theme was "Keeping the Bounce in Life without Getting Bounced." Somehow I'd woven Jesus, Joan Rivers, and Tigger into a light-hearted romp of a retreat, while my own depression had stomped out the bounce in my life and left me dazed.

Spirit was like a second home to me. I started coming to church camps here when I was in the fourth grade and fell in love with the beauty and serenity of the landscape. Here, in the plains near Arkansas City, Kansas, are crags and cliffs and forests and trails and lots of secret, quiet places to dwell in solitude. It was here I learned about the radical love embodied in Jesus, learned about the nature of trust in relationships, the gift of vulnerability in strengthening the soul, and the power of opening myself to the presence of creation in its many forms.

In the quiet of my room, I sat down at my desk and began to write. It's the only thing I knew to do to help crack open my mind. I wrote about the broken chalice that had become the symbol of my life. I had brought it with me on this retreat as a visual reminder of my deep pain. Everything around me disappeared as my mind emerged on the paper.

What was it about that chalice? Was it the jagged edges of its wounds, the sharp corners exposed beneath a fired finish, baring themselves like ferocious teeth? I kept writing.

I am the brokenness. Those broken pieces are my broken pieces. I left them lying on the floor. I didn't want to pick them up or look at them.

I didn't want to pick them up or look at them. The chalice was in the next building, part of the makeshift altar we'd created for the retreat. I'd shown the chalice and its shards to lots of people, inviting them to look into their own brokenness. It was better that way, holding it away from the body, at arms' length. I'd treated it as a fragile treasure, gently wrapping each shard in its own tissue, placing each one into the hollow of the stem, and then wrapping everything in several cloths, like a swaddled child.

I got up from the desk, walked next door, and carried the chalice back to my room. I placed it in the middle of the desk and took each shard out of the cradle. I looked at them, scattered across the desk: five pieces, each a different shape. One still rocked on the surface.

The broken stem was dusty, the room dim. I moved it to a different place on the desk, out of the shadow, to catch light.

Three days passed before I could write again. When I met with my therapist following the retreat, she asked if it was all right to be broken I said no. *Why?* Because everything is supposed to be fixed, whole and perfect. *Where did this come from?*

I kept writing. The skeletons in my closet were clamoring to get out, to rattle all the little cages that held the broken pieces of my life, and present them to me in this nicely packaged cradle of emotional stem and shards. I was reading *The Ragamuffin Gospel* by Brennan Manning, and I came across these words: "Mark notes carefully that Jesus picked them [children] up *one by one, cradled them and gave each of them his blessing.*"[2]

The game was up. It was time to bring the brokenness out of hiding. My mind told me differently: Don't do this. If you do this, you'll regret it. You think you're hurting now? Wait until you start looking at all this crap and how it hurts everyone else. You think you feel bad now? You'll really feel bad when everyone else is mad at you and ashamed of you.

Then a gentle voice, something like how I imagine Jesus sounds, said: *Be kind to yourself. I'm here, to listen to you, to cradle you, to bless you. I can help transform this brokenness into healing. The shame you feel can be turned into blessing. The darkness you dwell in can be turned into light. The struggle you have with homosexuality can be turned into delight. The loneliness you know can be turned into solitude. I picked up those broken pieces off the floor. I cradled them in the chalice. I put them in a safe place until you were ready to begin the journey to wholeness, to rediscover who you are as beloved. I am here, now, as you begin.*

I looked at the stem and what I once saw as deep brokenness, I now saw as outstretched arms. *The arms aren't smooth or muscular. They are rugged, uneven, raised to different levels. The inside of the arms, the cradle, shiny and smooth, holds a pool of darkness at the base.*

I looked at the shards. The first was larger than the rest, and included part of the rim of the chalice. It had sharp edges and broken veins beneath the finish. The fire of the kiln had protected the finish until it cracked open.

The second shard was from below the rim, right above the stem. The design on its interior looked like a rainbow, with layers of black and green. This shard was the roughest of all with every side jagged, as though every turn was a new experience in brokenness, one continuing journey through the valley of the shadow. The sharpest point of this shard hurt to touch.

The third shard was smaller. At its top was a small portion of the rim, which gave way to something deeper, connecting the edge to the center.

Henri Nouwen, in his article, "Moving from Solitude to Community to Ministry," writes: "Sometimes I think of life as a big wagon wheel with many spokes. In the middle is the hub. Often in ministry, it looks like we are running around the rim trying to reach everybody. But God says, 'Start in the hub; live in the hub. Then you will be connected with all the spokes, and you won't have to run so fast.'"[3]

That shard pointed me to look inward, to live with my brokenness and be with my pain, and learn from where it led me.

The fourth shard was small and shaped like a check mark. Its edge looked like a tack, or the sharpened edge of a knife ready to cut deep.

The fifth shard was the smallest piece and was shaped like a V. Held one way, it looked like what a shooting pain must feel like inside. Held another way, it looked like a mountain.

Questions, questions, questions (Joe)

November 1997

Sometime after I told Leigh Anne about my indiscretion with the man at the singles meeting, I wrote these questions in my journal:

- What contributed to the "fling"? Was the fling a desperate attempt to feed my false self? If false self is impostor, then no. Now I see clearly, face to face, as Paul says in his first letter to the Corinthians. This was my true self, the self that had been buried so deeply in the shadows that when a light began to shine through the eyes of another man, I could only meet my longing with guilt.
- Am I wrestling with my shadow?
- Am I wrestling with God?
- Am I trying to secure a blessing?
- Am I ready to surrender and be pinned to the ground?

Then, in an ironic twist, I found myself writing, "come out of hiding." Right there in green ink (I wrote in different colors to reflect what I was doing or trying to do—green, growing; red, bleeding).

Come out of hiding. Name the impostor. What is an impostor? One who pretends to be someone they are not. One who lives in such a way that they are not true to who they are. How can someone be an impostor if the way they are living, even though it's not reflective of who they truly are, is defined by societal realities and myths?

I had no healthy role models or people to talk to about my identity. My shyness, introversion, and reflective nature made it difficult to talk to anyone about anything. In the early stages of revelation, I was trying to make up for eighteen-plus years of development in a few short weeks. Emotionally, I felt like a sixteen-year-old boy in a thirty-five-year-old body. The leadership at the church I was serving wanted a time frame for my healing to determine whether I would be able to stay on staff or leave. How can healing have any sort of time frame?

51

The last sermon I gave at the church was "Let's Get Passionate." The sermon was based on a text from Mark's gospel, the story of a woman who emerges from the shadows, stepping out of hiding, and anointing Jesus with pure nard. Coming out of the shadows, uncovered and vulnerable, she breaks open an alabaster jar, pouring its essence, her essence, onto Jesus.

I wanted to break free of my shadows, especially the ones mired in guilt and shame. I called my mentor, Rev. George Gardner, and he agreed to meet me and talk. That evening, as I explained the heaviness of the shame in my life, George invited me to look back over my life experiences and sexual experiences, not as good or bad, but as moments of living. He asked me to explore these moments with love, sifting out what was covered in shame, and what could be opened as gift, and I discovered that my sexual longings were natural and my attractions to men natural.

Only the outsides touching (Leigh Anne)
1996

Work was your mistress,
TV your best friend,
but neither of those could touch you.
You came to me
to satisfy your need
and I thought I was supposed to.
Your mouth suffocated,
your hands, how I hated
the way they seemed to take from me.

Sex came to be
so painful for me

with only the outsides touching.

Healing palm (Leigh Anne)
1997

> *Numb with pain,*
> *I cannot pray*
> *there are no words but "help me."*

> *Aware*
> *that there are others*
> *who care for me*
> *I beg to receive*
> *their prayer for me.*

> *I breathe.*
> *My room becomes a holy place*

> *God's hands*
> *beneath me as a bed,*
> *above me as a blanket.*

> *I rest*
> *and healing begins.*

Serzone, namaste and transformation (Joe)

During one of my therapy sessions, my therapist asked me to spend some time writing about my adolescent sexual experiences. That week, I wrote and wrote, filling page after page of how I was introduced to sex by my neighbor, and then the man he introduced me to, how I fantasized about men.

In our next session, I read what I had written and felt exhausted. With my therapist's encouragement, I went to see my doctor and ask about treatment for depression. She prescribed Serzone, an anti-depressant she believed I would best respond to, and talked with me about how to ease into it. We also discussed possible side effects including lack of sex drive, vivid dreams, and difficulty sleeping.

That evening at supper, after taking my first pill, I felt a lightening in my spirit. I was with Taylor and thinking about the way he greeted me when I got home—the way he always greeted me—a huge smile, a delighted "Daddy!", a run toward me, and a hug. On the way home that afternoon, Leigh Anne told me Taylor had asked if I would be home. When she said yes, he said, "I'm gonna give him a great big hug and a kiss."

A friend once asked in conversation, how do you greet the one you love? The question stirred a remembrance of the Bible story of the prodigal son and his father who runs to embrace him—a parable about unconditional love. Buried in depression, I was numb to unconditional love. I no longer recognized it and believed the only way I could receive it was to earn it. The lightening of my spirit came through the simple gift of my son's greeting. He showed me divine love in its purest form and blessed me with a gift that began restoring joy in my soul.

While light and love were creating new hope in my life, I was still wrestling with some fierce obstacles. In therapy, I was revisiting experiences related to orientation, identity, and sex, and sorting through what was gift and what was shame. It was exhausting. Moving through a mass of shame was akin to trying to stay afloat while being pulled back by a strong undertow.

I've seen this played out with parishioners and friends in similar struggles. When a series of good things happen, an internal valve shuts down, discounting and diminishing all the good and deserving of good, and the goodness is sabotaged.

The light at the end of my tunnel was a vision of belovedness. I had grown up hearing the story of Jesus' baptism, his going into the water, the dove descending, the heavens opening, and a voice saying, "You are my beloved, my child; with you I am well pleased."

These words became flesh, connecting with the vulnerability of human nature, and the core of my nature, leading me to realize that more than anything else I longed to know I was beloved.

Whenever I found myself in the unique position of encouraging others to welcome their most vulnerable neighbors as people of value, intrinsic worth, and dignity, my own value as beloved was deepened. I was not "better than," but "one of." Not only can an individual grasp this gift and be cradled in it, but a community can be transformed by its power and presence.

The ancient Sanskrit greeting, *namaste*, introduced to me by two different friends over a span of years, is a bold reminder of this transformation. The greeting is offered with hands clasped in prayerful posture in front of the chest, accompanied by a humble bow. With the bow comes the spoken word, which translates, "the divine in me greets the divine in you." Recognizing our varied names for the divine, I adapted the phrase to say "the beloved in me greets the beloved in you." *Namaste*, then, is a sacred greeting of equality. We acknowledge the light and love in each other and this act honors the space in which we gather.

Honoring the beloved in ourselves, and each other, creates a light that banishes the shadows of shame. We are not to be covered, but to be invited, over and over, into a light that releases shame from darkness and into the light of gift.

My body, my temple (Joe)

For the life of me, I have always struggled with accepting the goodness of my body. Looking in the mirror, I have glanced and thought, "I don't fit the image of a beautiful man." I'm too skinny. I'm skinny fat. I'm not muscular. I could go on, but won't.

When I was young, I was around other boys who were muscular or had hair growing on their chests and their legs. I had neither. I wanted both. I would sit in the locker room, looking awkwardly at my peers, thinking, where did they get all that hair and where did those muscles come from?

I was never rugged or masculine. And never had a lot of body hair. Dad took me to the drug store in high school to buy me an electric shaver for my beard. I remember asking him, "What beard?" "You'll need it," he said. My beard started growing in college. I felt more feminine than masculine, with soft skin and fair features. Gym class was my worst nightmare. I didn't like undressing in front of the other boys. I felt embarrassed, less than.

One afternoon during sophomore year in high school, after P.E. class, I was on my way to the shower and felt my penis begin to grow. I carried the beginnings of an erection into the shower. I became the talk of choir practice next hour. One of the other guys was happy to show, with his finger, what my penis had done on its own. Completely embarrassed, I had no words of retort.

I'm not embarrassed by my penis. My penis is one of my gifts. However, that moment in gym was one I tucked away in my secret catalog of shame. All I wanted to do was get through high school.

When I brought this topic into a conversation with my therapist during our intensive work in November 1997, I explained how confusing arousal, attraction, and my struggles with orientation had been as an adolescent. She explained that arousal does not necessarily indicate sexual orientation or identity. It is natural for human beings to be drawn and attracted to beauty. And a normal response to beauty, regardless of gender, is arousal. (In my various forays into dating girls, kissing and embracing would inspire physical arousal, but beyond that there was no chemistry.)

I wondered how this translated during sex with my older male partner? Arousal motivated me. He was interested in my body. He thought I was beautiful. He found me sexy. He wanted me. I wanted sex. The state of arousal was clear. What I wasn't clear about was his motivation.

Was he an abuser? Had he taken advantage of me? I had been fully aware of my arousal, but emotionally immature. When he took the Polaroid photo of me I felt like a disembodied object.

That disembodied feeling carried over into my religious life. During my sexual adventures in high school, I maintained my "good boy" image in school, at home, and in the youth group at church. We didn't talk about sex in church or youth group. My pastor was a gentle teddy bear of a man, one I enjoyed talking to. He exuded love and I felt safe in his presence. But I couldn't talk to him about this part of my life.

I'd read scriptures about the body being a temple of the Holy Spirit and how to treat it as such, but the concept always seemed abstract. That day in therapy I wondered: if my body hasn't been treated as a temple, have I not treated my body as a temple? How I treat and perceive my body is a reflection of how I treat and perceive myself. In subsequent reflections on this observation, I wrote in the margins: *our sensuality is our body imagery. Sensuality is one of the components of our sexual self, impacting our desire and desirability.*

From what I was reading and hearing, sexual orientation was being increasingly confirmed as biologically based. I welcomed the idea that my orientation could be genetic, the way I was wired.

A promise of friendship (Joe)

November 17, 1997

Leigh Anne shared with me her greatest fear: "I'm concerned that through all of your searching, you'll stay with me not as a whole person, denying your true identity."

"I don't want to lose you," I answered.

"You'll never lose your children, you'll never lose me—I'll always be your friend."

Her words became prophetic for me. Though it wasn't easy for her to say, she was encouraging me to stay with the search and be honest with myself and with her.

Depression: Sifting through (Joe)

In November, the days were getting shorter and I was in a deep depression. I was home most of the time and scared to share much with anyone. The church I was serving was concerned about me and wondering what they could do to help me and our family. They sent hundreds of cards to give some tangible expression of encouragement, prayer, and hope. I opened every card and read every letter, grateful and unable to respond.

Over the next few months I placed all of the correspondence in a clear plastic storage box and put it away.

Twelve years after I first opened those cards, I went up to the attic to retrieve the box. After years of carrying it from place to place, I decided to open it.

The box was filled with cards and letters from a faith community that dug down deep into its heart to express love and care. Many of the writers encouraged without a compass. They didn't quite know what to make of my absence, nor of the condition I was reeling from. "I don't know what you're struggling with," some wrote, "but take the time you need."

One card arrived filled with notes on small notebook pages written by youth in the church. The first one, from a boy named Matthew said:

Joe, we think of you in our prayers. We want you to know that you are missed, and we hope you can come back ASAP. Take as long as you need though, you have a very difficult job. Remember with time, God will heal your pain. Keep him in your every thought and you will heal.

Another letter from a clergy colleague, Trey, was carefully written to include Emma and Taylor. Toward the beginning the letter read,

Emma and Taylor, you probably know that something is bothering your daddy, and has been for a while now. If you sometime have occasion to read this letter, I want you to know that I was thinking of you.

Then, later he addressed me,

Joe, since I do not know, nor would the details make any difference to me, I can say that you are an exceptionally fine person. All of us have pieces of our lives of which we are not proud and/or cause us pain for other reasons. The things

which are our past are just that, they have shaped us into whatever we are for good or ill. So long as they haunt us, they can prevent us from doing our work well...

Trey's words, along with hundreds of others, reassured me of my inherent goodness, while I struggled to be honest with myself and Leigh Anne.

One card, sent by Ann, carried a handwritten quote attributed to Dame Julian of Norwich, 13th century:

All shall be well,
And all shall be well,
And all manner of
things shall be well.

Rereading these notes helped me remember what I couldn't grasp then. The human community, in faithful ways, wanted to connect. When one is suffering, we all suffer. When one is broken, we all feel broken. Even as I was drowning in depression, the community appeared in my mailbox.

When nature meets facade (Joe)

In the early winter months a lot of struggles came to bear. One was the dilemma of being in a public ministry while caring for a private matter. As I began to write a letter to the staff/parish relations committee and the church, I kept the tone honest and upbeat, acknowledging struggles, but remaining vague. If my life at this time was an onion, this was peeling the first layer of skin. I wanted to invite people in, to connect in some way through mutual struggles, but also keep them at a distance.

I also became astutely aware of my introverted nature battling with my practiced, extroverted nature. This paralleled with the wrestling between my innate nature as a homosexual and my practiced nature as a heterosexual. What happens, I wondered, when nature meets facade?

I live in a society that is gender-specific, heterosexual-specific and procreation-specific. Any variation leaves you on the margins, in an "alternative" lifestyle, out of the puritan mainstream. This is how I was raised. This is what my parents knew.

The lessons in elementary school went something like this: I am a boy. Boys have penises. Girls have vaginas. When a boy falls in love with a girl, they get married. They have intercourse. How, you ask? The boy puts his penis in the girl's vagina and his sperm fertilizes her egg. They make a baby. This is called a family. See, everyone is smiling. Being a family makes us happy. We all need someone.

But life isn't this cookie cutter. Life is filled with struggle and with ambivalence. Nature has a way of shifting and evolving and we humans experience it right along with all of creation.

In a move of honesty, vulnerability, and great risk, I decided to tell my clergy colleagues about my indiscretion with a man the year before. This was a turning point. After consultation with my colleagues, a meeting was called for early December with the staff/parish relations committee of the church to more fully explain where I was in my healing process.

I was meeting regularly with my therapist, discussing a plan of return, setting personal and professional boundaries, and putting into place the care and tending necessary to heal and serve. When I revealed to my colleagues the nature of my indiscretion, they were concerned that I was dealing with issues far deeper than just a short time away would resolve.

Sometime in the blur of those days, Leigh Anne and I met with two of the clergy. They were concerned because of the depth of my issues, particularly regarding self-care and identity/orientation. They strongly urged me to consider taking a voluntary leave of absence.

The ramifications of this were significant. Not only was I in a physically vulnerable state, but this decision would also place my family in a financially vulnerable position. I would be without income within a month. We would be able to stay in the parsonage until the next pastor was appointed. This would mean looking for a place to live, looking for employment, and, along the way, nurturing our family and sorting through my issues of identity. Meanwhile, Leigh Anne would be present at the church, continuing to do her music ministry. The bottom line: in taking a voluntary leave, I was leaving everything I knew.

Transition and healing (Joe)

December 21, 1997

For anyone who has ever attempted to make the shift from pastor to participant in a congregation, there are many stages in the transition.

During our first meeting with our colleagues, we talked for a long time. I cried most of the time and felt numb. I mostly nodded in agreement, not having the energy to offer anything other. I simply wasn't prepared for the wilderness.

In the weeks following, we made plans for a healing service on the Sunday before Christmas in the sanctuary of the church.

Three days before Christmas Eve, on a snowy evening, hundreds made their way inside the sanctuary. I was overwhelmed with the show of love and support and couldn't stifle my sobs. The sanctuary was filled with soft light and music that was healing in its tone and spirit. We prayed, shared communion, and listened. I talked that night about those two special chalices—one, broken, the pieces cradled in a stem; the second, whole, blue, reflecting still waters, an invitation to healing, given to me by Leigh Anne's parents. I spoke the only truth I could speak that night: that I was hurting and broken and in need of healing.

This sacred moment was a goodbye of sorts, and also part of a long path toward opening my closet door.

Who else do I tell? (Joe)

In the next month, I shared the image of the chalices in a letter to my clergy colleagues in the larger conference. Pondering what to write, I wondered, what do I share? How much do I share? In attempting to share insights about my journey, how much do I open myself and how do I prepare myself for how the letter is received?

It's one thing to write about brokenness, healing and the search for wholeness. While all of these are spiritual realities, they only tap the surface. I wasn't in a place to share it all, but I wanted to share something. The experience was like watching the swirling energy of whitewater rapids. You know there are boulders underneath, shifting the movement of the water. Could I write about the boulders, where the real churning was taking place?

I'd already taken a major risk in telling my closest colleagues. I wasn't ready to take the greater risk of being completely honest and vulnerable with a larger group of colleagues. Even in a communion of clergy, vulnerability is a risky venture. Colleagues who appear to be supportive will drop like flies when the truth emerges. It's the old tale of how truth makes us look at our own vulnerabilities. If I open my closet door, someone may come knocking on their closet doors. And, where there are closets, there are shadows and there are fears. What does personal and professional honesty convey to others? Especially in an environment where sexuality is not openly discussed, other than in debates at annual conferences about homosexuality, whether openly gay clergy can be ordained, who's in and who's out, or in seminars on sexual misconduct.

Time and again I had witnessed clergy struggle with infidelity, struggling with the aftermath of affairs, some quietly covered up, others turned into scandal. Some clergy, after confessing and seeking repentance, were sent to the far reaches of the conference, and allowed to return if they behaved themselves. This was the ritual for clergy who were heterosexual.

Those who were homosexual were not so easily forgiven, whether openly "out" or silently "out" like me.

I focused on resting, relating to my family, and caring for myself.

The charm of the forklift (Joe)

One day, out of the blue, I received a phone call from the director of United Methodist Urban Ministry (now Open Door) in Wichita, Kansas. He told me he didn't know what my situation was or why the church, in his words, had "fired" me, but he had two jobs available at UMUM and I could have either one.

The first was a forklift operator in the commodities warehouse. The second was coordinator of volunteers. I told him I'd think about it and get back with him.

Being a forklift operator sounded pretty great. This coming from a guy who quit being a waiter after dropping a tray of meals in front of a full dining room at an exclusive country club—how wise would it be to operate machinery that lifted heavy pallets above everyone's heads? The appeal—absence of interaction with people, going in, doing my job, and leaving. Man and machine.

The charm of the forklift didn't last long as I began thinking more about the volunteer coordinator position. This was a natural fit—I would have some solitude and some interaction. I could inspire and encourage people, educate and delegate, and help others make a difference. I could create spiritual community.

The greatest challenge would be balancing my mental health, continuing my inner work, and doing meaningful work for the agency. In conversation with my therapist and Leigh Anne, I decided to take the job and started at 30 hours a week. This allowed me the chance to ease back into work, check myself on boundaries of self-care and work, and create a new way of being. All the while, I was attempting to stay connected with the church and figure out how to *be*, rather than *do*.

For the first time in my professional life, I had no compass, other than simply being. There was no ladder to climb, no "larger" church to aspire to, no sign with my name on it. I was in between. Everything.

Somewhere in the middle of in between, I read *Between the Dreaming and the Coming True* by Robert Benson. The depth of his writing moved me. His vulnerability, and his candid discussion of his own depression, gave me an anchor to cling to. I gave copies of the book to my three clergy colleagues.

There was much that touched me, and one phrase, toward the end of the book, lives with me still:

"The journey between the dreaming and the coming true is a journey made on holy ground. It is a journey made through silence and longing where, if we will listen, we can hear the whisper of the Dreamer echoing deep within us, calling us to become what the Dreamer sees when our names were first whispered..."[4]

It was time to go deep and live between the dreaming and the coming true.

A series of events at the table, Part 1 (Leigh Anne)

December 21, 1997

The occasion: a service of healing and wholeness with anointing and laying on of hands in prayer. It was Joe's opportunity to address the congregation about his departure from active ministry. He had written a vague letter of explanation to the clergy in the conference and this was his time to talk with the congregation face to face before he took leave. Of course, it was politically impossible for him to be candid about what was really going on, so depression and burnout were the words used to describe the reason for his leave.

Joe spoke about a chalice that he had recently discovered broken in his office and saw as symbolizing his brokenness at that time. I was in the congregation that night, seated far to Joe's right, out of his line of sight, biting the inside of my lips to keep my mouth shut. "Why don't you just tell these people the truth?" I was screaming in my head. I was so worn out from keeping his toxic secrets that I didn't want to cover for him anymore. When Joe came out to me, he yanked me into the closet with him. I was in that dark closet most unwillingly that night, seething with anger as all the attention and compassion of the church focused on him, while I sat there in the pew, coming unglued.

I remember three things about that service. First, when I came forward to kneel at the communion railing for healing, anointing, and laying on of hands, our colleague Nancy, who knew the truth and who understood the profound depths of my suffering that night, prayed for me with such compassion that I experienced the healing closeness of Christ's love. Second, when everyone came forward as Joe knelt to receiving healing, anointing, and laying on of hands, each one placed a hand on the shoulder of the person in front of them and together we made the shape of a huge cross, with Joe at its center. Finally, when the meeting was over, one church member, a woman, who seemed to be a magnet for misery, stood entirely too close to me, held me entirely too long and stayed in my personal space until I felt invaded. It was not the only time I felt invaded in that dark time, or felt powerless to protect myself from people who seemed to be drawn to my misery. Part of my healing process was to learn to set a more impermeable boundary, to take care of myself.

My overriding response to this experience was how disintegrated it was for me. I knew the truth, but the truth was not told; people were understandably moved to compassion for Joe, but because he was not honest, I could not be honest and I could not avail myself of the compassion and understanding that I needed so desperately. I felt isolated, save for the ministry of our two clergy colleagues and my therapist. Each one was a lifeline for me. I would write in my journal afterwards that I felt "as if I were covered in a dirty, wet, cold blanket." No one could see me there and I could not reach out. It was an excruciatingly lonely place.

A deep sense of consolation came as a gift from God for me shortly afterwards, in a Sunday morning communion service. It was the custom in our church for most parishioners to receive the Lord's Supper in the pews and those who felt a need or desire to come forward to kneel at the communion railing could receive the Lord's Supper there. That Sunday, I made my way down to the railing, knelt, lowered my head and prepared to close my eyes. I was astonished by what I saw before me on the metal communion railing. It was a drop of oil, which remained from the healing and anointing service for Joe. At that moment, it seemed that this drop of oil was intended just for me, a sign from Christ himself, that in spite of all the half-truths that had been spoken, Christ knew the whole truth and understood my private anguish, He knew all the details and loved me and desired for me to find healing as well. I wiped the drop of oil from the railing with my fingers and rubbed it on my hands, lifting them, awestruck, in gratitude as the bread of life and the cup of salvation and the healing compassion of Christ were offered to me.

The stomping box (Joe)

1998

One of the creative gifts I received during my struggle with depression was a large brown box with the following instructions:

Joe—this box contains game pieces for "STOMP." PLEASE DO NOT OPEN AROUND CHILDREN.

Rules:

1. Put on shoes (size 17 preferably)
2. Lay bubble wrap pieces flat on <u>hard</u> surface
3. **STOMP**
4. Smile and giggle
5. Repeat as needed

Refills available.

Giggles, grins and the colors of God's love in a bubble.

Jane

A letter to my colleagues (Joe)

In the weeks following my voluntary leave of absence, I went to intensive therapy sessions twice a week, considered new employment, continued treatment for severe depression, and wrote two letters—one to the church I had served thanking them for their outpouring of love and support, and one to my clergy colleagues.

In part, I was attempting to clarify my own struggles by sharing them with others. There was a risk in opening myself to greater vulnerability while trying to quiet my life and listen. The other risk was telling my story, albeit metaphorically, in hopes that others might find some spirit of solidarity and the courage to share their own story.

I wasn't sure how my colleagues would respond, but knew that I wanted to share with them in a way that could prompt meaningful conversations about some of the challenges of ordained ministry that aren't often discussed.

Dear Friends and Colleagues,

As of January 6, 1998, I am on a Voluntary Leave of Absence, granted by the Board of Ordained Ministry and the Cabinet. Prior to that I was on a personal leave from the church I was serving, with support from staff colleagues and the Staff/Parish Relations Committee.

On my desk at home I have two chalices: one represents for me the brokenness in my life and the healing promise of God's grace; the second represents for me the waters of renewal and wholeness.

The first chalice is a stem, cradling many broken pieces. At first, all I could see was brokenness: recent emotional trauma triggering the memory of abuse from a stranger in my adolescence; a shame self-image; depression and burnout; a struggle with setting boundaries; a sense of

69

losing myself in the chaos. I was broken and vulnerable. Thanks to the great help and care of my colleagues and church family and friends, I was able to see this chalice as a cradle of love, held by God's loving arms. On December 21, the church held a Service of Healing and Wholeness, for me and for the church. During the service, as I shared the story of the chalice, I began to see the cradle attached to the stem as a smile and symbol of hope.

The second chalice is new, given as a gift from my in-laws. Both the outside and inside are filled with blue, symbolizing the healing waters of new life and the possibilities of wholeness. As I look into this chalice I am drawn more deeply into these waters.

As I enter these waters, I go longing to discover who I am and who God is calling me to be. In many ways it's like going into the desert stripped of "fluff" and clothed only with the vulnerability of life. Yet, I am learning that vulnerability, though feeling like weakness, is actually strength.

I would gladly welcome your calls and/or words of encouragement. Leigh Anne continues to serve on staff at the church. Out of care for her, ask how she is doing. And, most certainly, hold each of us in your prayers, especially our children, Emma and Taylor.

Thank you for your love and care as we share this covenant of ministry together.

Shalom,
Joe Cobb

Survival, renewal (Joe)

Spring 1998

After I left the church we had both been serving, Leigh Anne remained on staff, continuing her music ministry, while I attempted to make the transition from being a clergy in the church to a participant. I sang in the choir and welcomed the opportunities to be connected to the community.

Life was based in survival. I started my new job at Urban Ministry at thirty hours a week, and continued practicing new ways of living. Leigh Anne and I honored our decision to be celibate for a time while sorting through our questions, emotions, and the rawness of the hurt each of us was experiencing. Gradually, we began holding each other and listening in ways we hadn't before.

I remember wanting the healing process to happen faster than it was. I felt a new intimacy with Leigh Anne. We began talking about renewing our wedding vows, a short three months after my confession and the beginning of my work in therapy. While neither of us was remotely ready for this step, I remember looking at new rings in a James Avery catalog and approaching our colleague, Nancy, about presiding at our vow renewal service.

When Leigh Anne broached the subject with her, Nancy asked if I had fully examined my own issues of sexuality from both perspectives (heterosexuality and homosexuality). In my journal, I wrote: "I know I haven't. I love Leigh Anne. And I want to share my life with her. I also know that the value of growing in myself can be the greatest gift I give to her."

Depression's dreams (Joe)

As much as I appreciated the effects of Serzone in boosting my seratonin level, my depression was still taking me for a ride. Every morning was an adventure in analyzing the terrifying dream from the night before.

One night I had a dream that frightened me so much I wanted to forget it, but couldn't. In the dream I was searching for my son, Taylor. I walked past a pool, peered in, and couldn't see him. Then, I saw a lake, next to my brother's house. Alan came outside, and I told him I was looking for Taylor. He dove into the lake but couldn't find him.

I ran to the next lake, dived in and saw Taylor. He was submerged, his eyes closed. I was afraid he was dead. Alan dived in too, rescued Taylor, and lifted him to the shore. I pulled Taylor into my arms and held him. I noticed a tooth missing in his mouth and that he was wearing braces. When Taylor came to, he complained that he wanted the braces off where the tooth had come out.

Taylor had actually been sick, so I knew in part where the dream came from. On another level, I felt as though I were gradually losing everyone and everything in my life that was meaningful and loving.

When I shared the dream about Taylor with my therapist, we discussed some interesting interpretations. We talked about Taylor as a symbol of my male self and the struggle of both losing and regaining my self-identity. I feared losing everything in losing identity; I also realized there is a price to pay in regaining a new sense of self. In looking for my lost self, I needed help. I couldn't do it alone.

Viewed through the lens of abuse, the dream of Taylor symbolized my lost inner child. I had felt helpless to save myself or stop myself from going into deep waters, well above my head. I was overwhelmed and couldn't summon the power to help my healing or know where to turn.

Talking about this dream helped me identify certain realities. I struggled in making decisions, particularly involving the next stage in therapy. I knew I must continue to explore my sexuality and body, reclaiming the goodness of both, while working through the feelings of guilt over my relationship with the older man in high school, and the broken trust in my relationship with Leigh Anne.

It was far easier to identify areas that needed attention and far more difficult to celebrate the progress I was making. Among the best things that were happening, I was learning to listen to my "inner voice," trusting my feelings and intuition, and making decisions that were helpful in my healing.

A day later, I had another startling dream. I remember watching as an older man had anal sex with a boy. During the act, the man held his hand over the boy's mouth. Other people were in the room, oblivious to what was happening. I was sitting next to the bed, stunned by what I was seeing, glued to my chair. Following the act, the man, dressed in a military uniform, got up to leave. The boy pulled a video camera from his leg. The dream ended.

Therapeutic review (Joe)

February 1998

Leigh Anne and I met with the therapist to review where we'd been and where we were going. This review took place three months after I started therapy and was an important step in my healing. I was also ready to begin work with a different therapist, a man specializing in marriage and family therapy. I wanted to shift my work to exploring issues of male identity and formation and believed that a male therapist could help me.

During the session I wrote down areas of improvement and areas needing attention. Next to the improvement category, I wrote "setting boundaries—personal and professional" and the word "huge." This included caring for myself, easing back into work and a new job, and saying no, a lot. I felt more in tune with myself, listening to my inner voice and giving myself time to pause and reflect. Reflection was a rare commodity in those days, and even giving myself time to reflect made me feel uneasy. Knowing that reflection can be the birthplace for new life, I followed four basic steps: listen, stop, evaluate, and act. (The acting step doesn't always involve doing something. It may mean saying "no, thank you.")

I began valuing myself more. I began trusting my feelings, not treating them as marginal. I began listening to my body, at a basic level. When I craved rest, I rested. I established a pace of life that was both comfortable and energizing.

As my world was turned inside out, I was working from the outside in. I was moving away from the idea that external demands alone define me. The reverse is true. What is within defines who I am. Where treasure is, there my heart is.

I reflected on a long list of risks I had taken over those three months:

I shared my struggle with homosexuality.
I told my spouse.
I told my colleagues.
I requested a personal leave.
I wrote about my depression and abuse.
I took a voluntary leave of absence.
I was leaving my vocational work.
I dared to give attention to my inner life and family relationships.
I asked specific questions about sexual identity, orientation, and what these questions meant for me and my relationships.

As I reflected on the list, I compared perceived fallout with actual reality. One of the discoveries I made was that the risks I took were health-based, rather than fear-based.

One of the spiritual dimensions of this reflection was forgiveness. I simply could not forgive myself. I had become less hard on myself, but I struggled with actual forgiveness. To reach a new vision of myself, I had to work through the barriers of shame, guilt, and anxiety.

Some of the tangled undergrowth needed to be cleared, including depression, with its roots and feeders. I would discover that depression isn't something that can be quickly eliminated, but more often is managed, its power diminished through medication and meditation.

Another category for review was my journey toward sexual identity. I wasn't sure I could trust the changes that were occurring within, because they made me look at myself in a radically new way. I felt pressure from many angles and from many people, including myself. There was so much at stake— a family, a future—and none of it was clear.

With one way of my life closing, and depression keeping me from seeing a way that was opening, I had many unanswered questions:

who am I, really?
can I keep my attraction to men in check?
am I truly gay?
will I ever feel passionate again? about life,
about self, about another, about what I am called to be and do?

The questions were all important. At the close of the session, my therapist's instinct was that I needed more "desert time" to learn and explore, in order to arrive at some clarity about the direction of my life and relationship with Leigh Anne.

The deeper, authentic life I longed for couldn't begin until the external stuff was stripped away. On that day, I knew I had to be completely naked. I needed to learn to love the whole of myself, the whole of my body.

Sharing secrets (Joe)

March 1998

Today I told Leigh Anne secrets I'd been holding. My fear of sharing had been a wall of isolation. The freedom i ⸱⸱sharing was liberation. I told her about a dream, a sexual f ntasy. I was receiving pleasure from a man. I didn't remember the face of the man. Was this a breakthrough in feeling good about pleasure received and offered? Was this an indication of my orientation? I didn't remember how or if she responded. I do remember that she listened.

The sharing brought relief. I told her I had thought recently what my life would be like as a single, celibate man. We both desired wholeness, including sexual wholeness. I prayed for clarity, for a clear vision of sexual wholeness, for healing of our relationship, and for direction regarding my call in ministry.

When I met that day with my therapist, he invited me to hold my sexuality in a cradle of humility—not to approach it with ready-made convictions—but to cradle it as a gift of God's creative act, to treasure, nurture, respect and nourish. We also talked about holding and cradling my marriage as a gift with possibilities for healing.

Eight days later I had another dream. I was standing in a shower, soaping and washing, and a man—a very strong man—was standing outside the shower stall reaching in. He was taunting me, as if to pick a fight or wrestle, and saying, "You are homosexual," over and over. I remember feeling the muscles in his arms, but I heard my voice, trembling with frustration and anger, say, "I am not homosexual. Go away and leave me alone."

Following this dream I tried to remember the first time Leigh Anne and I met, the moment when I knew I loved Leigh Anne. I wanted to remember something good. I wanted to name the gifts of our relationship. But, the harder I tried to remember these gifts, the more I realized I was running away from my very real sexual wholeness and attraction to men.

During these days of struggle I also became keenly aware of what our children were wondering about. Emma, quite out of the blue, talked about divorce. For a while she mentioned it frequently and when I asked her questions about her feelings, she talked about our neighbors. The woman had moved out a year earlier and Emma was aware of the change in their household.

Curious conversations (Joe)

During lunch one day, a clergy colleague and I discussed a new round of resolutions being proposed for our United Methodist Annual Conference on "transforming" issues regarding gay and lesbian persons in ministry. Many of these resolutions were "wolves in sheep's clothing," their ultimate tone one of exclusion. I had always been intolerant of an exclusionary gospel, because it seemed to counter what Jesus modeled.

The next day at a Lenten luncheon, I was talking with a friend who expressed her feelings toward what she observed as increasing religious intolerance. "If the picture of heaven passed on so frequently—that of those sifted through the judgment entering and the others left outside—I'd rather be on the outside helping those who were excluded."

In conversation with my doctor, we agreed to switch my anti-depressant from Serzone to Zoloft.

Becoming friends (Joe)

I am holding Leigh Anne, standing in front of the window, looking out at the trees, and listening to her voice. She says, "I feel like we're becoming friends. We've been physical lovers and now we're becoming friends." Physical love is no longer the end. The end of our desiring is to love as friends who can reach into the depths of our hearts with complete trust.

A wink and a smile (Joe)

On the evening of our thirteenth anniversary, Leigh Anne and I went out to dinner and then to Borders Books and Café to browse.

One year after my self-revelation, we were still working with a marriage and family therapist seeking to determine the best way forward in our relationship. I was still torn by hope and fear.

My hope was to find clarity regarding my sexual orientation. My fear was everything else: radical change, an unknown future, endings that I couldn't comprehend.

I went to the poetry section and picked up Emily Dickinson.

Hope is a thing with feathers
that perches on the soul
and sings the song without the words
and never stops at all[5]

Leaning against literature, while reading poetry,
I looked down the aisle of science fiction and mystery.

A clerk walked toward me followed by two men.
The third man wore a red bandanna,
brown curls of hair peeking out from beneath.

As he turned the corner between mystery and science fiction,
he winked and smiled.

I nearly dropped Emily Dickinson.

I had no words,
only a reality,
a knowing.

This will be the terrible and liberating gift.

COMING APART

I am more attracted to men (Joe)
August 14, 1998

I' m sitting in a chair facing our therapist. Leigh Anne is seated next to me, in another chair. The therapist has worked hard to restore our marriage. I've worked hard to learn about distinctions between attraction, orientation, identity, and intimacy. After the wink and smile in Borders Books and Café, I'm on edge. I open my book of revelations and speak one to break the silence. "I'm more attracted to men." Thirty-six years in the making. I say it and wait.

From my journal that night: *I'm totally wasted tonight. Feel like a washcloth hanging on its last thread after being soaked, rinsed, and wrung out. Courageous is the word Leigh Anne offered. Shitty is what I feel. The honest truth. It doesn't get anymore barren than this in the desert. I've said that before.*

Earlier that day, while reading *Listening to the Desert*, I came across a story about a restless Abba (monastic leader) who went to another for advice. "Abba Poemen said to Abba Joseph: Tell me how I can become a monk. And he replied: If you want to find rest here and hereafter, say in every occasion, who am I? and do not judge anyone."[6]

I was innocent. I was guilty. I was my own harsh judge. Every step I took toward understanding tapped into my guilt. I had a harder time recognizing the healing that was taking place.

Some things were becoming clear and I uttered them through a cascade of tears. I have struggled with my sexuality—during our marriage and before. I am attracted to men more than women. I'm scared shitless about all of this.

And I have lots of questions: Am I gay? Am I confused? Who the hell am I? Why did I marry Leigh Anne? Did I need someone to care for me? To bring security and stability to my life? To love me from the inside out? To discover that a loving relationship is not based on secrets, guilt, and shame, but on love and truth?

As I kept thinking, I thought about the man I had sex with throughout high school and the secret power he held over me. Twelve years after telling Leigh Anne the partial truth about my relationship with the man, I remembered the rest of the secret.

In 1990, five years after I received his last letter, one in which he forgave me and said he looked forward to meeting my new wife, Leigh Anne and I were living in Lyons, Kansas. Wichita and the surrounding area had been ravaged by tornados, and after returning from a trip there to see my parents, we came home to a message blinking on the answering machine. "I thought you'd like to know I'm still alive." *Click.* I recognized his voice, knew that he lived in one of the ravaged areas and realized that the forgiveness promised was conditional. I erased the message.

Two years later, another message: "I thought you'd like to know I mailed the photos to get published." *Click.* The only photo I could remember was the Polaroid he took of me. I was naked. He thought I was beautiful. Let me take a picture of you, he said. All right, I said, reluctantly. He held it as it developed. There I was, naked.

Had he taken other photos without my knowledge? I erased the message.

He was like a gnat that wouldn't go away. If I could've swatted him, I would have. His voice also served as a reminder of an inner voice I was working hard to keep buried.

Three years later, in 1995, shortly after we moved to Wichita, I was in the dining room with our one-year-old son, Taylor, and the phone rang. "Hello," I answered. It was his voice. Every urge in my body wanted to hang up, but I listened. "What do you want?" I asked.

"I just wanted to call and apologize for all the trouble I've caused you over the years," he said. "I hope you can forgive me."

"I forgive you," I mumbled. He kept talking. He told me he and his lover had gone to Colorado for a holy union and they had experienced a great spiritual moment. Then: "And I wonder if you would be willing to come to our house and bless our union." I was dumbfounded. I looked across the table at Taylor and wanted this voice, this man, to go away.

"I'll have to think about it," I said, when what I really meant was, there is no way in hell I'll do it. I took his phone number. And lost it.

Cross to bear, Part 1 (Leigh Anne)

The year that Joe was working to determine his sexual orientation, we bounced from one extreme to the other in marriage counseling. We learned early on that our therapist was truly called and committed to saving marriages. He saw his job as helping us work it out. He did his job well. There was a point early in the process when we were ready to renew our wedding vows. We didn't go through with it. The therapist talked with Joe about impulse control. His recommendation regarding sexual desire that wanted to be expressed outside our marriage, whether heterosexual or homosexual, was simply, "Don't act on it."

The therapist talked with me about the Kinsey Scale, describing how sexuality in the human population is expressed across a wide scale, from 100 percent homosexuality at one end of the scale to 100 percent heterosexuality on the other end of the scale, with bisexuality splitting the middle. At my final appointment with him, he said to me, "Joe's homosexuality is your cross to bear." At that moment, utterly defeated, I bent over, hanging my head between my knees and holding my face in my hands. I said, in a voice loud enough only for me to hear, through gritted teeth, "That's a cross I do not choose to bear." Neither Joe nor I felt a need to go back to marriage therapy again.

Waiting for the decision (Leigh Anne)

After Joe told me his secrets, I pledged to stay with him as long as he was in therapy to figure out if he was gay or straight. The hardest thing about that period was the total unknown of the future. I had meant it when I said "I do" and "until death us do part," and I had never thought of not spending the rest of my life with Joe, raising our children together and growing old together. This was the life that I wanted, the life that I chose and the marriage to which I was committed. Not knowing what the future would bring, whether I needed to prepare myself to support myself and my children alone and let the dreams for our future together die, was a tension that left me feeling shredded.

I did my best to stay neutral, supporting Joe in therapy and taking care of myself the best I knew how through therapy, journaling, prayer, and enjoying my children and my job.

Some days were easier than others. I was afraid of being alone. I didn't want to feel like a failure in the most important relationship of my life. I didn't want to damage the children any more. I didn't want my dreams for our future to die. I wanted Joe to come out on the other side of this discernment with a new commitment to our marriage.

At the same time, I began to have long talks with myself. "If Joe is gay, is there any way I could stay married to him?" I would ask myself. I was so lonely in our marriage. I knew that if he said he was gay and wanted to stay married anyway that the choice would then be mine. Could I live as a straight spouse with a gay man? It did not seem to me to be what God intended for marriage.

I went over the vows that I made with all of my heart, soul, mind, and strength at our wedding, asking myself, "Is this what 'for better or worse' means?" I finally came to the conclusion that I made our marriage vows with the complete confidence that we were two heterosexual young adults. When Joe confessed that he was not heterosexual, the foundation upon which we made our vows collapsed. Staying together, if he were gay, would not be an option for me. So I simply waited until he could come to a conclusion.

One Saturday in late summer, Joe's indecision very nearly killed me with emotional whiplash. As we sat at the table finishing our breakfast and the children watched cartoons in the next room, Joe announced that he was leaving us and going to take a job in Nebraska. He quickly left to go to the bookstore, while I wept and began to think about what life would be like and what steps I should take next, since I was going to be on my own. He came home mid-day and said that I was the best thing that had ever happened in his life, that we were the most precious gifts in his life and there was no way he was going to leave us. I drew in my breath, my tears, my plans and thoughts and looked for solid ground. Before the day was over he was ready to leave again. That's when I exploded.

"Don't you see that you are playing ping-pong with my entire life, my emotional health, my future? You have got to stop this and make up your mind." I really didn't think that he had any idea of the emotional upheaval he was causing that day because he was so focused on himself.

Desert (Joe)

August 12, 1998

I'm drawn to the writings of the desert mothers and fathers in early spiritual history. They represent mystery—their mystical journeys, pathways into intimacy with the divine. Some of these early mystics became so disturbed by the realities of the world that they fled to the desert to become hermits, stripping away everything that wasn't ultimately essential to their spiritual lives.

These ancient sages fasted, prayed, studied the scriptures, and opened themselves to one purpose: becoming one with the divine. Henri Nouwen, writing in *The Way of the Heart*, described the journey in three movements—to flee, to be silent, and to pray—"three ways of preventing the world from shaping us in its image and thus the three ways to life in the Spirit."[7]

As a disciple of Nouwen, intrigued by desert spirituality, and anticipating a trip to the desert in a few months, I was eager to learn from those who had gone before me and discover what parallels there might be with my own journey.

I made my way to Eighth Day Books in Wichita for a quiet retreat. The shop is in an old house, with books in every niche, and a table in the front, just right for silence and writing. As I walked through the front door and across the creaking floor, many thoughts were swirling: the wink and smile on the evening of our anniversary, the encounter with a man a year earlier on our anniversary, a desire to make our marriage work, my continuing wonder and confusion as to how all of these decisions would unfold. In the quiet of the moment, my mind was anything but.

I remembered conversations our church staff had about discovering our spiritual types, based on a book and model of the same name by Corrine Ware. Through a series of questions, we learned about ways we approach and perceive the divine in our lives, and how we most naturally grow in our spiritual lives.

These reflections, along with the quiet of the day, led me into reading about kataphatic and apophatic spirituality. Kataphatic is to say yes, to assent to the divine through the mystery of images (like praying with our eyes open). Apophatic is to say no, to seek the divine through the mystery of unknowing (like praying with our eyes closed).

Unknowing is not a practice taught in school. *Unknowing* flips everything on its head, shakes it loose, and drops everything unessential. We may be able to see, but one of the challenges of *unknowing* is to let it go. The practice is a lot like meditation. To quiet the mind, we must anchor in our breath, and let all of our thoughts pass through like a parade, letting them go on their way, and not follow them.

Unknowing begins by removing layer after layer, revealing the mystery at the heart of existence. Who am I, really? What is my purpose in life? How do I begin letting go of what I'm struggling with, layer after layer after layer? The practice comes in looking at each layer, and receiving it as a gift. Hold it, bless it, break it, and give it away. Let. It. Go. Holding on takes up space and clutters the soul. Letting go opens the soul to new depths of growth and life.

As I explored this unknowing, I was distracted by everything else happening in my life: moments that were both within and beyond my control. I began analyzing everything, and the darkness grew dense.

My greatest desire was stillness. My reality was chaos. I wanted to be like my ancestors, the desert mothers and fathers, and flee. I thought the silence and prayer could come later. I'll go to the desert, immerse myself in apophatic spirituality and become a hesychast. I came to understand hesychasm as peace and stillness of the heart.

I wanted to dwell there, in the peace of the heart. To get there, I had to travel a journey fraught with danger. With the danger was silence. And silence creates space for prayer. Solitude is a gift of God, designed for the creation of silence, with prayer an expression. In this silence the gifts of prayers are born and given.

A wink and a smile: the discussion (Joe)

On the night of our anniversary, I talked with Leigh Anne about the wink and smile. The next day, she shared a vision from her own silence: the wink was an expression of my internal arousal. She saw this as a way for me to honor myself in beauty. The vision was lovely and scary. Arousal had not been a friendly companion. It had resembled more of a curse, a deeply imbedded secret, worthy only of existing in shadows.

Throughout the year of therapy, the curse was being lifted, the blessing being opened, and signs of wholeness beginning to emerge. Little things. I stopped biting my nails. I became interested in caring for my body, what I was eating and drinking. I was taking the time to listen to my body and pay attention to its messages. This was all part of discovering hesychia, stillness in God. I wanted to reach for a place of being, to be in prayer all the time.

I learned, like those who ventured into the desert, that this doesn't happen overnight. Wherever I wanted to be, I needed to stay focused on my inner work—to listen for and discern my inner voice and honor it in relation to my family, others, and myself.

But, instead of clarity, I experienced distraction. I paid attention to anything that would distract me from going deeper into my work. A job offer in Nebraska. A new book to look at on stillness. I had faced so much pain and change, I felt exhausted.

Two days after our conversation about the wink and smile, I was sitting at my desk looking at three chalices. The first was the smiling stem cradling the broken shards. The second was tarnished silver, showing its eighty years, holding a note of gratitude from its giver, Betty. The third, a beautiful, deep blue chalice, shimmered, as though light were dancing in healing waters.

These chalices spoke to me of solitude, silence, and prayer, gifts preparing me to be a sanctuary, dwelling in the one thing necessary.

Conversation in sanctuary: Poustinia (Joe)

Three days after I spoke my truth of being more attracted to men, Leigh Anne and I shared lunch at Poustinia in the Marketplace, a lovely, peaceful sanctuary in downtown Wichita. My spiritual director, Virginia Winters, owned the space and set aside a room for us to experience some solitude and conversation.

We talked about our fears, about feeling alone. We were both feeling vulnerable and isolated. I had a few friends I could talk to, and Leigh Anne, who had kept much of her/our struggle inside, realized it was time to tell her story. She needed to come out, open up, and share with her family and colleagues.

I listened as she described my early experiences of sex not as orientation, but abuse. Several months earlier, when I shared my story with a close friend, she asked how old the man was. I told her he was ten to twelve years older than me. When I told Leigh Anne this, her face changed. "You were sexually abused." While there was truth to this (he and I met and became sexually active when I was a minor and he a legal adult), I had never considered it abuse.

I had something he wanted and he had something I wanted. We were both pleasure seekers. He became my pleasure teacher. But beyond the sex, there was never a healthy relationship. I didn't know what "relationship" meant, and he didn't know what boundaries meant. I don't know if my age ever registered with him, but it clearly didn't matter. He lived in his lair of a garage, and I made my way there to receive whatever I could learn about sex.

Sex became our secret. And shame became mine.

The veil lifted (Joe)

September 4, 1998

I feel very distant, confused and worthless. Leigh Anne is telling her truth: to the full staff at the church, and to her family. The secret veil has been lifted. I want to sleep and wake up from this nightmare.

I want to hurt myself (Joe)

September 5, 1998

I wanted to hurt myself tonight. To take all of the shame and inflict an internal wound in my soul. I went to Borders

Books and Café to find gay literature. I read an erotic story. In a searing surge, my penis grew erect with the intensity of the literary encounter. Why go on?

I put the book away and walked to music. To Arvo Pärt and John Tavener. To the mystical. To the mystery of my life, and love and release. My mind and spirit soared with the music, but I couldn't get the erotic out of my mind.

Letter to the Taylor family (Leigh Anne)

Labor Day 1998

Dear Mamma and Daddy, Mike and Kat, Butch and Ruth, John and Donna,

I'm writing you all under the same salutation so you'll know that I'm sending you all the same letter. I'm mailing them all on the same day but I doubt they'll all arrive on the same day, so give each other a few days before you start calling each other.

I need to let you all know the details of what Joe and I have been going through since last November. I am choosing to break my silence because I need you to know what has been and is going on and I need your love, support, and prayers and I need them now.

I took myself to the therapist last Halloween when I recognized signs of depression in myself. Joe asked what he could do to help me. I asked him to go to the therapist too. After we had both been to one session, Joe confessed to me (Nov. 4) that in his late teens and early twenties, he had been in an extended sexually abusive relationship with a man. He also confessed that he had had sex with a man in August of '96 at an event in St. Louis. You will remember that he was dealing with two antagonists at church at the same time. They were the ones that took the public blame for his leave and subsequent leave of absence status from the appointive process but the damage of the sexual abuse, the shame of the affair, and the ongoing confusion of his sexual identity were the real causes. He has remained in therapy but has only in the last month come to the realization that he can go no further, can not get well, until he faces the sexual abuse and the identity question. He says he doesn't know if he's gay or straight. He is extremely wounded, broken, and confused. He does seem to be able to function at work. He is continuing under the care of a physician and a therapist, and is taking an anti-depressant. He is not suicidal. We have both been tested for HIV and both of us are negative.

I am writing because I need you to know the hell I've been through and the uncertainty of our future. I need you to know because I'm taking control of my role in our relationship. I will not be held hostage by Joe's secret shame any longer. It's not my shame. Joe knows I'm writing to you. Perhaps he will have the courage to write you himself eventually but I'm not planning to wait for him anymore. I have told Joe that I hate what has happened to him, I hate what he did to me, but I don't hate him. I love him and I am committed to working as long and hard as it takes to get better. I want to be married to Joe and to raise our children together. I also have made it quite clear that if he needs to be with a man to be whole, I deserve to be free. That's what I need you to know.

I don't know where my marriage will be in six months or a year. I really can't tell where Joe will be in six months or a year. I am crushed to think what divorce would mean for Emma and Taylor. I don't like to think what my life would be like as a single mother but I will not stay married to a gay man. He may come out on the other side of this straight but there is no guarantee. So pray for Joe. Pray for clarity in his therapy. Pray for me and Emma and Taylor.

I am leaning on you now and I feel extremely relieved because you know.

I have been taking care of myself. I am continuing to see a therapist. I can confide in my colleagues, my friends Anne and Marion in England and my friend Anne in Nashville. This past week I told the members of Core Staff at church what I told you and those wonderful people are holding me together in their love, support, and prayers. I trust them to guard my privacy. I do not plan to tell any others at church unless it comes down to divorce. At this point, Joe's family does not know and I will not tell them. He will have to do that himself but I'm not going to cover for him any longer.

I am doing my best to eat, sleep, and exercise. I do find joy being with my children and am pretty happy at work. It's a challenge to concentrate.

Emma and Taylor seem oblivious but I don't know how much they are picking up. I think it's going to get worse before it gets better and I worry for them a lot. Pray for us to be good parents.

What I don't need right now is criticism of how I have handled this. You will fault me for not telling you sooner. Perhaps you will fault me for telling you now. All I can say is, I've done the best I could do under the circumstances. Help me go on from here.

I love you all,
Leigh Anne

Telling the Cobb family (Joe)

Labor Day 1998

I called my mentor, George, and asked if I could meet with him. I needed his listening ear and wisdom to help me inch toward some clarity about the path ahead. I was filled with questions, reliving the "wink and a smile" moment in the bookstore, realizing that Leigh Anne and I needed to make some decisions.

As I talked, he listened with a wise and welcoming heart. Several realities began to emerge: *I know I need to be on my own. I don't know whether I'm gay or not, but I do know I need to erase the shame and embrace the treasure of who I am. I need solitude.*

When I revealed my struggle with homosexuality, George acknowledged he had sensed it for a long time. He wasn't surprised. I asked what he meant. He said, "intuition," that he had perceived an "aura" about me. "You have a keen sensitivity and gentle spirit." It felt as though he was identifying a connection between my spiritual life and being gay.

I wondered if leaving was escape. I wasn't running. I was finally feeling peace. Leigh Anne had reached the stage of acceptance. She had written a letter to her family. I was going to talk to Mom and Dad the next morning and look for a place to stay.

Some things in my life still needed to be secret. It was all right to have questions, not answers. This was part of my desert: learning to be alone, moving through my fears of being lonely to finding peaceful solitude. I couldn't describe the relief I felt saying, "I need to be on my own." This was the first decision I'd ever really made for myself.

When I got home from my conversation with George, feeling confident about what I needed to do, I quickly became defensive when Leigh Anne asked about the conversation. Rather than speaking from a peaceful place I longed to know, I spoke from a tortured soul. I was angry that Leigh Anne was taking control of her own life and feelings. I looked for ways to blame her for how I was feeling. I told her that she seemed cold and uncaring.

The next morning I woke up feeling uneasy. I was determined to tell my family the truth. I called Mom and Dad and asked if I could come over. They were in the kitchen when I arrived, concerned.

The risk of telling everything carried the risk of disconnection and rejection. Walking into the kitchen that morning felt like walking into a wilderness without any sources of strength or nourishment. I was afraid of how my family would respond.

After a few moments of awkward silence, I opened up and told them that I had had a fling with a man, that I was pretty certain I was gay, and that Leigh Anne and I were separating.

Dad didn't say much. I spilled everything out and it was still dancing around the room, taking its sweet time in landing. Mom came and sat beside me, gently reassuring me through her own tears. No matter the depth of hurt, her love was like an anchor, a sure and certain hope. In those moments, Mom, in her words, and Dad, in his stillness, were the Word made flesh, dwelling with me.

After her tears subsided briefly, Mom said, "Joe, I don't have a problem with you being gay. I have a problem with you getting a divorce."

When we finished talking, I called my brother, Alan, and his wife, Holly, and asked if I could come over and talk with them. I stood, embraced Mom and Dad. I wanted to share my truth in person, with each of my family.

When I got to Alan and Holly's house, I sat down on the couch in the living room. Their two youngest children were also in the room. I took a breath and told them exactly what I told Mom and Dad. They held me, and their children circled around me, climbed on me, and hugged me. I paused enough in the telling to remember that their youngest was to be baptized that Sunday in church. In preparing for his baptism, we had taught him to say to the pastor, "Thanks for the water."

Next was my youngest sister, Peggy. I called her and asked if she was home and made the next leg of the journey. If there was any blessing in all of this telling, it was that my parents and two of my siblings all lived within two miles of each other. Not much time passed between each stop.

As I told Peggy, I could tell she was having a hard time hearing my confession. She didn't want to know about the affair. She talked about Exodus, a transforming program for homosexuals. I wondered how she knew about this program. I tried to listen, but felt agitated. I wanted to leave. But I stayed. She needed to say what she was feeling and I needed to listen. Her greatest concern was about my leaving the marriage. She also told me that she didn't believe a single event or even a series of events define a person.

As I sat and listened, I reminded myself to hold the memories as gifts, open them to new understandings, and gradually remove the power of their shame. And in the gifts, I would find my gift and my heart. Confession digs out the dirt, turning secretive family systems on their head, opening the way for true treasure, filled with gifts of a life yet to be lived.

I thanked Peggy, and left. I would call my other sister, Nancy, who lived in Pratt, Kansas, when I got home. Completely exhausted, I got in the car. As I was driving along Kellogg, a major highway through the heart of the city, I began to sob, great heaving sobs, tears drenching my face to the point I had to pull over and cry until the tears subsided.

I sat there for a long time. Everything I'd kept intact that morning, so that I could speak truth after truth, broke. My eyes were red, my cheeks puffy, my face wet, and my spirit empty.

I slowly pulled back onto the highway and drove the rest of the way home. I called my best friend, Gayla. She came over immediately. I sobbed so much I ached. I told her about feeling totally helpless and filled with anguish. I was angry toward my abuser and told her how my youngest sister talked about considering prosecution. Gayla sat with me, listened to me, emptied her pocket of fresh Kleenex for me.

I knew I shouldn't be alone, because I felt incredibly lonely, desperately alone.

"You must live in confession for a while until you are empty enough to receive the Word."[8] I wrote this in my journal later that day. Being empty to receive. Trying to see a path ahead through a sudden downpour of cleansing tears, I could not travel on. I had to sit a while and bare my soul. Gayla was Word with me. I called my therapist. Gayla drove me there and waited.

――――――

Is there a sweet sound in grace? The music of my family's love and their heartfelt encouragement to love myself and forgive myself was surely a blessing. Talking with them the day after was much easier, the heaviness of a secret now divulged. At least for a moment, a spirit of grace had created an atmosphere of pure, honest conversation.

Mom talked with me about the image of the woman at the well and the power of forgiveness. My sister, Nancy, spoke words of strength, bravery, and courage. My body ached with fatigue. I knew grace was near, yet it also seemed so far away.

Every day I felt Leigh Anne's anger and my own discomfort in seeing her angry. It was hard for me to be near her anger. I knew it was justified. I knew it was important for her to express her anger. It had been welling up for some time. The intensity of it was alive in her eyes and in her voice. She was angry about my betrayal. She was angry about my difficulty in making decisions. She was angry about my keeping my secret under wraps, and denying her own voice in the process. Every step I had taken was one she needed to take. I didn't know how to respond, other than to listen, to receive, to let her be angry.

Livid (Joe)

Journal, September 9, 1998

Leigh Anne is livid right now. It's hard to see, but understood. I'm trying not to respond, only listen. I don't know if there's hope. I sense that whatever I do, it will never be enough. Do I want to spend the rest of my life continuing to live under shame? I do feel a victim, not of Leigh Anne's anger, but of shame I'm trying to overcome. Dammit, I'm a good person, a gentle person, a loving person. Do I want to share the rest of my life with Leigh Anne? I honestly don't know. I love my children. I love Leigh Anne. I am anguishing over the direction of my life. I feel totally drained of energy and I'm tired of being tired. I feel as though a cloud is hovering wherever I go. It is an internal cloud I can't seem to shake. It's scary. Leigh Anne wants me to decide, and even though she says she has patience, I don't feel it. I don't blame her. Our families think we should stay together for the children. I think we should be honest and love our children.

Moving out (Joe)

October 3, 1998

All week I wondered how to tell my beautiful six—and four-year-old children that everything they knew about their family, everything that felt safe and loving and reassuring, would change. I wept every time I thought about it. Of all the decisions I ever made in my life, this was the most heart-wrenching.

The day before, I sat down with Emma, Taylor, and Leigh Anne and told them I was moving out of the house. Leigh Anne and I had talked earlier about how to share this with the kids. We wanted to make it as positive as possible, and make sure the kids understood and could ask any questions they wanted to. We knew the conversation would be difficult.

We sat in the family room, close to each other, near the fireplace. I told Emma and Taylor how much I loved them, and that the best way I knew to take care of myself, to heal, and to be loving to Mommy, was to move out. We wouldn't live together anymore. I told them I would be staying with some very good friends who loved me and would take good care of me. We all sobbed. We talked about what was scary. We talked about what hurt. Emma ran to her room, crying. Leigh Anne went to her and found her kneeling by her bed, praying.

We held each other, cried some more, and talked. I felt empty. I felt as though I was abandoning everyone I loved. The only piece of hope that kept me going that night was knowing that if I abandoned embracing who God created me to be, I could never be whole, and my family could never be whole.

We gathered some toys that I would take with me, so that when we were together, away from home, the kids could play with something familiar. They both disappeared into their rooms and brought some toys out to the family room. Emma and Taylor came to me, hands extended, cradling a piggy bank. Emma told me I could put money in it for them. As they extended this precious gift to me, they smiled.

Leaving that night was deeply painful. As I walked out the door to my car, I thought, what have I done?

The weekend he left (Leigh Anne)

I knew I couldn't be in the house when Joe moved out. My sister-in-law Holly invited the kids and me to come over for the weekend and I took her up on it in a heartbeat. I remember very little about the time at Holly's except that the kids and I slept together on the fold-out couch. I wanted to have them close to me and for once, I didn't mind the sharp elbows, knees, and all that breathing. The kids played happily with their cousins and Holly made a chicken artichoke pasta dish for me that I make to this day when I want someone to feel loved.

The first thing I did was create beauty (Leigh Anne)

I did not take the children with me the first night I returned to the house after Joe moved out. I knew that I needed to feel the shock of being in the house without Joe, without Joe's belongings, by myself. I did not want the children to see me if I came unglued, and when they did come in, I wanted to be available to them if *they* came unglued.

The first thing I did was to create beauty. We had a planter by the front door that we had not planted anything in yet, so I bought yellow mums on the way home and the first thing I did, even before I unlocked the back door, was to plant and water those yellow mums.

I went from room to room, opening every window and every door. We had painted the house recently and some of the windows were stuck shut, but I got a piece of two by four and a hammer and opened every one. I was determined.

Next, I lit a candle, held it in both my hands and began to move slowly, deliberately through every room of the house, beginning in the mudroom, moving to the kitchen, living room, office, family room, and bathroom, finally ending in our bedroom. As I walked through each room, I held the candle up in front of me and prayed out loud, "Holy Spirit, this is your house now. Spirit of depression, spirit of anxiety, spirit of deception, you get out of this house! You are not welcome here! You have no place here now!" I prayed each room clean of dark spirits, imagining them as dark shadows seeping out of the windows, and I prayed the light of the Holy Spirit into each space. As I prayed, I asked for angels to guard every window and every door so that the dark spirits would not be allowed to re-enter.

This prayer became harder and harder as I came to the places that Joe inhabited. It was especially hard as I prayed in his bathroom, his side of the closet and over his dresser (I opened every drawer and prayed each one clean). I nearly came undone as I prayed over his side of the bed. I knelt there and prayed for cleansing as I held the candle over the middle of his side of the bed. I knelt on my side of the bed and prayed for healing as I held the candle over the middle of my side. I wept as I prayed. When I began to be afraid that I might set the bedclothes on fire, I placed the candle on my bedside table and turned to lay my head in the seat of the rocking chair that sat beside my bed. It was the chair I had nursed and rocked both our babies in. One that Joe had bought me. At this moment, this chair became a lap for me to collapse in and release the depth of my sorrow over losing Joe, and the devastating loneliness that overwhelmed me.

What happened next, I cannot explain, I simply know it that it happened. My grandparents came. I did not imagine them. They came to stand with me. To love me. To let me know for certain that I was not alone. All four of my late grandparents came in an instant, for an instant, not clearly visible but utterly recognizable, standing side-by-side, just above and beyond the headboard of the bed. I did not need to see them clearly to know that I was loved, that I was not alone, that I could get through this.

I was comforted. I did not need to cry anymore. I got up, dried my face, and went about rearranging things to suit me, including shutting the door to Joe's bathroom, which I never set foot in again until the day the kids and I moved out.

It's time to go (Joe)

The journey from leaving home to coming out began by moving in with friends. I moved my belongings into a garage. Every day was a new adventure in being raw. I lived with my friends for about seven weeks. They created a space for me to be—to sleep, rest, focus on getting acquainted with all of the transitions happening in my life. In the sanctuary of their home, I was able to share my struggles with honesty, deepen my vulnerability, and eat lots of homemade brownies. Comfort food made being comfortable with myself a little easier. And I knew that soon I would need to find a place of my own, to be alone.

As I began to look for a place to live, I did so with a sense of hope and the realization that I was beginning to feel better inside. I didn't feel pushed out or pressured to leave, because my friends wanted me to be ready. Yet, my inner voice said, *it's time to go.* A lot like my mom ushering me out of the car on my first day of college: *Joe, it's time to go.*

It was time to face the reality of my situation. Being alone. I knew I could call Gayla any time. I knew I could call countless other friends. But there is this crazy dance of the mind that says, yes, even though you have friends who truly love you and don't want anything to happen to you, you probably shouldn't call them because you don't want to be a nuisance: blah, blah, blah.

I looked at several apartments. The first was a cool one-bedroom, downtown, a few minutes from work, in a renovated warehouse. Lots of light, space for the kids to stay, and managed by a friend. The rent was reasonable, but the application process got tied up in red tape. I looked next at an apartment close to my friends, a garden-level one-bedroom, freshly painted, with decent light, intimate. The rent was just right.

Little boy (Joe)

From my journal, written in non-dominant left hand,
October 1998

I feel vulnerable
lost in a cavernous space
wondering who I can reach
out to
and who will hold me.

Like the little boy
climbing the huge steps
of the big yellow bus,
I look to see
who is steering
this bus.

Can I trust him?

Suddenly,
I feel sorrow,
aching,
for a young father
who never held his son,
who watched from a distance

waving to him as he is
placed in someone else's
arms,
as he takes his first
steps
into someone else's
embrace,
as he climbs the huge steps
of the big bus
into an unknown driver's
care.

He looks to see
how this driver is
gripping
the wheel,
how this driver will
receive this child,
once a vibrant
presence,
now a distant
apparition.

There is much
distance now
between the silent,
waving father
and his little boy.

The rumor mill (Joe)

Within two weeks of moving out, I began dealing with the rumor mill. A colleague and I met for coffee and she expressed genuine concern for me. She had received a call from a clergy serving a parish I had previously served, who shared with her that people there were asking questions about our situation, the issue of homosexuality, and what friend I was staying with.

I was befuddled.

I was not surprised people were talking. That's what people do. In my own frustration, my first thought was to point a finger at Leigh Anne. We had decided, whenever anyone asked, that we would answer, "we mutually agreed to separate" and that I was staying with friends. Yet, even with our direct response, many began speculating the true reason for our separation.

I was the only one who could tell my story. And Leigh Anne was the only one who could tell her story. We both needed people to tell who would listen. My rational, objective mind knew this. My protective, defensive mind didn't want anyone to know.

I was concerned that whatever was shared, even if it was brief and vague, would mushroom into some large tale. The other complication was that I had decided to leave the church where I had been pastor and look for another church to attend. I had tried to stay on at the church as a participant, rather than pastor, but the boundaries were too easily blurred. The transition from pastor to participant hadn't worked. Leigh Anne was on staff, in a very public ministry, and had financial stresses and enormous responsibility, including the primary care for Emma and Taylor. I was torn. I did everything I could to support her and the children, but was angry about how many people were talking about our situation. At one point, I met Leigh Anne in the parking lot of the church and said, "I need for you to stop talking to others about me." I was trying to communicate a boundary, but it came off sounding selfish.

Through my experience as a pastor, and personally, I learned that human beings don't have a natural inclination to talk directly with each other about conflict or anything troubling. It is easier to talk to others, to commiserate and to seek understanding. Sometimes people just wanted me to know they cared. While I knew that and appreciated it, I wanted them to come to me and ask me. Or go to Leigh Anne and ask her.

In those days, I did a lot of writing with my non-dominant left hand. This practice was recommended by my therapist as an alternate way to enter my mind and let the child in me open up. One of the entries, in a legible scribble, said this:

I feel angry.
I feel like an object
of discussion,
not affection.
I feel sick.
I feel tired.
I need rest.
I just want to sleep
and sleep
and sleep.
I want to be left alone.
I want to be held.
I want to understand.
I want to be understood.

The following day I went to Emma's school to assist her first-grade class. The children were writing letters. One little boy was writing a letter to his brother. He began to write a sentence out of his writing book: *My dad is tall.*

I asked him, "Is your dad tall?"

He answered, "My dad is dead."

Being separated from my children began to hurt even more.

Thrown into work (Joe)

Over the next week, work at Urban Ministry was the calm in the storm, along with additional evenings working at two local, independent bookstores. I would split the week between Watermark Books and Eighth Day Books.

As a long-time customer of Eighth Day Books in Wichita, I had asked the owner if he needed any extra help. We worked out a schedule and I immersed myself in a place I'd come to love.

My first night there I learned how to enter brief descriptions of new and used books in the database. The titles were fascinating, each one a new adventure. I flipped through pages, eager to get a feel for each writer's focus and style. I wondered about each writer's passions unveiled in words. I imagined their different approaches to writing, something similar to the labor in giving birth.

Holding used books, I was intrigued by their previous owners (wondering what led them to this book, imagining their first time holding the book, wondering whether they read it or not and what the experience meant to them, wondering why they let it go), lives intertwined with books. That night, I learned about hinge cracks, broken spines, chips on dust jackets, texts in "fine" or "very good" condition, what qualifies as "rare."

Some books captured my interest, inviting me to go deeper. Others, with a glance and a catalogued description, were placed in a stack, with the recognition that someone out there may be searching for just that book.

Sitting alone among the quiet stacks, my mind would wander to another search I'd begun in my life, for my origins as an adopted child. This search coincided with my search for wholeness as a gay man and I was filled with questions: Was my birth mother out there searching for me? Where could I share my life that she might find me? Would I find who and what I was looking for?

Those days were filled with conversations. Friends checked in. How are you? Is there anything I can do for you? Strangers wanted to help. One man shared the story of his journey through a serious nervous breakdown. A friend from a previous church called to share her concern, her own pain over our separation, and her love for us all that would never change.

All of us were struggling with how to sustain rituals of comfort, when everything was utter chaos. On the nights I went to the house to spend time with the kids, to read stories and sing songs, Emma and Taylor fought going to sleep. They used to go to sleep knowing that we would be there when they woke up. Now going to sleep had become scary. I had trouble sleeping, too.

"Work it out with her," someone challenged me. "Divorce is hell."

So is pretending. I tried the non-dominant hand exercise again.

Left hand:	*Right hand:*
work it out with her.	*work it out with your soul.*
divorce is hell.	*dishonesty is hell.*
I feel torn.	
am I a new creation	
being shaped and sewn	
with new thread?	

Am I torn apart
lying in tatters,
in need of mending?

The fabric has been
torn...
ripped.
The pieces
can never return
to their original design,
yet they now resemble
something new.

Like the pieces of
my chalice
will they always be
"broken"
or
be held
cradled
as new images
of beauty?

Leigh Anne and I were still finding ways to express love to each other. I was preparing to go for a weeklong retreat at Ghost Ranch in Abiquiu, New Mexico. We had discussed going together, but as events unfolded, and as we separated, Leigh Anne opted not to go.

She encouraged me to go. She perceived that the retreat would be significant in my life, bringing much into focus. As with so many of her perceptions, even in her own anguish, she was a prophet for healing.

Embodiment (Joe)

As I prepared for my week in New Mexico, I found one of Chris Glaser's books in a local bookstore. In the preface of *Coming Out to God*, Glaser writes: "When we allow the Lord of the Dance to lead, sexuality becomes responsible and spirituality becomes responsive. Sexuality becomes responsible by becoming centered, and spirituality becomes responsive by becoming embodied."[9]

I was ready for my own incarnation. Word becoming flesh. Flesh becoming word. Sensual, spiritual self. Embodiment.

Having lived with spirituality and sexuality disconnected for so long, their separation had become normal. Living felt like an out of body experience, as though I were looking at my sexual experiences through someone else's eyes. Look at that boy having sex with that man. Oh, that's me. Look at that man having sex with that woman. Oh, that's me. Disembodied.

Going through the motions is not a fair assessment. I didn't understand love with him. I did understand love with her. The love I came to embody, through Leigh Anne's embodiment, was a love centered in Spirit. With everything she had, even in her unknowing, she taught me about loving my true self.

Nearly everything about our marriage was compatible, everything but my deepest longing—to know and be known as my authentic self. While I grappled with separating from Leigh Anne, I began to wonder about how I could mend and heal my inner separation.

The first step came in calling a new therapist and setting up an initial consult. She was my third therapist that year and came highly recommended. After Leigh Anne and I both agreed not to return to the previous marriage and family therapist, I wanted to meet with a therapist who could simply help me embrace my authentic self and celebrate my beloved nature. I was ready to release all the damned shame and guilt. But it's never that easy. Both love to dance around in the mind, wreaking havoc, leaving a trail of debris. I was tired of picking up after them.

The second step I took was connecting with actual, living, "out" gay people. A friend arranged dinner with a male couple who had been in a relationship for years and were happy to listen and guide me. I wrote down some questions I wanted to ask them: When did you know you were gay? What signs and experiences helped you along the way? Did you have support from your families? What experiences were harmful along the way? What was it like for you to come out? How did you tell your families and friends? How have your struggles helped in your own wholeness? How did you meet? What's it like to love a man?

The questions brought relief and restlessness. I wanted everything to move quickly, and had to remind myself that it was all a journey, and many of the steps would be slow and plodding.

After the high pitch of hurricane winds the week before, I now felt closer to the eye. There were moments of calm, but a very clear sense of the storm around me. This was my first sense of what it might be like to live from a still center.

In his book, *Reaching Out,* Henri Nouwen describes it as an invitation "to convert my loneliness into a solitude that can be shared."[10] By entering into the solitude of my own heart and the hearts of others, my racing, restless loneliness gradually turns to calm oneness. Communion.

Moving to the center, or the eye of the storm, and seeking to live from there, opened me to an element of surrender. Initially, surrender felt like life was being taken away bit by bit. Far from giving up or giving in, surrender instead became letting go: letting go of the debris of shame and guilt; letting go of the false separation of spirituality and sexuality; letting go of the voices keeping me from authenticity.

During these discoveries, I had a dream that Leigh Anne and I were in a casual, enjoyable conversation with her mom and dad. Her mom asked me, in light of people's concerns about our sharing a bedroom at the beach, if she should make reservations for one or two bedrooms. I responded with silence. And then, "I don't know."

My subconscious confirmed my conscious reality. Here I am. I don't know. Anxiety emerged any time I thought of others' perceptions. Reducing the power of these perceptions and their paralyzing effect was a difficult exercise.

Ghost Ranch (Joe)

November 1998

> *Ubi caritas et amor*
> *Ubi caritas Deus ibi est.*
> *Where charity and love prevail,*
> *God is there.*

Ghost Ranch is a retreat center in a valley between two red mesas in northwestern New Mexico. The land is enchanting, rugged, a teeming wilderness. When I arrived one late afternoon, an ominous, deep blue sky beckoned me to enter the landscape and rest for a week.

I didn't know what to expect, so was filled with wonder. I was there for an immersion in the writings of Henri Nouwen, led by Chris Glaser, who studied with Nouwen at Yale and who, ironically, is a gay man who has written extensively about the unity of sexuality and spirituality. The writings and spirit of Henri made me feel welcome and Chris made me feel at home.

I checked in, found my room and took a walk. On the path leading from the dining room to the sleeping rooms, I met a stunning man named Chad, with dark brown hair, a swimmer's build, and a sparkling smile. We stopped and introduced ourselves and discovered we were both participating in the retreat. "It's a man," I exclaimed under my breath, remembering Dorothy's thrill at discovering the Tin Man. The retreat was already off to a great start.

When I reached my room, I met another lovely man, Bob, older and wise, his eyes gentle and spirited. We shared some of our stories and he told me of his marriage and his identity as a gay man, showed me a picture of his family and his gay lover, and described the journey he and his wife had made in deciding to acknowledge their differing sexual orientations while staying married.

The retreat hadn't yet begun and I'd already received two significant gifts. Could it get any better?

Twelve people from across the country gathered in a rustic, intimate room, placing symbols of our lives on a long wooden coffee table. Draped down the center of the table was a rainbow cloth. I placed my broken chalice among the objects and wondered what stories would begin to fill the room.

Chris welcomed us and invited us to sing *Ubi Caritas*. We introduced ourselves and shared the stories of our symbols. I spoke of my recent journey in coming out, and moving out. Someone asked why I didn't glue the chalice back together, and I talked about seeing the beauty in the broken pieces.

In every session during the week, we received printed quotes from Nouwen's writings and took turns sharing. On the first night, as though Henri was sitting next to me, gently nudging me, I read these words from *Reaching Out*: "To wait for moments or places where no pain exists, no separation is felt and where all human restlessness has turned into inner peace is waiting for a dream world. No friend or lover, no husband or wife, no community or commune will be able to put to rest our deepest cravings for unity and wholeness."[11]

In this place of solitude, I realized I was entering a journey through loneliness into discovery of my own solitude. I couldn't rely on or require anyone else to make the journey for me. I could, though, travel with these companions for a week, and let the gifts of their lives help me along the way.

As the leader of the retreat, Chris created a sacred and safe space in the room where we met. Soft lamplight shone from four different tables, surrounded by soft leather couches and chairs. In the center of the room was the coffee table we had converted into an altar. Chris also made himself available to talk one-on-one with each of us throughout the week.

Following the first session, I spoke with him and we agreed to meet the next day and go for a hike up to Chimney Rock. We set a slow and steady pace, taking in all the beauty along the way, giving attention to small details, noticing geckos slithering over rocks and into deep crevices, and eventually reaching the top. We sat down, and he invited me to lean back into his embrace. The sacredness of being held was a gift beyond measure. He prayed for me and with me. He held me and I rested in his arms. Our embrace helped me recognize the importance of touch and opened a new door to intimacy. We exchanged a holy kiss, as new-found friends on a faithful journey to authenticity, and sat in silence letting the beauty of the sky warm our souls.

When I returned to my room following our walk, I noticed a book on my pillow. My roommate had given me *The Word is Out: Daily Reflections on the Bible for Lesbians and Gay Men*, which Chris had written. I read some each morning, discovering the liberating power of sacred scriptures shared in a new way.

At the beginning of many of our sessions, Chris introduced us to songs inviting us to open our hearts and minds. Early in the week, we learned new words penned by Holly Whitcomb to the familiar tune for "Morning Has Broken."

I am the glory.
I am the dwelling.
Incarnation,
Body and Soul.
None other like me,
I am precious.
Gift of creation,
Honored and whole.[12]

As the words filled my mind, long after our singing, we shared our personal stories of belovedness. I remembered how many people, including Leigh Anne, had extended love and care through my journey in coming out and how much this meant for the journey ahead.

Later that day, we shared in an exercise of blessing based on affirmations from Nouwen's writings. We were each invited to take turns sitting in a large brown leather chair, the kind you can sink down into and rest. When my turn came, I sat down, then sank in, and extended my legs onto the adjacent ottoman. Everyone stood around me, touching me gently. Each person shared an affirmation of blessing, followed by silence to let the blessing rest on me.

At the close of the blessing experience, I let the stillness hover.

"This is great," I said. "It feels like a womb."

One of my new friends, Sharon, said, "I'm glad it's not mine!"

We burst into laughter. Chris then chimed in and said, "Joe, it's time to be born!" I opened my eyes, and smiling, said, "Welcome home, Mommy."

We explored what it meant to find our sacred center through solitude, community and care and remembered that in vulnerability our convictions can convey our deepest yearnings. Yet, in our deepest yearnings we shouldn't expect another person to give or satisfy our every need. We should instead celebrate the gifts as they arrive in our lives.

This is the spirit in which I welcomed the company and presence of the man I'd met earlier in the week, along the path. While I was hesitant to risk getting too close to anyone I'd likely never see again, I wanted to get to know him. We spent a lot of time together, holding each other, talking and kissing. The gift he gave me that week was a new recognition and acceptance of my own beauty, a feeling of being attractive, and the beginning steps of realizing the beauty in male relationship and intimacy.

Late one afternoon, I approached the labyrinth shaped out of native stone, near the creek below a steep cliff. I entered and slowly walked the winding path, opening to what Spirit and breath might bring my way. As I walked I began to sing the hymn *Sanctuary,* written by Randy Scruggs and John W. Thompson. I sang softly, to not bother the other traveler in the labyrinth.

The words took me back to the moment when my daughter, Emma, came to visit me at my new job in Wichita at the community food warehouse of Urban Ministry.

She was accustomed to seeing me in sanctuaries with pulpits and altars and rails and pews. The day she pulled open the glass door and entered a hall filled with blue plastic chairs and a wooden table with clipboards on top, she ran to me and shouted, "Daddy, where's the sanctuary?" I paused to welcome the full effect of her question, and then realized that the place we were standing *was* sanctuary, just as the rocks on which I was walking and singing at Ghost Ranch were sanctuary, just as my heart was sanctuary.

The weeklong retreat closed with a meditation on Nouwen's book, *Can You Drink the Cup?* Following the three movements

Nouwen writes about, we spent time reflecting on holding, lifting, and drinking the cup. These movements are familiar to Christians in the sacrament of Holy Communion when we symbolically remember Jesus's last meal with his disciples.

On this occasion, Chris asked us to reflect in these ways: "When you hold the cup, look at your life and claim who you are; when you lift the cup, offer a toast to your life and the life you can offer to others; when you drink the cup, take in the whole of your life and anticipate what is yet to be."

In celebration of the moment, I spoke aloud these words for the journey ahead: *Holding the cup, I am a beloved, beautiful child of God; a tender, loving man; a wonderful daddy and a minister of hospitality; lifting the cup in blessing, dance, dance!; drinking the cup, I look forward to a new life filled with honesty, courage, joy, and lots of writing!*

I left Ghost Ranch with a new spirit and hope for the days ahead. I would need it.

You have no idea how right it feels to be with a man (Leigh Anne)

After we were separated, but before we were divorced, Joe sat in the chair in the living room of the house that we had shared. I sat on the couch. He said to me, "You have no idea how right it feels to be with a man."

It was all I could do not to stand up on my couch and scream, "You are damned right, I have no idea how right it feels to be with a man! I have been faithful to you since the day we started dating and you are the only man I have ever known! I have no idea how right it feels to be with a straight man! All I have ever known is what it is to be with a gay man faking straight! I have no idea how right it feels to be with a man and I have you to blame for that."

I have no idea where the self-restraint came from, but I said nothing. I was more certain than ever that we were making the best decision for both of us.

Confidences kept, trust broken (Leigh Anne)

I was surprised when I began to tell the story of our separation to my inner circle of friends, surprised by reactions that helped and those that hurt. One family member was immediately interested in getting Joe involved in Exodus Ministries. I knew that if twelve years of marriage to a straight woman who loved him and whom he loved had not "made him straight" that no amount of prayer or brainwashing would have any effect. Another friend I confided in went home and called her pastor who was a United Methodist colleague of ours. He, of course, called his district superintendent, who then called me. So much for letting Joe be in control of sharing his story with his colleagues. It was a consequence I should have anticipated, but did not. I regretted the day I took her into confidence. Many other friends were wonderful, too wonderful and too numerous to count. They are the ones that got me through.

A barrage of questions (Leigh Anne)

There were two women in our church who seemed to be attracted to me during my time of sadness. In fact, they seemed to be attracted to me because of my sadness.

Sheila, who was about my age and had children about the same age as my children, came to visit me repeatedly in my office at the church. She never called for an appointment; she just barged in with a barrage of questions. One weekday, soon after Joe and I separated, Sheila came into my office at church, obviously upset, and asked me, "How am I supposed to keep my marriage together if you can't?"

When I recovered my ability to speak, I mumbled something like "my marriage is not about you, Sheila," but she was not satisfied. She started asking me why we were separated. I remained silent, honoring Joe's dignity and our privacy. She went away frustrated but it didn't take very many days for her to come back. At least this time when she came through the door, I knew what to expect. This time when she barged in, she demanded answers, "Is he an alcoholic? Did he have an affair?" Still I remained silent. The third time she returned, she exclaimed as she came in through my office door, "He's gay, isn't he?" I remained silent again. "I'm right, aren't I?" No response from me. She read my silence as a "yes." She seemed oddly triumphant that she had figured it out. I wondered if I was on the set of a bad daytime soap opera. I felt like a six-year-old on the playground whose nosy friend found a way to lift up my dress day after day to see what color panties I was wearing.

Marsha, an older woman whose husband sang in my choir, was invasive in her "care" but in a different way. She visited me several times in my office or caught me after services to share in my sorrow. She did not seem to be interested in offering consolation or encouragement at all; she wanted company for her own deep sadness. When she came, she physically sat too close to me, shared too much of her personal story, asked too many probing questions about mine and stayed too long. When she sat down beside me, I felt like she grabbed my hand, jumped down a well and yanked me down into the darkness with her. This deep sharing of sorrow seemed to create a level of intimacy that she needed. It left me feeling claustrophobic, invaded and used up. I was in such a weakened and vulnerable position that I did not have the strength to set a boundary to protect myself from either of these women.

Broken ritual (Joe)

Emma and Taylor loved bath time. From the moment they heard the water running in the tub, clothes came off, and leaping and splashing commenced. These were gleeful times.

Amply soaked, they stepped from the tub into their warm towels. Then pajamas. Then bed. Then stories. We read a lot of stories together and it was amazing to see their level of discovery and involvement increase over the months and years. I watched them shift from points and grunts to recognition of objects with matching words to reading sentences together. With each story, we entered a new world together.

One of our favorite books was a collection of old nursery rhymes. *Hey diddle, the cat and the fiddle, the cow jumped over the moon. The little dog laughed to see such sport*—and about this time Taylor would get so excited I'd turn to him and say, *and the dish ran away with the*—and he would shout— "poon! Again! Again!" And we'd say it again and collapse in a giggling heap.

When we put the books away and turned off the lights, I would continue another nightly ritual: spinning tales of a special underwater creature called the Purple Beet Juice Fish, inspired mostly from my imagination and my dad's dislike of beets. This fish lived deep in the sea in a world of underwater kings, queens, princes, and princesses. Emma and Taylor became characters in the plot I created as I told the story and every night was a new adventure.

Regardless of the characters or interesting twists in the tale, the story always culminated with the Purple Beet Juice Fish leaping out of the water and giving an unsuspecting character a surprise, slobbery, raspberry zerbert. Again. And again.

Then we would sing: *Skidamarink a dink a dink, skidamarink a doo, I love you. Hush, little Emma, don't say a word, Daddy's going to buy you a mockingbird. Hush, little*

Taylor, don't say a word. You are my sunshine, my only sunshine. As we wound our way closer to sleep, and especially on the nights we read Robert Munsch's *Love You Forever*, I created a tune for the oft-repeated refrain:

I love you forever,
I'll like you for always,
As long as I'm living,
My Taylor/Emma you'll be.[13]

Then hugs and kisses and "Daddy don't leave." Emma always fell asleep as soon as her head touched the pillow. Taylor chattered on until there was silence. His imagination and words carried him into dreamland.

Everything changed the night I told them I was moving out. The ritual was broken. I tried to be there as many nights as I could. Leigh Anne knew this was important. I also knew that our life as a family was changing and there had to be some space for this to happen.

I spent a lot of time wondering how to create new rituals in the face of trauma, especially for my children. The night I moved out, Emma went right to her room, knelt down by her bed, put her hands together and prayed. This is what we had taught her to do, to take her heart to God's heart, the One who loves more deeply than even her parents. She prayed and she cried.

I don't know what she prayed about. I can imagine. I prayed that she and Taylor would be okay. That all of us would heal. That someday the hurt would soften and happiness would return. That ritual would return in new ways, in new stories and new songs. That a Purple Beet Juice Fish would jump out of the water and surprise and splash us all and make us laugh.

Light in here (Joe)

Shortly after I moved out of my friends' home and into an apartment of my own, Emma and Taylor came to spend the night. The apartment was described as garden level, which meant that the windows were at sidewalk level and everything else was underground. Looking back, I'm certain my deep depression determined my choice of where to live.

Before going to bed that night, I closed all the drapes on the windows, partly out of a desire for privacy, and, subconsciously, to keep the apartment dark. We all cuddled in bed together, reading stories and singing songs, until I turned off the light and we fell asleep.

The next morning, Emma awakened cheerful, happy and ready for a new day. She went into the living room, climbed up on a chair near the window, grabbed the drapes and flung them open. "Daddy, we need some light in here!"

October therapy (Joe)

My journal is opened to an undated entry—notes about being adopted, climbing onto a school bus at age five carrying a big airplane, breaking tradition and expectations in family systems and church systems, and going against the flow of who I am.

These packed notes are from a session with my new therapist. She's the third in a year. Each one has helped along the way. The first, a woman, listened as I named my struggle and began loving myself. The second, a man, helped me struggle with identity, orientation, and whether or not I could be authentic and stay in my marriage. With the first, I spoke truth: I struggle with homosexuality. With the second, I spoke more truth: I'm more attracted to men.

The third therapist is challenging me to look at my earliest moments of life. She's helping me understand the experience of being adopted, how natural feelings of abandonment may have shaped my life, and why I chose to go into ministry.

I wondered, if I have abandonment issues, how are they being re-opened as I leave my family to be who I am? Do abandonment and authenticity go together? How do I explore the nature of my inner sexual orientation in relation to my call to ministry? How do I bring into focus a very personal, private reality with a very public, often judgmental, vocation?

Call to ministry (Joe)

January 1981

I was a freshman at Southwestern College in Winfield, Kansas, and had recently taken a job as a youth director at a small, rural United Methodist church. On a January night, I was sitting in the sanctuary, listening to the district superintendent lead the annual church conference, and I experienced a moment of intense, inward focus. It was as though every part of my being was dwelling in my heart, and I received a message: "I want you to be a pastor in a church."

Everything was beautifully clear. Prior to that moment, I didn't have a clue what I was doing or where I was headed. During my senior year in high school, Dad asked what I planned to do with my life. It was his gentle way of kicking me in the ass—*you need to think about it, Joe.*

I chose Southwestern because my parents attended there. They met there in chemistry class in 1954. I also chose Southwestern because it was a well-respected United Methodist liberal arts school, and I was a good United Methodist boy. I enrolled and set my sights on a double major in vocal performance and accounting. Being an accountant would pay the bills and singing would keep my soul alive.

I loved numbers. In sixth grade, we had addition competitions between the classes, writing out long rows of numbers, then seeing who could add them the fastest. I was the champ. In junior high, I loved drafting, and learned different ways of writing numbers. On the side, I created all sorts of number games with a deck of cards. I would spend hours immersing myself in these games, designing chart after chart of numbers. In high school, I took an accounting class and excelled.

But when I arrived at college, I felt lost. My nest had changed. I went from having my own room to sharing a room. Mom and Dad did everything they could to make the transition easier. Mom and I picked out a bedspread and linens, and she even designed a matching carpet to go between my bed and the desk. They helped me unload and set up my room, and we went to lunch. That first day I tried everything I could to extend their stay. Finally, Dad pulled up in front of the student union and parked. From the back seat, Mom said, "Joe, it's time to go."

I went forth, with much reluctance. Everything was out of sync: my body, my focus, my sexuality, my spirit.

As the first semester rolled on, I needed some extra money, so I started looking for a job. I found a posting on the library bulletin board for a youth director at a small, rural church near Winfield. The posting listed the school's librarian as the contact. I went to the library and talked with him.

He introduced me to the pastor, who then introduced me to the pastor-parish committee. They interviewed me and hired me to work two Sundays a month, creating and leading a youth program. I loved the job and it seemed like a natural fit. After all, I grew up in a church, was involved in youth fellowship, was a leader in the church, preached, and loved serving on church committees.

So, sitting in that pew in the back of the church and feeling my heart leap with the promise of a future direction, I was ready to go. I switched advisors and majors. Southwestern didn't have a degree in religion, so I majored in philosophy. I worked in as many United Methodist churches in Winfield and Wichita as I could. I learned from many pastors and Christian educators. I deepened my love for God, and for the church, and was approved for candidacy in ministry by my home church.

My struggle with sexuality continued to create an undertow, but I did everything I could to set it aside and focus on my goal of becoming a pastor. I finished college in three years, packed my little Toyota Corolla to the gills, and drove to Dallas, Texas to begin seminary at Perkins School of Theology. Four years of seminary and I would be back in Kansas serving as a pastor. That was the calling and the mission.

God called me. Why would I question the call? I didn't conceive of a moment when, like Samuel, I wondered who was calling me or what the direction of the call meant. The direction seemed very clear and I never considered the possibility that I had misinterpreted its meaning.

Sometime in the heat of re-examining my call into ministry, I had a conversation with Todd, who had been my roommate for a year and a half in college. He remembered a conversation we once had about my entering ministry. "Are you doing this to get away from your sexuality?" he had asked. "Yes," I answered.

I had tucked that conversation far, far away, hoping to never revisit it. In part, I could just imagine the ordination interviews: "So, Joe, why are you entering the ministry?"

"To be honest, it's the best way I know to escape my sexuality."

As I shared some of these insights with my therapist, she posed some additional questions: why would you choose to go into such a highly charged, judgmental atmosphere to run from yourself? Are you running against the flow of yourself? Then I wondered, having been active in ministry for eighteen years, had the ministry been a "running away from" or a "coming home to" the person God created me to be?

The tidy package I created of my life was ripped open. Everything was thrown out. I could go around and pick up the pieces, but everything was different. Everything was new. My friend, Ann, reminded me of this when I left the United Methodist ordained ministry in 2001. "Joe, you'll always be a minister. Even if you're a brick layer, you'll be a minister."

The legal document (Leigh Anne)

I felt I had to take the initiative to file for divorce. Joe was in a terribly passive mode. He would not do it. He would wait for me. I would have to do it and pay for it if I wanted to have it completed. I did not like taking the initiative. I felt it was cowardly on Joe's part not to take the lead. I wondered if he was waiting for me to file for divorce so he could blame me— "my wife divorced me," a passive stance, the victim mode.

I hated every bit of the process. I hated calling an attorney friend in the church to get recommendations for divorce lawyers. I hated the phone calls, the visits to the divorce attorney's office, the envelopes that held the official documents, the crushing feeling in my chest, and the tears as I read the draft of the legal document that would end our marriage. I hated the bills from the attorney.

On May 19 we signed the document that ended our marriage. Two days before my birthday. A fitting present: liberty. One that I gave myself.

Late to church (Leigh Anne)

It was an unbelievably busy time. On Sunday, December 20, 1998, the Cobb family would gather for our family Christmas celebration. On December 21, all of the choirs I directed would participate in a huge Christmas celebration during worship at church. That afternoon, the children and I would board a plane, without Joe, to travel to Virginia to celebrate Christmas with my family. As a beautiful kindness, our pastor had offered me Christmas Eve off and I was looking forward to a week of vacation and rest at home.

Saturday was a crazy jumble of packing suitcases, wrapping gifts, cooking for the family Christmas dinner, preparing to endure the awkwardness of the first family gathering after our separation, leaving the children with Joe and going to church to prepare for Christmas worship the next day. When I went to bed Saturday night, I had accomplished everything I needed to do that day, including laying out my clothes for Sunday morning.

I accomplished all but one thing. I failed to set my alarm. Since I was exhausted, I slept very well that night. I didn't have my all-too-common work-anxiety dream of showing up late, moving in slow motion as I followed the choir at a great distance down the center aisle, music floating out of control onto the floor and my half-on, half-off robe flapping in the breeze as I raced after them.

This Sunday the dream was reality. The phone woke me up. "Leigh Anne, are you coming?" asked my senior pastor.

"Shit." I could count on one hand the number of times I had used that word in my life at that point. I could not believe that I said it to my senior pastor at 8:00 a.m. on December 21. "I'll be there in 20 minutes."

I got ready in no time flat, drank a glass of water on my way out the door, and arrived at church during the prelude music played by the youth handbell choir. My colleague Scott met me in the hall with my robe and baton and gave me a big smile as I walked into the service, taking over from a generous volunteer who had stepped up to direct the youth in my absence. We stopped, started again and the service went forward without a single hitch. After the service was over, I apologized to the choirs and was able to laugh at myself as I told them about oversleeping. They were loving and forgiving and we repeated the service for a live television audience later that morning.

Home for Christmas (Leigh Anne)

This was only the beginning of an amazing Christmas for me.

When I came home to Virginia, I found time to be alone and pray on Christmas Eve. Everyone in the family was busy so I had two uninterrupted hours of contemplation in my favorite chair in the living room. It was a perfect day. Snow was falling gently enough that I could see the mountain through the curtain of white. There was a fire in the fireplace, the Dale Warland Singers' Christmas concert was on the radio and I was sitting in the swivel rocker in my parents' living room. I felt comfortable and comforted.

I sat there with a map of Virginia open in my lap, talking with God.

There is only one thing I know right now, God. I want to come home. I need to come home. I can't stay in Kansas. I want to come to Virginia, but where do I go? I have to have a job. I can't just come home without a job. I will not live with my parents, not at this age and not with two kids. What kind of job could I have? My resumé only says one thing—church music. I don't have any idea how to find out about church jobs in Virginia. Who do I know who would know? How do I find out where church music jobs are posted in Virginia?

I looked at the map and my eyes focused immediately on my small hometown. Then my eyes moved to the left and I saw Blacksburg, a university town about twenty-five minutes from my childhood home. I remembered a lovely medium-sized church that I had visited there and I said to myself, "That's too good to be true. Besides, I have never known them to have a full-time position in music." I looked at Norfolk, Richmond, Washington, D.C., and Winchester, thinking that I'd have to look in a large urban area to find a church large enough to hire a full-time musician. I gave in to the idea I would end up several hours' drive from my parents, consoling myself with the thought that I'd be close enough to drive home in a day. Better than being halfway across the continent. Just the right distance from my sorrow, I thought.

I sat quietly crying for the devastating beauty I saw and the disorientation I felt that day. As I sat, too tired to cry anymore, I suddenly remembered my friend Rev. Barry Whitcomb, who was a campus minister at the university in Blacksburg. I had known him since I was a teenager. He had directed a choir for years. Surely he knew prospects for church music jobs in Virginia, or would know the right person for me to talk to. I stood up from my prayer chair and gave him a call. It was Christmas Eve and he wasn't home so I left a message on his answering machine. I let it go after that, determined not to worry about the outcome, and enjoyed the peacefulness and rest of the holidays with my parents and extended family.

A week later, on New Year's Eve, I got a call from Barry. I picked up the phone.

"Leigh Anne, I thought you were calling about the University United Methodist Church job."

My jaw nearly hit the floor.

"What University UMC job?"

He went on to tell me that University United Methodist Church in Blacksburg had created, for the first time in its history, a full-time minister of music position, that the job was currently posted in all the professional journals and that they were accepting applications until February 1. Barry gave me the name of the search committee chair and encouraged me to talk with her.

On New Year's Day, I called Hannah Brown and talked with her for an hour and a half. She was lovely and we had an almost instant ease. When I hung up the phone, I had a deep intuitive sense that God had made a way for me to come home and have a job too. I just needed to convince the folks at University that I was the person they wanted to hire.

I got back to work on my resumé and a video of my conducting as soon as I got back to Kansas. I was fortunate to have the resources that I needed right at my fingertips. At Crown United Methodist Church in Wichita, we were televised live every Sunday so finding tape of my conducting was no chore at all. I simply needed to get in the studio and tape an introduction. Peter, the producer from the local TV station, was a wonderful help in this process. Linda, the assistant to our senior pastor, was a consummate professional who had given up a six-figure salary in corporate life to serve God, and had also been through a divorce when her children were young. She understood my position and the importance of this next step, took me under her wing and helped me prepare the very best possible resumé and cover letter. I am forever indebted to these loving people for their help.

While I was in Virginia over Christmas, Steve Rogers, the father of two of my youth choir singers, an alumnus of the youth choir and a dependable choir tour chaperone, wrote an astounding prayer for me. While Steve was attending worship at Crown United Methodist in Wichita on December 27, the Sunday between my prayer and my call with Hannah at University United Methodist, he had a deep sense that I would be leaving. He wrote down this prayer for me and gave it to me when I returned to Kansas early in January. His prayer became my daily prayer, portions of it in the form of breath prayers (breathing in a phrase, then breathing out a phrase), not just for a day, a week, or a month, but for years.

I pray for you a strengthening prayer,
one that you will feel rumbling in your toes!
I pray for you a holding prayer,
one that will wrap your innermost worries and fears.

I pray for you a singing prayer,
one that will run through your heart
and pour out songs of Living Water.

I pray for you a healing prayer,
one that will bring breathtaking hope and embrace all of
your tears.

I pray for you an encouraging prayer,
one that renews your walk and brings you purpose.

I pray for you a laughing prayer,
one that sparks your joy and explodes your spirit.

I pray for you an unending prayer,
one that is ceaseless in its need to uplift and sustain you.

I pray for you the Presence of Christ,
a friend and intercessor that never leaves,
a grace and love that never ends.

I pray for you a strengthening prayer,
one that rumbles clear to your toes!
to set you free to run the race ahead:
Feel! See! Taste! Hear! Know! Embrace!
the Eagle's leap
and the breath of wind
that has come to lift you up,
to remind you,
in a whisper and a smile,
who and whose you are.
In our prayers lie all the hopes and dreams of Heaven,
breathing to be born.

I pray for you,
a strengthening prayer,
that another will enjoy the miracle that is you.

Mr. Steve
"A Prayer for All and Each"

For the first three weeks of the new year, I worked on my application materials. I sent my resumé, my video, and my cover letter before the February 1 deadline and waited, worried sick about how it would be for the children to make this enormous move to Virginia. Hadn't they moved enough? Hadn't they been through enough transition? How hard would it be for them to live so far from their dad, their cousins, with whom they had spent so much of their time? How hard would it be to start all over again in a new town? A new church? A new school?

I was desperate with worry for them because I knew at the core of my being that the move would be right for me. I had a deep sense of sorrow for the pain it would cause them and a growing sense of assurance that this was the right thing for me to do. For the first time in my life, I understood the meaning of the phrase, "If Mamma ain't happy, ain't nobody happy." In other words, it began to dawn on me that if I took care of myself first, I'd be better able to take care of them. I cried over it, sitting on the fence between the pain it would cause them and the opportunity for healing that it would offer me.

I let go and let God have the application process, the kids' emotional transition, and my emotional work for them. I began to trust that whatever happened, Jesus Christ would embrace us all and we'd be able to make it through.

The application process moved rapidly. I had a phone interview on a Sunday afternoon late in winter and was invited to come to Virginia for an interview and audition scheduled during our spring break. I was told that the committee would make a decision in May and that I could expect a call after the top three candidates had made their visits, so I was surprised and overjoyed when Hannah called the Monday of Easter week in April 1999, to offer me the job. They had decided not to interview the other top candidates until they had offered it to me first. I literally danced for joy, all over the house. I whooped and hollered and danced from room to room, thanking God for making a way for me to come home to the love of my family and my Virginia mountains, to breathe fresh air and put my life back together again.

We celebrated Easter at the end of that week and it meant more to me than it ever had in my life. Though I would never compare my sorrow with Christ's suffering and death, I had experienced such a period of loss and dying with the end of my marriage that this new possibility truly felt like new life to me. I had a new understanding of resurrection and salvation because I had been saved from the sorrow of my life. Now I had a hope and a future. And I was going home.

Magnolia (Leigh Anne)

The huge magnolia in my parents' yard
must be as old as I am.
We've grown up together, she and I.

I have always admired her waxy, strong leaves
that stay green throughout the winter,
the intoxicating scent of her enormous white blossoms
and her abundant offering of them.

One winter her crest was broken off by ice.
That same winter, I was broken by divorce.
She stood as sentinel to survival for me that year.
I kept her image in my mind to give me strength.

The following summer she welcomed me home.
Although disfigured by her loss,
she stood strong, sensuous, dignified,
her inner beauty bursting forth,
profusely blossoming,
reminding me that my summer too, would come.

The fence (Leigh Anne)

After I applied for the job in Virginia, I began to have second thoughts about taking it. I was so depleted, emotionally and physically, that I didn't see how I would I have the energy to pack up our house and move our belongings halfway across the country. I felt overwhelmed by the thought of selling and buying a house. I cried every day; tears mostly of grief and fear for my children. It seemed like we had just gotten settled in this house. How could I move them again? How could I take them away from family, and make them change schools on top of all the other changes? How could I support the children through all these changes when I barely had enough emotional or physical energy to make the changes myself? Somewhere beneath the fear and grief, I knew that if I took care of myself, things would be all right for them eventually, but that thought was not enough to quell my fear and grief.

I was sure that I needed to go home. I needed to climb into the cradle that had rocked me to knit my life and my heart back together. I had to have a better-paying job. With rent taking half of my paycheck and little help from Joe at the time, I knew I had to earn more or downsize our living expenses in a big way.

So each day I cried. One exhausted Saturday afternoon when the children were with Joe, I lay down to rest, tears still wet on my cheeks. In my sleep, or in a waking vision, I'm not sure which, I dreamed that I sat alone, on a wooden fence, with my head in my hands, sobbing.

The setting of my dream was a place I remembered well. My dad and brothers and I had worked together to build this fence the summer I was ten years old. I had carried lemonade up and down the hill to the men as they dug holes for the fence posts by hand and hammered the boards into place. Later I would paint this fence, first with white paint, years later with black. The summer of my sixteenth year, I had stood alone at this wooden fence that bisected the acre of my parents' well-tended, sloping front yard and our neighbor's cow pasture. Standing with my face toward the west on a warm summer evening, surrounded by the green of grass and trees, the blue of distant mountains, breathing the scent of freshly cut grass and pungent pasture, listening to the song of crickets and birds, I watched the sunset paint the clouds shades of golden yellow that changed to pink and blue outlined in brilliant red-orange, until the sun sank behind the mountain and the colors faded into the deep blue of night. As I watched the changing canvas that God was painting right before my eyes, I joined my voice with the voices of nature all around me and made up songs of praise to God for the beauty of God's creation. The place itself felt holy. I sensed God's presence there.

In my dream, I sat on that same fence, in the same spot that I had felt God's presence so near to me in my youth, with my head in my hands, sobbing. I lifted my head from my hands and I saw Jesus in front of me, kneeling on the grass with his arms reaching up to me. We held each other's gaze. He said, in a voice I could hear with my heart and my ears, "When are you going to get off that fence and trust me?" His face was expectant and his question was gentle, without judgment.

In the next scene, I was standing in front of Jesus with Emma and Taylor on either side of me. Jesus, still kneeling in front of us, reached out and gathered all three of us in his arms. When I woke up from that dream, I stopped crying, I stopped grieving, I stopped being afraid. I knew I could trust Jesus to care for me and my children. I was not afraid again.

Too much help (Leigh Anne)

In the winter of 1998, after Joe began his official leave of absence from his job at church, we were both vulnerable. He was depressed and not able to work. I was overwhelmed and doing the best I could to deal with my own emotional turmoil, my work, the children, and our family life. I was attempting to make our home life and the upcoming holidays as peaceful and predictable as possible for the children.

135

We knew that we would not be able to stay in our house for long, since it was provided as a benefit of Joe's work at the church. His leave of absence status would end in June and after that he would need to look for a job. We did not know if that job would be in ministry or if he would need to start something new. We had no idea what he would do for a job, what we would do for housing or how we would pay for it. The church allowed us to live in the parsonage for six more months while Joe was on leave of absence and we were in transition. We had not saved enough money for a down payment for a house because we had lived in parsonages all of our married life. Joe's salary was on the low end of the clergy pay scale and we intended to be in ministry for another thirty years. We had plenty of time to think about saving for a house of our own later. Or so we thought.

A generous group of people from the church then did an amazing thing. Headed up by Sam Neighbors, one hundred people each gave one hundred dollars to us so that we could make a $10,000 down payment on a house. I was overwhelmed by the generosity of the gift and extremely thankful for it, but receiving this money never felt honest or completely right to me. At the same time, I didn't think we could or should refuse it. I was so conflicted over it that I never could bring myself to look at the list of names of people who were so generous to us. I wondered if they would have been so generous if they had known the whole truth. I knew the truth but had no liberty to tell it, which left me feeling trapped and ashamed. Joe kept the list of names and I let him write the thank-you notes to everyone. I never knew if he finished. I didn't ask. Sam suggested that we host dinner parties at the house for all the donors who contributed, to thank them for helping us buy it. Under different circumstances, I would have loved to have done that. I never had the words to explain to him that we barely had enough emotional energy to survive, much less entertain people in our home. I never had the words to say that it was too hard for me to know the truth of Joe's situation and be in close conversation with people and not be able to speak about it.

During that vulnerable transition time for our family, Sam went the extra mile to help us. He had lots of connections. He had an elderly client who had died and he made arrangements for us to buy both his house and his car at a good price, solving two very big problems at the same time.

I could not articulate it at the time, but I was uneasy about how much Sam was doing for our family. It seemed to me that he was "over-functioning," which enabled us to continue our "under-functioning." He was playing the role of rescuer opposite our role of damsel-in-distress. I did not want to be rescued. I wanted Joe to step up and take care of our family. Joe was not able to take care of us and neither was I. The vacuum of leadership continued to attract Sam, and Joe and I both continued to be needy.

This imbalance in our relationship righted itself a year later as I became stronger and began to make arrangements to move to Virginia. After I had accepted the job in Blacksburg, Sam offered to help us sell the house that he had helped us buy a year earlier. Instead, I asked another friend, Elizabeth, a realtor with whom I had worked closely in the church. While giving me ample support and expert guidance, she expected me to make my own decisions and did not do for me what I could do for myself. When Sam found out I had contracted to sell the house with someone else, he visited me in my office at church. His final words to me as he exited my office were words of admonishment, "You *take* help when it is offered." The words did not bother me as much as the smack he gave me on the derrière with the notebook that he was holding in his hand.

"Yes," I thought to myself, "Elizabeth was the best choice for me."

Our family's story (Leigh Anne)
January 15, 1999

As I lay down to take an afternoon nap, I fell asleep asking God to help me talk to our children about our decision to divorce. I woke up with this story fully formed in my mind. I jotted it down in a little notebook as fast as I could, afraid I would forget it. I read it to them the day Joe and I told them about our decision to divorce.

To Emma
To Taylor
January 15, 1999
Leigh Anne Taylor

Most of the time, little boys grow up and want to be with women.
Most of the time, little girls grow up and want to be with men.
They get married and have children and live together until they are old.
These women and men are called heterosexual.

Some of the time, little boys grow up and want to be with men.
Men who want to be with other men are called gay or homosexual.
Some of the time, little girls grow up and want to be with women.
Women who want to be with other women are called lesbian or homosexual.

When Daddy was a little boy, he knew that when he grew up, he wanted to be with men.
But he didn't know anyone who was homosexual.
He felt different. He felt afraid.
He thought his mommy and daddy would not love him if he were different, if he were homosexual.
So he hid all of his thoughts about being with a man down deep in his heart.
He thought if he didn't think about them, they would go away.

They did not go away.
They made a broken place in Daddy's heart that has never gone away.

Daddy wanted his mommy and daddy to be happy.
So he went to elementary school, to middle school, to high school and to college.
He was a good student and he made his parents proud and happy!
Daddy was happy too, except for the broken place in his heart.

When Daddy was in college, Daddy decided to become a minister.
This made Daddy happy.
It made his parents happy and all of Daddy's friends happy.
Daddy was so happy he could almost forget the broken place in his heart.

When Daddy was in graduate school, he met Mommy.
Daddy loved Mommy.

Mommy loved Daddy.
They decided to get married.
They did!

A few years later, God gave Mommy and Daddy a daughter named Emma.
Then, God gave Mommy and Daddy a son named Taylor.
Mommy and Daddy and Emma and Taylor were happy, for a while.

But, the broken place in Daddy's heart kept getting bigger and bigger.
It made Daddy feel very sad.
Daddy had to give up his job.
Daddy had to go to the doctor who helps heal the broken places in our hearts.
Daddy finally realized that the broken place in his heart was because he had been hiding his thoughts and fears about being homosexual down deep in his heart.
He finally realized that he had to talk about it so he could feel better.
He told the doctor the truth.
He told Mommy the truth.
Now Daddy wants you to know the truth.

Now that Daddy knows the truth about himself, he knows that he can't be a good husband to Mommy.
Now that Mommy knows that Daddy is homosexual, she knows that she can't be a good partner to Daddy.
Mommy and Daddy are both very sad because now they know that they cannot stay married.

They are both very sad because they know that it will make Emma and Taylor very sad to have parents who are divorced.
Mommy and Daddy believe that getting divorced is the kindest thing that they can do for each other and for our family.

Does Daddy still love Emma? YES!

Does Daddy still love Taylor? YES!

Does Mommy still love Emma? YES!

Does Mommy still love Taylor? YES!

Can children get divorced from their parents? NO! NEVER!

Mommy and Daddy will always love Emma and Taylor, no matter what.
But they will never all live in the same house again.

Do you feel like you are the only boy or girl whose parents got divorced because their dad realized he was homosexual?

How does that make you feel?

Do you have a broken place in your heart?

Do you wish you could talk to a doctor who helps heal the broken places in your heart?

What do you want to say to Daddy?

What do you want to say to Mommy?

What does Mommy want to say to Emma and Taylor?

What does Daddy want to say to Emma and Taylor?

What does God say to us all?

I love you.
I created you.
I will never leave you.
When you are sad, pray to me.
When you are angry, pray to me.
I love you just the way you are,
married or divorced,
homosexual or heterosexual,
young or old,
mad or sad.
I love you.
I will help you through the pain of divorce.
I will help you make a new start.
Depend on me.
Trust me.
Tell the truth.
I am with you.
Love,
God

What do you want to say to God?

Daddy is gay (Joe)

"Why don't you live with Emma and Taylor?" my six-year-old nephew Gus asked into the space of my car. "Because Daddy and Mommy are getting a divorce," six-year-old Emma answered for me.

"Why?" asked Gus.

"'Cause Daddy is gay," answered Emma.

"What does that mean? Is he going to have another girlfriend?" Gus asked.

"No," answered Emma. "He needs to be with a boy the rest of his life."

A prayer for Leigh Anne (Leigh Anne)

My friend and colleague Micki sent me this prayer at just the right time. She told me that she had been inspired to pray this for me while seated on an airplane and felt compelled to send it to me upon her return. I read it, memorized it and prayed it many times in the months and years ahead. I drew great strength from praying this prayer.

Leigh Anne,
You are enrobed
with the brilliant light of God in Christ.

You are a strong woman of God—
a woman of hope,
a woman of wisdom,
a woman of power,
a woman of passion.

God has created you good, whole,
beautiful and strong.

The light of Christ is your guide and your shield

And, through the power of the Holy Spirit,
you are sustained and upheld for the Journey.

Peace

Unavailable (Joe)

We met during a Walk to Emmaus. He was tall, with brown hair, brown eyes, and a bright smile. His name was David. He carried a lot with him.

I was the new associate pastor at the church he attended. David was married and had three young children.

I don't remember who called whom. We met for lunch at Chili's, with no attraction other than an idea that we could learn a lot from each other and become good friends. Over lunch we talked about family, about hopes for the church, about my work with young adults. The conversation took lots of twists and turns, eventually shifting to social issues, and revealing strong opinions about certain topics. I don't remember who brought up the topic of homosexuality and the church's stand, but I know we both agreed it was time the church welcomed all people, regardless of orientation.

As a general rule, especially as a new pastor getting acquainted with members of the church, it was not my general custom to discuss the church and homosexuality. However, our conversation was easy, as though we had been friends for ages.

I rarely developed close friendships with men. It was not for lack of interest. Sometimes I found it difficult to move beyond my attraction for men into the idea of sharing the intimacy of a caring friendship. I also wanted a friend I could be completely open and honest with, someone who would listen and let me step outside of my pastor persona.

This burgeoning friendship grew. We went to lunch together, caught an occasional movie, and always talked about ways we could support each other. When I entered the darkness and depression knocked me out, I turned inward; so deeply that I didn't want to see anyone or talk about what I was facing.

David didn't ask questions. He just showed up. To see if I was okay. To ask if I needed anything. To check on me. There were no trappings, no hidden motives, no long-term desires, no passionate attempts to take me away and seduce me.

He was my friend, my best friend. It took me a year to share my struggle of sexual identity with him and utter the word that came up in our first conversation. He listened and embraced me. Then, one day, he told me, matter of factly, "I know something about the journey you are on."

I was silent.

One morning, months after this conversation, I called him to see how he was. We both wanted to talk, so he came over to my apartment. He was happy to see that I was feeling better, and noticed my smile had returned.

David and his wife, Sarah, had helped us paint the house we moved into after I took a voluntary leave of absence from the church. He had helped me move the two times it took to get into my first apartment.

On this day, after talking for a while, I went to the kitchen to get a drink of water. I was leaning against the sink. He was standing across from me and reached over to me and took me into a hug. When we separated he kissed me.

We stayed in the embrace and touched each others' bodies, briefly, then stopped in fear: I, who had been practicing setting boundaries, and he who was deep in his own struggle with being gay and married.

He left to go home. I went to visit Leigh Anne and see the kids. I shared with her some of what had happened. I told her I thought I was in love.

She listened gracefully. Then the phone rang. It was David and his wife. They told her I seduced him.

A series of events at the table, Part 2 (Leigh Anne)

Joe was the first one to tell me about kissing David.

We were separated and I had filed for divorce. He was living on his own and we were settled into our groove of trading children back and forth for visits. He was living in a new apartment, working at a new job and getting on with his life as a gay man in a limited circle of family and friends. I was getting on with mine. I had applied for the job in Virginia and was charting a new course for my future.

Joe came to the house one afternoon in the spring to drop off the children and he took his usual place in the brown rocker across the living room from where I sat on the couch, for the conversation that we typically had after the kids visited him. He told me about how helpful David had been when he moved into his new apartment, how they had talked about their friendship, and how they had kissed each other while he was there. He seemed surprised and pleased by the encounter. I couldn't stop thinking how weird it was to hear him talk about kissing a man, much less a mutual friend who was married to a woman.

We had known David and his family since the week we moved to town. They had brought us a meal of homemade lasagna and brownies the week we moved into the parsonage and we had enjoyed their company ever since. Their children were about the same age as our children and we enjoyed spending time together as families eating pizza and watching movies. I had always admired the thoughtful contributions David made to the discussions in our young adult Sunday School class and we had enjoyed going out to dinner together as couples.

I was utterly confused that these two men were attracted to each other and I wondered if they had been secret admirers during our social times together before Joe and I separated. I had to address my own inclination toward feeling betrayed. "I have no right to feel betrayed," I told myself. "We are nearly divorced. I will have to get used to the idea of Joe being in a relationship with another man."

What I said out loud was, "It's too hard for me to hear about this right now Joe, especially with David. You'll need to confide in someone else about your relationships with men."

David was the second one to tell me about it. He sat in the same brown rocker as he confided in me about kissing Joe and what it had meant to him. I had a deep sense of compassion for him as he described the pain and struggle of his long years repressing his homosexuality. I had an idea of the challenge that was ahead of him, since I had observed Joe's struggle. I wished him well.

Sarah was the third and last one to talk to me about it. She invited me out to dinner and asked me a lot of questions about how I had handled Joe's coming out. She was hurt and angry. I felt a deep sense of compassion for her as well. I was only a few steps ahead of her on my own challenging journey and I understood her pain intimately.

I couldn't help but think how bizarre it was for all three of these people to seek me out to tell me their version of the story. I was too wounded to be much good to anyone and I knew that I could not continue to listen to the details of their story. The thousand-plus miles from Kansas to Virginia looked more and more like just the right amount of distance between me and my soon-to-be-former marriage.

The next and only place I encountered David and Sarah before I moved to Virginia was at the communion table in the sanctuary at Crown United Methodist. On Friday of the week that I was offered the job in Virginia, Pastor Nancy asked me to stand beside her and help her serve Holy Communion at our Good Friday worship service. It was the last time I would serve communion there before I moved to Virginia. Again and again, I repeated the words that I had heard all of my life to the people who came forward: "This is the blood of Christ poured out for you and for many, for the forgiveness of sins."

About halfway through the service, I saw David and Sarah and their three children get up and take their place in the line to receive communion. My knees began to shake so that I could barely stand up as questions shouted inside my head. *Can I say, "This is the blood of Christ, poured out for you for the forgiveness of sins," to David, and mean it? Does Christ's forgiveness cover this? Will the words come out of my mouth?*

My mouth completely dried up and a lump the size of Texas grew in my throat as David and Sarah approached. I told myself that this sacrament was not about me or my knowledge of this couple, or my connection with what was going on in their marriage; it was about forgiveness from Christ, which was not mine to choose whether to grant or withhold. I told myself that this was not the first time God had forgiven such sins in the sacrament, nor would it be the last. I did speak the words of forgiveness to David and his family. Later, I realized that there was a hidden and unexpected gift in it for me. I had a very real sense that Christ himself had given me the opportunity, before I left Kansas, to let go of any feelings of betrayal that I might have had toward David and to simply pronounce God's forgiveness toward him. I could only hope that David and Sarah would be able to forgive one another.

A pilgrimage to the past (Leigh Anne)

My final spring in Kansas included a road trip to our alma mater, Perkins School of Theology at Southern Methodist University. I was the alumni representative from the Midwest Conference of the United Methodist Church and as such, my one job was to attend the Perkins alumni weekend. I was reluctant to make the trip. It would become a pilgrimage to the place where Joe and I had met, where all of the memories of our meeting, our courtship, and our early marriage were made. I had never been there without Joe. Memories of him lingered on every sidewalk, in every classroom, in the chapel, and in the echo of every hymn I sang there. I felt terribly alone and lonely as I returned without him.

The road trip to Dallas was surprisingly therapeutic. The anonymity of the road and the privacy of my car invited an unexpected verbal explosion of pent-up anger. I yelled, I screamed, I swore in language that I had never used before and have rarely used since. I raged in a voice that I had never heard come out of my mouth at a level of intensity that I had never felt before. When my anger was spent, I felt better, lighter, stronger somehow, and certainly more honest with myself.

There were two memorable moments on that weekend. One of the keynote speakers, Dr. Thomas Boomershine, had preached the sermon at my ordination in Kansas, which had left a very deep impression on me. I was happy to see him again, though I was certain that he would not remember me. I had a chance to greet him privately between workshops. He asked me how I was doing and I surprised myself by telling him that I was about to be divorced from my husband, whom I had met here, and how difficult it was to be back. He looked at me with the kindest eyes, and, touching my arm gently, said, "There is dignity in the place where you are." I felt as if I had been truly seen, truly accepted and truly loved with the divine love of God in that moment. I looked back on it for comfort many, many times in the months that followed.

The other memorable moment came during an informal meeting of all the alumni representatives. I stood in a group of pastors who had graduated across a number of years, so few of us knew each other well. Our leader asked us to introduce ourselves and to tell the story of our names. I could hardly breathe as the people before me spoke. I was choking back tears and wondering if I could or should be truthful to this group of strangers with the story of my name. When it was my turn, I said, "My name is Leigh Anne Cobb. I was named for my mother Ora Lee and my paternal grandmother Ann Gertrude. I have always been grateful that my parents chose to pass on the Leigh Anne part and not the Ora Gertrude part to my generation!

This is the last place that I was known as Leigh Anne Taylor. I met my husband while we were students here and in a couple of months, when our divorce is final, I'll be taking Taylor back as my last name."

This circle of strangers looked at me with such compassion and love as I spoke, my voice constricted by spasms in my throat, tears streaming down my face. Even though I had made the trip alone, I did not feel forsaken. I was not alone, not in this room of strangers who welcomed me.

COMING THROUGH

A new vow (Leigh Anne)

The day that Joe and I signed the divorce papers, we met in the formal living room of our house on Herschel Road. While we were talking, a realtor was showing the house to the couple who would ultimately purchase it. It was awkward to have such an intimate and difficult conversation with strangers wandering through the house, but we did it. In doing so, we set the course for the next season of our lives, a course that enabled us to write this book ten years later.

When we signed the papers, we vowed to "speak and act in loving ways toward one another and about one another," especially in front of the children, and for the sake of the children. This new vow, which was as important as the one we made on our wedding day, had the same guiding and restraining power that our wedding vows had had for me.

I was unfaithful to this second vow only once, when I spoke bitterly about Joe with a girlfriend. I was ashamed of myself for blaming Joe as soon as I said the words. It was enough to stop me in the future, to cause me to measure my words, to give Joe the dignity that he deserved and to take the high road of mutual respect and honor. I did not have the power to do this myself. I wanted to blame, to suffer, to play the victim, to invoke pity from others. I did not have the power to speak and act in loving ways toward Joe and about Joe within me. I had to pray and journal daily to work it out, to ask for help, to halt my bitter thoughts and tongue. I could not have done it without daily spiritual, emotional, and psychological work.

A new vow (Joe)

Some time after Leigh Anne interviewed for and accepted a new job in Blacksburg, we discussed the reality of her moving with the kids to Virginia. The thought of being so far from the kids was devastating to me, but I also knew how healing the move would be for Leigh Anne. I couldn't imagine limiting her or them in any way. One of the papers I had to sign, since we agreed on joint custody of the children, was my consent for them to move with their mother to another state.

While I felt as though I were signing everything away, I knew this would be a step toward all of our healing. I also knew that we would do everything we could to ease the distance for the kids, planning visits and lots of phone calls, and making space for each of us to grow into our new lives.

The day we signed the divorce papers is a blur in my memory. Our house was on the market, Leigh Anne was beginning to pack things for a move and finish things up at work, and I was trying to be supportive, while grieving along with them.

What I do remember is that, even with the reality of the papers in front of us on the coffee table, there was such love between us. The pain of signing papers legally ending our marriage was transformed into a buoyant hope as we spoke new vows, to speak and act in loving ways toward each other and about each other, for the sake of the children and for our health and wholeness.

Though we didn't write the words down and sign them as an official document, they were etched in our souls, and set as a seal of honest, authentic love.

After they left (Joe)

When Leigh Anne and the children left in early June to make their way to Virginia and a new home, I was alone. The papers sealing our divorce were signed and presented in court. The mandatory two-week session, "Children of Divorce," was completed.

The initial shifts in ritual were abrupt and required new thought and initiative. The first wave came in October when I moved out. The second wave came in making time to be together, listening to and living with the wide range of emotions all of us were experiencing. Now, with Emma and Taylor traveling to live twenty hours away, the third wave pounded on my heart. We had to devise a new plan of visitation, shaping our time together around four extensive visits.

In our conversations over the summer, Leigh Anne and I agreed that I could come and visit in the fall, after they found a place to live. Then, in the winter, we agreed to drive halfway and meet somewhere in Indiana or Illinois. We chose a hotel along the interstate, with an indoor pool, and a place for the kids to unwind after the long road trip. We had dinner together, and the kids stayed in my room, giving their mom a break.

My primary ritual that summer was to stay busy. I had just been hired as the new director of development for Urban Ministry and I learned how to create an annual fund campaign and how to ask people for money. Tell the story, make a connection, ask for a gift. It was the last part that I struggled with the most. I found it easier to ask someone for money in writing than I did in person. Some of this was my introverted self and some was my feeling of inadequacy in the work I had taken on.

Adding to the insecurity I felt in my new job, I felt inadequate in another way. I felt as though I had abandoned my children. As an adopted child, I had been talking with my therapist about the role feelings of abandonment play in a child's life. Though our children weren't adopted, I wondered how my own feelings about this over time were impacting what I was feeling now. While I never felt abandoned consciously, I certainly felt it subconsciously, often wondering about the circumstances in which my birth mother let me go. Now, as a parent trying to guide two young children through the divorce of their parents, I wondered how to continue the intimate connection I had with them while not losing sight of my wholeness.

I struggled internally with knowing that the decision we made to divorce and to open the way for Leigh Anne to move east with the kids was not only right, but necessary. She needed a healing place and so did I. I knew the children would be surrounded by love from their grandparents and extended family. I knew that I would work overtime to provide for them from a distance and to stay in touch with them on a regular basis.

While I knew I hadn't abandoned my children, I was determined to make the time we did share together, through phone calls and face-to-face visits, as meaningful and special as possible.

When not working, or missing Emma and Taylor, my evenings were generally free and very quiet. I would often light candles and listen to meditative music. I wasn't eager to be alone, but had to learn how to be alone. Sometimes the silence was deafening.

Rather than staying up late, I went to bed when I felt tired. Falling asleep was difficult, so I added pillows and embraced them. I played CDs to help me fall asleep. A favorite was

Return to Pooh Corner by Kenny Loggins. The music became my lullaby.

After one too many moments of being jarred awake by a loud persistent beep of the alarm clock in the mornings, I bought a new radio with a CD feature. The soothing melodies of Arvo Pärt's *Sanctuary* became a welcome wake-up ritual.

I began dating. I dated a mortician for a month. He was a beautiful man who excelled in make-up for the deceased. At the end of the month, right after we watched a romantic movie, he looked at me and said, "I'm not falling in love with you." I tried not to take it personally, but I felt like lying down and having him do my make-up.

I met another man, sweet in spirit, gentle as a teddy bear, who disappeared after two dates. The idea of being with a preacher was more than he wanted or needed. Our mutual love of Whitney Houston, combined with my gift to him of *The Preacher's Wife* soundtrack, sent him running. In my ideal world, I wanted to be out enough as a gay man to enjoy my life and honor my calling and vocation as a pastor. I wanted to meet someone who could share this hope.

My voluntary leave of absence was now in its second year. I began pondering a return to ministry, weighing my pastoral calling with my sexual orientation and the risky consideration of serving a church whose language and judicial process had not been friendly to gay and lesbian persons.

The United Methodist church had adopted an unwritten rule, a religious "don't ask, don't tell." The official language said I couldn't be a self-avowed practicing homosexual and be ordained. The "don't ask, don't tell" implied an even more oppressive stance, requiring that I live out my call through "singleness in celibacy."

This was my dilemma: I was an ordained clergy on voluntary leave, working in a United Methodist agency, coming out and into my own as a gay man, attempting to create new relationships and friendships, beginning to date men, conflicted about being completely honest and vulnerable about my sexuality, knowing that I'd either have to check my sexuality at the door and announce with blood oath that I was single and celibate, or keep the secret of my heart buried in the oppressive silence of the church.

How many men, I wondered, would run from the preacher by day, gay man by night routine? How much longer could I live this divided life? What challenges would I face in attempting to live out my calling as a pastor, while acknowledging the concerns of others that my lifestyle was a liability and danger to their own well-being and their own secrets?

All of this kept me in an active state of depression. I kept taking my medications, but between making new friends, being uncomfortable in my new job, drinking and eating without concern for health or diet, I became lethargic and gained weight.

Welcome home (Leigh Anne)

When I got to Virginia, I had six weeks to rest and recover in the cradle of my parents' home before I started my job at University United Methodist Church. I had one very important job on my to-do list during that summer: I had to find a place to live. I was glad to have a temporary respite in my parents' home but there was no way in the world that I was going to stay any longer than absolutely necessary.

My dad enjoyed the process of driving me around to look at houses with the realtor. He was with me the day that I visited the two houses that I will never forget, each one because of an intense intuitive experience, one negative, one positive. House hunting would never again be such a supernatural experience for me, but my intuition was the guiding factor, and I was satisfied with my choice for a long time.

My first house visit started out like all the rest. I studied the landscaping on the way in and noticed the immature trees and the need for lots of attention to the yard and garden. I confidently walked through the front door and began to study the floor plan. "Nice and open," I thought as I noticed the vaulted ceiling in the living room. I started up the stairs toward the bedrooms and about halfway up, a cold chill went down my back and caused my feet to stop. I had a sudden, strong feeling that something bad had happened in that house. Shuddering, I immediately turned around, walked down the steps and straight out the front door.

"Let's get out of here," I said to the realtor, without an explanation. I was sure she would think I was crazy if I tried to explain why I left in such a hurry, so I didn't try. We didn't waste any time moving along to the next house on our list.

I liked the house on Broce Drive immediately. Two giant maple trees, blooming azaleas and mature rhododendron grew in the front yard; I liked less the overgrown prickly bushes that crowded the sidewalk and front porch. I liked the hardwood floors, the bathrooms that reminded me of the house where I grew up, and the size of the house, which seemed perfect for a mom and two kids. I didn't like the unfinished basement and copious amounts of turquoise paint that I would have to strip. The house was two minutes from the elementary school and six minutes from work in a neighborhood where I knew we could be happy. The price tag seemed too high to me and I had no idea if the bank would approve a loan for that amount based on my salary. I was unsure as I went home at the end of the day. I was terrified of the process of getting a mortgage loan. I was afraid this was too big a financial responsibility to assume alone.

I went to bed that night afraid and worried.

During the night, I had a dream. In my dream, I approached the house, parked in the driveway, walked along the sidewalk under the maples to the front door just as I had done earlier in the day. This time as I approached the front door, it opened. Jesus was standing there. He extended his left arm to me and his right hand into the house. Smiling, he said, "Welcome home!"

I got up the next morning, called the realtor, and made an offer on the house. I didn't have to wait too long to hear that my offer had been accepted. I felt a deep sense of peace.

The day at the attorney's office was a different story. I never realized how much a person's signature was worth. I was well aware of the enormity of what I was promising to do. I had a migraine when I went home, one of only two or three in my life. Mom and Dad had planned a celebration dinner for me, complete with a babysitter for the kids. When I got home from the attorney's office I went straight to bed. A two-hour nap released the tension in my head and we went out for dinner at Chateau Morrisette in Meadows of Dan, just off the Blue Ridge Parkway. With a gourmet dinner and a glass of our favorite local wine, we raised a toast to my new home. I think my parents were as happy as I was to be one step closer to self-sufficiency and out of their house!

The kids and I loved the house on Broce Drive. It was nothing special, but it was ours. We loved the hardwood floors, the ancient kitchen appliances, the picture window that looked out over the maple trees and the way they turned our front room yellow in the fall. We loved our yard, our flower garden, our neighbors across the street, the neighborhood walks and bike rides, and our proximity to the elementary school, grocery store, and church. Best of all, we loved the fact that we were only a twenty-five-minute drive to my parents' house.

We felt as if God had made a place for us to heal, to make a life for ourselves, a life that we could enjoy.

Just happy (Leigh Anne)

The kids and I were riding in the car to my parents' house. Everyone was grumpy, including me.

I could not tolerate the continuous whining tone of the children's voices. I asked them if they were anxious about Daddy coming.

"No," they replied, "just happy."

I told them that I was glad he was coming to see them, but that I was also sad and angry, and that was why I had been grouchy.

Taylor said, "You know what I do when I feel sad? I ask a friend to play with me. It happens a lot at school."

In a brief attempt to do what Taylor suggested, I experimented with internet dating.

On my one and only date with Bachelor Number One from Bristol, Tennessee, whom I affectionately named "Norge," I got more than I bargained for when he turned to get out of the car in too-snug jeans that didn't meet with his too-short shirt tail in the back. I don't enjoy the sight of cleavage in males or females, in front or in back, accidently or on purpose.

On my one and only date with Bachelor Number Two, from Pulaski, Virginia whom I affectionately named "Comb-Over Guy," I endured an hour and a half of stories about how his ex-wife had spent every dime he ever made. When he asked me if I would go out with him again and I firmly said "no thanks," he asked me if I would give him a kiss anyway. I was all out of pity kisses.

On my third date, with Bachelor Number Three from Blacksburg, whom I affectionately named "Liar, Liar Pants on Fire," he made a fast exit from dinner out when "his mother called." He was stupid enough to tell me later that it was his ex-girlfriend who called and he left because he thought he might "get lucky." He was never lucky enough to date me again.

Three strikes were enough to prove to me that internet dating was not an effective method for me to find appropriate friends to play with.

I gave up this experiment and focused on other ways to open my life to love in all its forms.

First visit (Joe)

In September, I flew to Roanoke to spend a week with Emma and Taylor. I remembered the many times I'd flown into this airport, warmly greeted by Leigh Anne's family. I resigned myself to a brisk walk through the airport to the car rental booth, into a car and off to Blacksburg, another hour away.

When I emerged from the stairway leading into the terminal, I was surprised to see Leigh Anne, Emma and Taylor. They had come to welcome me, and their embrace extended a grace far greater than anything I could imagine.

This grace continued when Leigh Anne offered to let me stay with the children in their new home while she stayed with her parents. This offer was above and beyond anything I expected, but was a sign of Leigh Anne's spirit, even as she was struggling with seeing me, being around me, and creating a space for me to be with the kids.

The vow we made in signing our divorce papers, "to speak and act in loving ways toward and with each other and the children for our health and wholeness," had been tested in abundance. To make this vow a reality, we had to draw from the deep reservoir of love present in our lives.

On my first night in Blacksburg, Leigh Anne's youngest brother, John, called to talk with me. He was the only of her siblings to do so, and while the conversation was difficult, I was glad he called. As part of my own therapy that year, I'd written letters of apology to Leigh Anne's parents and brothers. I wrote as a way to let go, not building any hope on any future reconciliation.

John wanted me to know that he was uncomfortable with my being in Leigh Anne's home after all I'd done. He wanted me to know that he would do everything he could to make sure Emma and Taylor grew up in a healthy environment. I thanked him and told him how important it was for the kids to have him and his family active in their lives. But, I also said that Leigh Anne and I were their parents, that we made a commitment to love and nurture them, and that we were very capable of ensuring they would grow and thrive in a healthy environment.

His statements were painful because they questioned my ability to be a parent. They made me think about phrases often pinned on gay parents, based on negative and inaccurate stereotypes: "You're defective. You are pedophiles. You molest children. They don't need to be around your type and you should just leave them alone. Leave the raising of children to all the healthy and happy heterosexual people."

While I knew this wasn't true, I felt the need to muster some deep-down courage and speak an alternative word.

Somewhere, somehow, I did that night. I made it clear that Emma and Taylor were in good, loving hands, surrounded by an abundance of love and grace. Speaking this out loud, with the kids playing in the room, was a tangible way of living out this new vow I'd committed to on the day of our divorce.

I also knew that Leigh Anne was surrounded by a direct and protective love, as evidenced in John's intention in calling me. I was grateful then and am grateful now. I thanked him for calling, shed many tears that night and week, and savored the time with Emma and Taylor.

Addendum to Joe's visit (Leigh Anne)
Spring 2000

My prayer:

I'm smart enough to lean into this anxiety and learn from it.
I'm smart enough to slow down and do what I need to do to take care of myself.
Lord, Jesus, lover of my soul, help me through these days.
Help me to know how to relate to Joe.
Help me to be honest, to love myself enough to value my own feelings and state them as necessary.
But this visit isn't about me.
It's about the kids.

On the Friday night of Joe's visit, I needed to be at home, so he came to the house in the evening and did the nighttime ritual with the children while I was there. I went to my bedroom, turned the radio on, and tried to block out the sounds of him in the house. I felt a pang of sadness but was not overwhelmed by it. He spent the night elsewhere and returned the next morning for a hot breakfast feast at my table. It was the first of many meals to come. I was surprised by how comfortable it was having him there.

Back to Kansas (Joe)

Returning to Kansas left a deeper ache in my soul. I continued dealing with the challenges of work, dating, filling up time. There were three things that kept me sane that winter: my community of new friends and family, my faith community at Campus United Methodist and Urban Ministry, and the Pratt

Community Theatre production of Cole Porter's *Anything Goes*, a show my sister, Nancy, encouraged me to audition for.

On one of my early dates with the mortician, he took me to a party at Ralph's, a neighborhood gay bar in Wichita. The bar was hosting a karaoke contest, along with a great spread of food.

This was my first visit to a gay bar in Wichita. The place was small and dark, smoke hovering in the air, packed with a lively and noisy mix of women and men. I remember thinking how good it felt to be with other gays and lesbians. My date introduced me to a lot of people that afternoon, including two men who became close friends: Rod and Mark.

Rod loved to sing country tunes and Olivia Newton-John songs. Mark loved to sing Patsy Cline—"Crazy" is the one I remember most. That night, we got drinks, found a table and listened to the karaoke singers. I lost myself in the mix of songs and smoke and new friends. The karaoke host, Mel, kept the crowd engaged with her seductive, low voice and laugh, sparking laughter and celebration.

Ralph's became my neighborhood bar. At the end of the week, I'd go and meet the guys there, loosening up my straight persona and relaxing into myself. I started to sing again. Melissa, Mark and I created a trio out of "King of the Road," changing the lyrics to match our true inner longings, "Queen of the Road." Groups of us would pick out some great television classic theme song and make it our own.

For my part, I drifted to show tunes. Someone had to keep them alive. "I Could've Danced All Night," "On the Street Where You Live," and "Que Sera Sera" became core songs in my new canon of coming-out tunes. The more I sang, the more I opened up and began to enjoy and embrace my authentic self.

My family of friends grew, and late that summer, we began meeting for dinner on Friday nights at the Cactus Cantina, a

Mexican restaurant with big combination platters and incredible Long Island iced teas. Before long, we had twelve to fifteen people showing up to share dinner and friendship. These gatherings became my support system as I weaved my way through cycles of dating, missing my children and trying to be successful in my new job.

With my friends, I could relax, take off the masks, and be myself. They valued me as a person and friend, and recognized my work as a calling. They helped me discover that the path of loneliness is well traveled and does eventually lead to solitude. They helped me know they were with me along the way.

I'm sure I was wondering if I would ever meet anyone who would love me or even like me. When Leigh Anne's parents came to help her and the kids move to Virginia, my mom and dad helped them. Mom told me that Leigh Anne's mother said, "We hope Joe finds someone who makes him happy."

I left our marriage so I could learn to be happy with myself. Dating was a way to explore, have fun, and enjoy companionship. I wasn't looking for a long-term relationship. I was looking for friends who didn't freak out when I told them I was a pastor, or that I had been married to a woman and had two kids.

The friends I met that summer sustained me with their gift of presence, and they gave me hope and courage to continue on my way. They made my coming out easier by providing me a community of strength and support. They helped me learn that part of what makes marginalized people strong is their shared vulnerability.

————

Early in my leave of absence, I needed to find a new community of faith with which to connect. I had long felt called to shape spiritual community, and now was wandering aimlessly. One place I always felt welcome was College Hill United Methodist Church in Wichita, led by Rev. George Gardner, its congregation committed to being fully inclusive of gays and lesbians. I attended spiritual growth classes there, and was introduced to the powerful theology of creation spirituality by Matthew Fox, who had been marginalized by the Catholic Church for his theological work on original blessing (a major departure from the doctrine of original sin). I felt a kindred connection with his passion. George was a constant source of encouragement and helped create ways for me to be involved. Liz Lippoldt, who was directing their children's ministry, asked for my help in forming a young parents' class and teaching their sessions. This gift helped me keep my connection with my children alive while I helped other young parents find their way.

When my friend and colleague, Gayla, asked me to serve with her at Campus United Methodist as teacher-in-residence, I was thrilled. During the course of the year, I provided leadership in worship, preached on occasion, and created and led a variety of educational experiences that engaged people of all ages and interests. The church welcomed me in my searching, and created a space for my gifts to be shared. In every moment of teaching, I received the gift of learning in community. I was able to share openly and honestly about the struggles I was living, as were they. The year as teacher-in-residence became a gift exchange.

The third part of my faith family was the Urban Ministry community. From the moment I walked through the doors of the community food ministry in January of 1998 to interview for a job, I was on holy ground. The people, the staff, the warehouses, the vans, the volunteers, all of it, became living sanctuary for me. Even as I struggled with my work as a fundraiser, I kept at it because of my profound belief in the nature, mission, and focus of the ministry. Urban Ministry taught me how to be vulnerable, how to take care of myself, how to nurture relationships, how to establish and honor healthy boundaries, and how to fall in love with love. Urban Ministry saved my life.

For years, one of my wishes was to be in a musical with my sister, Nancy. Nancy often performed in the local community theater in Pratt, and would share wonderful stories about the productions. That fall, she told me that the community theater was holding auditions for *Anything Goes*. She urged me to audition.

I hadn't been in a play in years. During college I played the role of Lamar in *Godspell* as part of College United Methodist Church's dinner theater. Most recently, I'd taken on the role of an old, bitter codger with a bad attitude about Christmas, who through the gift of music and the gentleness of a child is transformed to a peaceful soul.

I drove to Kingman, about forty-five minutes west of Wichita, to audition and read for the part of Sir Evelyn Oakleigh, a proper British gentleman, smitten by the over-the-top and bawdy lead, Reno Sweeney. I touched up my British accent from the year I spent in England in the late '80s, dusted off my vocal pipes, and got the part.

Nancy was cast in the play as Hope Harcourt, but we were only on stage together in a few scenes. I looked forward to the drives from Wichita to Pratt, and I often stopped at the Sonic in Kingman for a cheeseburger and fries. I immersed myself in the part, becoming Sir Evelyn, austere and proper, yet very interested in "misbehaving" with Reno. I sang and danced and memorized all my lines. During one of the rehearsals, so careful to make every entrance, I was standing backstage in a robe and boxers, awaiting my next scene, and began hearing shouts from the stage. "Sir Evelyn, where are you?" I suddenly realized I'd missed my cue (and a costume change), and proceeded to march onstage, in my robe and shin high black socks. I stayed in part, even as laughter came from every angle.

The show ran for three nights and got great reviews in the local paper. I was even named "a new talent with a great voice." My friends and family came to the show *en masse*. Colleagues from work and faith communities showed up to offer their support. I felt a new sense of purpose in life. Getting out of my box in Wichita helped me open up and explore a new part of myself.

One of the unexpected, yet interesting challenges of the play and my life at the time was how I had to constantly measure my responses to the attraction of women. Since I was not fully out, I had to temper a lot of my conversations and ignore basic assumptions. I also had to acknowledge that throughout my life I always felt more at ease with women as friends. Conversations were relatively easy, fun, encouraging, and a source of strength, yet even in high school and college, when I ventured beyond friendship to anything physical, the relationships became strained.

Being an affectionate person, caring and nurturing, I wondered how to be present with women. I didn't want to send mixed messages. I was also aware of boundaries— hammered into me by training, and leaving a somewhat sour feeling that I could never get close to anyone.

Clergy, by ethical and professional standards, are trained to keep our distance. We are taught to build relationships that clearly define roles and don't blur the lines. When we leave a parish, we are to remove ourselves from any pastoral roles or presence with the congregation so that the next pastor can establish those roles.

During the course of this transition time, I became aware of some women who were interested in me. Having just left a relationship with Leigh Anne that would still have been intact, were it not for my coming out, I felt frustrated. I wanted men to notice me, not women.

A friend recently told me that part of the attraction women had toward me came from a search for meaning and depth in conversation and relationship. Often times, women saw in me something they didn't see in their spouses or in other men. Ironically, I think this is what brings straight women and gay men into such close bonds. We have gifts to share with each other that aren't entangled with sex.

The tug of war regarding boundaries also came up when my therapist asked me to talk about why I was drawn to men who were not available. I understood her question, but felt frustrated by it. One man, whom I knew only briefly, was in a relationship with another man, but made himself available to me. I was enamored, and open, and, frankly, needed and wanted to be held.

David, my friend and confidant, was married, yet making himself available out of his own longing and searching. It was he who kissed me that morning and we entered into a whirlwind.

Boundaries, Joe, boundaries, I told myself. Find them, keep them, practice them. I worked hard to stay away from unavailable men, and on many subsequent occasions reminded my friend that we were in different places on our journey and we each had work to do.

There was a connection we experienced out of our solidarity in the margins. We were both leaving comfortable, privileged positions in society as white, male heterosexuals.

Deep inside, I believe we both felt a calling to be present for each other, even if from a distance.

While I felt gratitude for this experience and understood it in a way that many others couldn't, I also acknowledged that I was still clergy and he a layperson. According to the church, this was an imbalance of power and I had to be held accountable.

Angry (Leigh Anne)

October 1999

I never saw my mother angry. It is safe to assume that she experienced anger; she simply did not express it in front of the children. Any anger she felt toward my father was worked out behind closed doors and I never even overheard raised voices from behind those closed doors. I grew up thinking that good, southern, Christian women didn't get angry.

It took some time for me to recognize and express my anger after our divorce. I was in touch with the depression, the loneliness, the sadness, and the hurt, but for the longest time, I was not angry.

By the fall of 1999, two years after Joe first said to me, "I don't know if I'm gay or straight and I've had an affair with a man," I was ready to express my anger and purge it from my system. I knew that no good would come from directly expressing it to Joe. I had no need to harm him; I only needed to state for myself in very clear terms the extent of the damage he had done to me, and to name for myself how that made me feel. The bile that had been simmering within me boiled over as I wrote a letter to Joe that I would not send. I was able, for the first time, to articulate in direct (and colorful, I'll admit) language all of the ways I felt hurt and betrayed. I enumerated the accumulated violations I felt had been visited on my body, mind, and spirit for the duration of our marriage. I wrote until my anger was completely spent. I wrote until I was able finally to write, "I don't hate you anymore. That takes too much energy. I'm certainly not in love with you. That died a sad death a long time ago. I don't wish you ill. I wish you well, for your sake and for the kids' sake. But I do wish you a life separate from mine."

A return to ministry (Joe)

While discerning a return to pastoral ministry, I made the decision to once again bury my sexual identity and orientation and continue living a divided life. As long as I didn't out myself, or wasn't outed by someone else, I could continue to work within the system to try and bring about change. I knew this was a risk, but I wanted to try. Mostly, I wanted to serve as a pastor again.

To come out of voluntary leave and be considered for an appointment to a United Methodist church, I had to go through a series of conversations and interviews. During those meetings, I spoke of my regular sessions in therapy, of realizing a greater sense of who I was as a person and pastor, and of developing a clearer understanding of boundaries. That said, I was still hiding an essential part of myself.

I chose to live separate lives. My spirituality and sexuality could dwell together, but only in the secret garden of my heart. I decided to guard my story and not tell anyone I was gay. I would present myself as a single, divorced man with a call from God to be a pastor. (I guess I considered myself fortunate that the church would consider appointing a divorced man.)

The doors opened, an unspoken trust (and unspoken sense of unease) prevailed and I was appointed to serve as an associate pastor at Three Crosses United Methodist church near Wichita. I became part of a staff of lovely and loving people who welcomed me and my gifts. The members of the congregation nourished and nurtured my soul through their presence, their openness to my creative spirit, their delight in growing spiritually, and their love for music and theater. Their delight helped renew my delight for ministry.

As part of my ministry, I auditioned for the role of Barnaby in the church's fall music theater production of *Hello Dolly*. In the spring I was asked to play the role of Pharaoh in the youth production of *Joseph and the Amazing Technicolor Dreamcoat*. My community of gay friends came to church, occasionally on Sundays, and to both plays to lend their support and presence. While I'm certain some people were wondering behind the scenes, the church graciously received them. In my own subversive, radical way, I began asking the question: What does it mean to be a radically inclusive church?

During my year at Three Crosses, I learned that a couple of people had approached the senior pastor asking about my sexual orientation. He fielded the questions, saying they weren't appropriate to ask. During that time, I often wondered how I would respond, if asked. I was never asked.

The beginning of my return to pastoral ministry also marked a newfound appreciation for my physical health. Shortly after I moved into the parsonage, I came across some photos taken a month earlier when I was preaching at a church in Wichita. My face was pudgy. My waist was evident over the edges of my pants. My clothes didn't fit.

Once I created a nest for myself in my new home, I began to walk regularly and then added mild runs. Over the next few weeks, I increased my running distances and eventually ran four miles, three to four days a week, in every season. Over the course of two months, I lost about twenty-five pounds and dropped from 195 (the heaviest I'd ever been) to 170. My friends were initially alarmed by my weight loss, expressing concern that I was ill, or, the worst-case scenario of the gay man's world, living with HIV.

I reassured them that I was healthy, just exercising. My energy level increased, I was eating well and had a healthy outlook on life. I was creating spiritual community, leading worship, writing, teaching Disciple Bible study, and learning and receiving as much as I was giving. The year I spent at Three Crosses United Methodist Church became the culmination of a two-year journey into my own health and happiness, and a catalyst for inner healing. This inner healing would prepare me for a journey I never imagined I would take.

What did you come to teach me? (Leigh Anne)

After I moved to Virginia, I began the long process of emotional healing from the wounds of divorce. I was troubled when a number of emotionally charged childhood memories began to demand my attention. I could not understand why they had come to haunt me now, after remaining dormant all these years. I had enough to deal with. I began to realize that each unresolved childhood wound held a key to helping me understand myself and could potentially give me valuable insight into my present emotional healing. As memory after memory bubbled up, often as the first thoughts I had when I woke up in the morning, I began to write them down in as much detail as I could recall. After I wrote them down, I would ask each one, "What have you come to teach me?" The answer did not always come at once, but it always came over time. This is the story of one of those memories and its lessons.

One snowy winter evening when I was about five or six years old, I bounced into the living room as usual, dressed in my nightgown, warm and toasty from my bath, ready for the familiar bedtime ritual of goodnight hugs and kisses with Daddy. Instead of the usual embrace, Daddy picked me up, carried me out onto the front porch and set me down in several inches of snow in my bare feet. I wailed. Laughing at my tears, he scooped me back up as I struggled in his arms.

Even at this young age, I was well acquainted with one of our family's favorite sayings, "We only tease the people we love." But as I stood in the snow in my bare feet on that cold night, I felt that the teasing had gone entirely too far. This did not feel like teasing; it felt like pure meanness to me. For the first time in my life, I felt powerless, voiceless, and too small to defend myself. I felt betrayed by my mother, who did not rescue me. In her defense, she was not close enough to the action to have prevented it. She came running from the back of the house as soon as she heard my cries—she just wasn't quick enough to save me. I felt betrayed by my big brother, who seemed to enjoy standing back and watching me cry.

There was no physical harm done. I was only in the snow for a short time before my dad scooped me up and attempted to comfort me. I would not be consoled by the one who tricked me. The harm was emotional, and it would remain unresolved for the next thirty years. As I healed the emotional hurt from that experience, I was able to see it for what it really was: a variation of the "ice cube down the back" prank. My dad had no intention of hurting me. There have been only a few other occasions in my life when I felt that my dad was teasing me beyond my comfort level, but by the time they occurred, I was able to defend myself.

When I pondered what that memory had come to teach me, I wondered if the feelings associated with my childhood experience were being echoed in my current life. I did feel betrayed by a man that I trusted, I did feel powerless, voiceless, and too small to defend myself against events beyond my control. Healing the emotional wounds of my past gave me power to name and heal similar wounds in my present.

One of the ways that I learned to process, heal, and grow from unresolved childhood wounds was to replay the memories in my imagination and alter the course of events into an outcome that I preferred. Sometimes in the imaginary rerun of memories, I accompanied my child-self as an adult, a champion who intervened to change the course of events on my behalf. Other times, my child-self had the power to think, talk, and act like an adult and she changed the course of events for herself. This second method was especially effective in healing that cold, winter memory. In my imaginary replay, my child-self spoke with authority to Dad, who respected her words and her wishes. I was amazed that a simple rewrite in the playback of this memory had the power to heal, but it did.

Memory by memory, over the course of five years, the healing work continued until I had the sense that every one of my emotional wounds from my childhood and my divorce had been healed.

Ignorant and innocent (Leigh Anne)

I didn't date a lot during high school. With forty-nine people in my small-town graduating class, there were just not many options. I always said that my favorite boy at our high school was my brother and I couldn't date him. I spent my summers as a volunteer counselor at the local United Methodist church camp and one my favorite aspects of that job was meeting the wonderful people who came to work for the summer. I usually ended up dating someone from camp into the school year. Because these were relationships maintained from a distance, I still had plenty of time to focus on homework, my after-school job, and music and dance lessons.

When I was in the fifth grade and had been invited to a friend's house for a party to which both boys and girls were invited, my dad told me, "Don't do anything you wouldn't do if I were standing in the room watching you." He had no idea how the vision of his head floating around watching me would haunt me for the rest of my young life. I would be kissing a boy goodnight in the car and the image of his head would pop up over the boy's shoulder. "I'm watching you" would echo in my mind. This certainly had the desired effect of reminding me that it was time to go.

This continued until one night during my engagement with Joe, when we were enjoying a level of sexual intimacy appropriate for an engaged couple, that I had to simply say to this vision, "Get out! I am an adult now and you are not welcome here. This is my private life and you no longer have any place here." Such was the pressure that I felt from my father to remain innocent and inexperienced until my marriage.

I made my own commitment to remain a virgin until marriage. When it came to sex, I was ignorant, innocent, and inexperienced and had never talked to anyone about sex. My only source of information was a copy of "Everything You Always Wanted to Know About Sex But Were Afraid to Ask" that belonged to my parents. I recall one time when the topic of sex came up at the dinner table at home, and my dad said, "Sex is beautiful." My mom blushed and didn't say anything. I learned sex is not a topic to talk about; it was even something for a woman to be embarrassed about.

When I was in college, I dated a fellow long distance for three years. We had met working at camp. We were not together very often and he did not seem particularly interested in close physical contact beyond the goodbye kiss. We agreed, at my request, to date other people during my senior year, and I enjoyed dating some boys who had a stronger drive to get close. That was when I discovered the lovely experience of what I called "horizontal smooching." Nice, and always fully clothed.

So by the time I was twenty-two and entering a relationship with Joe, I had very little idea of what normal, heterosexual sex was supposed to be like. And I had no ability to formulate, much less ask, any questions about homosexual sexual experience. The thought simply did not enter my mind.

I do recall the conversation I initiated when we talked about our sexual experience. I shared with Joe that I was a virgin and I wanted to stay that way until I married, and asked him about his experience. He was evasive, saying something that led me to believe that he had been hurt. I dared not probe and cause more pain. I cared about him too much to do that. In retrospect, I wish I had cared more about me. I gave him the benefit of the doubt, never dreaming that the cause of the pain was a long-term, abusive, homosexual relationship. I remained ignorant of his past, his hurts, his challenges, his wounds.

Ignorant and innocent: the dream (Leigh Anne)

The setting of my dream is a familiar-looking, traditional church sanctuary, though it is not one I have ever been in before. I walk in on the wedding of a couple I do not know, whose wedding is being officiated by an older female clergywoman who had been my mentor. I enter unobserved and find myself alone in the portion of the sanctuary where the grieving family sometimes sits for a funeral. I am wearing a white wedding dress with a red bloodstain in the center back of the dress. As I watch the wedding, I feel alone, sad, utterly disappointed, and shocked at the stain on my dress. I am confused why someone else's wedding is being celebrated and not my own. I rush downstairs in a fury.

The downstairs of the church is very familiar. I open the door to my left and see the room where I attended primary Sunday school. This is the place where I first learned the stories of Jesus and experienced the love of Christian community through my wonderful teacher. She helped us to make something special every week—Mother's Day cards and picture frames of popsicle sticks and glue. As I enter the room, I see my dad and Joe seated at the table where I had once been a student. By this time, I am no longer wearing the spoiled wedding dress. I am holding it in my hands. In a rage and feeling utterly betrayed, I throw the dress on the table in front of them and spit, "I was ignorant and innocent, just the way you wanted me to be!" and storm out of the room.

Feminine renewal (Leigh Anne)

My feminine identity
lay bruised, broken, bleeding.

Where is the infirmary
for physical and spiritual healing?

Healing began when I assessed
the nature of the wound, its causes,
reliving the memories and finally
grieving for my enormous losses.

Healing progressed as I allowed
my anger to take shape.

Where to go from here? I asked
and patiently I waited.
A simple ritual came to mind
for the final stages.
Beneath the water of my shower,
I call upon the power
of the living waters of baptism
and every morning
I am made anew.

"God, you created humankind
in your divine image.
Male and female
you created them
and you called them good.
Your divine being is both
male and female
and we are made like you.
I am created in your image
and I am divinely good.
I thank you for my female being,
physical and spiritual
and I accept from you this day
feminine renewal."

Shower prayer (Leigh Anne)

Spring 2000

I stand with the water pouring over my neck and shoulders.
I lift my hands three times.
I breathe deeply and lift my hands
the first time, praying, "I exalt you, Creating God,"
a second time, praying, "I exalt you, Jesus, Lover of My
Soul,"
a third time, praying, "I exalt you, Holy Spirit, Divine
Love,"
I ask the Holy Spirit to shower me, to fill me, to cover me.

I turn my back to the shower and enjoy the warm caress of
the water on my back and shoulders.
I pray, "Thank you, God, for all the ways you have cared
for all of my past days."

I pause to let some remembrance of God's care for me in my past come to mind.

I turn my body and face toward the water, extending my hands in front of me to cup its stream.

I pray, "I ask for the gift of faith."

I wait and watch as the water fills and overflows in my hands.

I toss the water in front of me, praying, "and I cast it forward as a beacon to light my way into all my future days."

"I trust you, God, to care for all of my future days."

I pause to consider something that I am worried about in the future and consciously release it into God's care.

I lift my hands above my head, praying, "I open myself to the divine love that you have prepared for me to receive today."

I allow the water to wash my mouth and eyes in a symbolic cleansing, praying, "Let me speak holy love today; let me see with your eyes."

Then, bathing, I thank God for the miraculous healthy functioning of my body.

I thank God that I am created in God's image, "male and female God created them, in God's image." I remind myself that God called all of creation good and that it is divinely good to be female.

As I step out of the shower, I pray, "As I step into this day, this gift from you God, bless all my steps that I may walk in the way of service that will honor you and your will for my life."

I come out of the shower feeling glad to be alive.

Lion/Loneliness (Leigh Anne)

It was one of those lonely Saturday nights when I was still too broken, too wounded emotionally to start building a social life or enjoy recreation with friends. I lay in my bed, crying, feeling sorry for myself and terribly alone. I drifted off to sleep and dreamed a dream that would be a significant step forward in my healing.

In the first scene of my dream, I am running up a steep mountain on a tree-lined road toward a distant cinder block shelter. I am being chased by a full-grown lion. I struggle to keep ahead of the lion and finally turn around to face the lion and demand, "What is your name?"

"Loneliness."

At that, the lion shrinks to the size of a kitten and runs into the woods. I turn to walk up to the cinder block shelter at the top of the mountain.

When I awoke, I was aware that this dream had been a wonderful healing gift to me. It had allowed me to name the fear that I was running from, the fear of being alone. It had also allowed me to be released from the power that the fear of loneliness had over me. From that day forward, even though at times I continued to feel lonely, loneliness never had power over me again.

Amaryllis (Leigh Anne)

Like a bulb beneath the soil,
I was hidden.
Covered by darkness, alone, cold, afraid.
But the instinct for life,
to reach up to the warmth of the sun
waited
behind a secret door of my soul,
bringing hope.

*As the promise of spring is awakened within by the warmth
of the sun,
the promise of life is awakened within me by the warmth of
Your divine love.
The secret door of my soul was cracked open,
the green shoot came up from the bulb.
Little by little the tender stalk grew,
and quite unexpectedly
blossomed.*

*Now I wonder,
does the amaryllis look down upon the soil that covered her
and curse it?*

*No.
She lifts her face to the sun,
extends her roots deep into the soil,
and draws strength and nourishment
from that which once covered her.*

Harbor (Leigh Anne)

September 2000

I was given an image of what married love can be like last night. It came like a dream, at the edge of sleep. The image reminded me of a walk I once took along the shore in Devon, England. I can see a couple at the top of a green hillside, high above a tiny village on the shore. They are gazing down on the harbor where several rows of boats are safely tethered to the narrow docks. Marriage, like a harbor, I am beginning to understand, is a place where one is wanted, where one's return is anticipated and joyfully celebrated. Marriage, like a harbor, is a place that fits just right, a place to rest from toil, a place to recreate and re-create; it is a place where one is accepted, barnacles and all. It's the fit that's so comforting, the welcome that's so healing, and the knowledge that tethered together and each shielding the other, both can withstand the storms of life—these are what make marriage a harbor.

When marriage is a harbor of love, it becomes a place where people can live, work, and play together, to become better people, to continue to mature, to yield to life's lessons and become more patient, more loving, more gentle, more generous to one another.

Holy Jesus, is this possible? I think so. You would not have given me this vision if it were not possible. Even with the love I had for Joe, our marriage was not a safe harbor. When truth came, I did allow myself to evolve, to yield to love rather than bitterness and hatred. I moved my boat to another harbor far away from the source of pain. I allowed myself to go through the horrible storm, sails set to your divine wind. You God, by your mercy and grace, brought me to this safe place, my boat, my harbor close to Mom and Dad's, not in it, just nearby. Today, I long for the sheltering, protective harbor of a man but I don't know if I'm ready to trust. I am ready to learn to trust.

Holy God, I yield myself, my love, my hopes and dreams, my longing for safe harbor, my present days, my future days, my wounded soul into the care of Your divine love. Hold me in the way my heart desires, renew my trust in men, heal the wounds of betrayal and deception and loss.

Bring about in my character the attributes that would please you most. Make me wise and loving, playful and able to trust and love again. I yield all of myself to you, Holy God. Transform me according to your will. Amen.

Cinder block house: the dream (Leigh Anne)
September 25, 2000

I am in the house where Joe and I lived in Lyons. This is the parsonage at Wildwood United Methodist Church, Joe's first church, situated along with the church and the cemetery on the corner of the Holtz' farm, with nothing in view but crops and a few wind-worn trees. In my dream, the house is made of cinder blocks. I am standing in front of the large picture window looking across the wheat field at an oncoming storm. I am holding an infant, a baby girl, in my arms, and an older woman with dark hair is asleep in one of the bedrooms. As I look out the big picture window in the living room, a tornado races toward us. I calmly watch as debris flies by the window. After the storm, several giant eighteen-wheelers come roaring across the wheat field with great clouds of dust billowing behind them. They are headed directly for the house, but they speed by without slamming into us. After the tornado and trucks pass by, the older woman in the bedroom wakes up. She comes into the living room and stands with me in front of the window. She calmly says, "Let's go outside to see if there's any damage to the house."

Cinder block house: reflections on the dream (Leigh Anne)

The more I think about this dream, the more its symbols reveal how far I have come in my healing process.

The house in my dream is a symbol for my heart: "Home is where the heart is." Its location in Lyons is a reminder that the pain in our marriage began when we lived in that house, but also of how I had been "lion-hearted," sustained by love that was fierce, strong, and courageous. The cinder block stones that make up my house/heart are hole-y/holy, reminding me that my heart is a place where God lives. These same blocks are made of cinders, reminding me of the mythological phoenix who rose up from ashes to new life and beauty. The three figures in my dream remind me of the fullness of who I am: part of me is like an infant who is vulnerable, underdeveloped, full of potential; part of me is like an adult who is able to hold, protect, and care for my vulnerable self, able to fully perceive what is going on around me (contrary to my previous pattern of denial); part of me is like a wise crone who is able to sleep through the storms of life and calmly determine what to do next. The tornadoes (twists in life that really suck) and loaded eighteen-wheelers (other people's baggage) that race toward me come very near to me, but do not harm me. My heart, the essence of who I am, remains safe inside my house made from holy stones. I am comforted by the fact that in this dream I can see and perceive what is coming at me. I am able to care for, and protect, my vulnerable self. I can even rest.

Before I dreamed this dream, I was reluctant to date because I did not trust my ability to choose a man who was good for me. If I was deceived before, what would prevent me from being deceived again? After this dream, I was no longer afraid.

When grace is a cover (Joe)

2000-2001, prior to Taos

The church has done a great bit of couching and covering of homosexuality in the name of grace. Some churches say they love the sinner, but hate the sin, certain that biblical scholarship clearly defines homosexuality as a sin. Some churches say that God's grace is available for all people, including people who identify as homosexual, as long as they don't act on their homosexuality. The United Methodist Church coined the phrase "self-avowed, practicing homosexual," saying that anyone who claimed this moniker for his or her life could not serve as ordained clergy. Some United Methodist churches won't even allow people to become members if they are openly gay.

This was a way of telling good little boys and girls who think they are gay, lesbian, bisexual, or transgender, "That's nice dear, now go out and play." The problem, of course, is that when they go out and play in ways that are natural for them, the church turns right around and slaps their hands for being sinners—but worthy of grace. The final caveat: whatever you do, don't play "gay" in the church. Don't bring what is natural and loving and grace-filled for you into our church because we might have to face what is unnatural, unloving and ungraceful in our own lives.

Going through a box of books on Methodism, I found several old volumes of *The Book of Discipline.* This is the rulebook for the United Methodist Church.

I used to collect these volumes, proud of Disciplines dating back to the mid-1860s, capturing in print the historical struggles of a movement and how, through quadrennial wrestling matches called General Conferences, the church codifies its rules. When I pulled the last Book of Discipline I purchased from a storage box, a bit of mildew and the year 2000 embossed in gold on its cover, I opened the book, fanning the pages to find the ones that ultimately excluded me from the institutional holy club.

The Discipline, much like the Bible, contains a small number of passages specific to homosexuality, open to wide interpretation, and often contradictory. Many of these passages reveal the church's ongoing struggle to live into its vision of open minds, open hearts, and open doors.

Principles (Joe)

In the United Methodist Church's *Social Principles*, a set of non-binding resolutions that seek to give guidance to the ideal mission and witness of the church, the section on human sexuality reads, regarding sexual abuse and protective services, "We insist that all persons, regardless of age, gender, marital status, or sexual orientation, are entitled to have their human and civil rights ensured."[14]

Then, following a brief section on "age appropriate and factual sex education," we arrive at this gem: "Homosexual persons no less than heterosexual persons are individuals of sacred worth... Although we do not condone the practice of homosexuality and consider this practice incompatible with Christian teaching, we affirm that God's grace is available to all."[15]

So, what is natural and a gift for me and countless others is incompatible with church teachings, yet within the bounds of human and civil rights. When we recognize sexuality as God's good gift and blessing to humankind, doesn't it make sense to look at the essence and nature of sexuality, both homosexual and heterosexual, through the same lens?

It became clear that part of my being was not compatible with the United Methodist Church, and that the church's Discipline was not likely to change any time soon.

I neared the halfway mark in my return year of pastoral ministry. I loved my ministry as a pastor and felt every confirmation that my gifts were meant for this calling. However, the pain of keeping secret a part of me that needed honest expression was beginning to take a considerable toll. Was my life compatible with the church's teachings?

I spent a great deal of time pondering the church's understanding of ordained ministry. When I was ordained as a deacon in 1985, then as an elder in 1991, I took seriously and with great loyalty my vow of accountability to the United Methodist Church. Part of my accountability was to live in covenant with my clergy colleagues.

Every time I read the section on ordained ministry stating "while persons set apart by the Church for ordained ministry are subject to all the frailties of the human condition and the pressures of society, they are required to maintain the highest standards of holy living in the world,"[16] I felt an appreciation for the very real challenges of being a clergy in today's world. I had lived through them and seen countless other clergy pulled under the tide.

But the following words always made my stomach and my soul ache with grief: "Since the practice of homosexuality is incompatible with Christian teaching, self-avowed practicing homosexuals are not to be accepted as candidates, ordained as ministers, or appointed to serve in the United Methodist Church."[17]

The church was and is in a climate, as are many churches, of great conflict, pain, and discernment over ordaining openly gay, lesbian, bisexual, and transgender persons with gifts for ministry. I was long past the years of being a candidate. I was not a "self-avowed practicing homosexual" in the technical sense that I had never spoken these words to anyone. And I was appointed and serving in the church.

My decision lay in my heart and whether or not I would "defect in place," as a dear friend had chosen to do, to leave in good standing, or to leave kicking and screaming. Part of my decision began to surface following a writing retreat I took in late January 2001.

Go gently (Joe)

January 2001

As a birthday gift to myself, I decided to attend a week-long writing workshop with Natalie Goldberg, at the Mabel Dodge Luhan House in Taos, New Mexico. Since my retreat at Ghost Ranch near Abiquiu, New Mexico, in 1998, I longed for another place apart to reflect, meditate, and write. I don't remember how I learned of Natalie's workshops, but I was excited and eager to spend some time in the desert and open my soul.

The experience was cathartic. Being introduced to writing practice opened my mind. I learned a new way of releasing and working through what Buddhism calls the "monkey mind," all of the loud, clattering noise of the mind voices that say, *you can't do that, what were you thinking?, are you crazy?, how stupid.* I learned that when these utterings grow loud, my mind is near a breakthrough and the most important thing I can do is keep writing. So, I wrote all week. And I shared my story. The hospitality and companionship of the strangers I met that week created a space for me to relax, open my closet door, and open myself and my heart in a new way. At the end of the week, I felt new and alive, full of hope. I also felt a twinge of sadness and fear, knowing that the experience of this nest was coming to a close and it would soon be time to go.

Driving through the mountains, east of Taos, toward home, every bend became a risk, settling into the turns, twists. I never knew what was ahead, but discovered new beauty at every curve. The heavy grip I held on the wheel began to loosen and relax into the rhythm of the winding roads.

Trust in what you love, I thought, even when you don't know where it will lead you. Love something, and let yourself love it completely.

On the edge of leaving, my writing friend, Hope, spoke a blessing: "Go gently." That which you give so generously to others, now give to yourself. I stopped the car and began to write.

Be (Joe)

> *Behold, child.*
> *Beloved child.*
> *Be gentle, child.*
> *Be restful, child.*
> *Be playful, child.*
> *Be hopeful, child.*
> *Be loving, child.*
> *Be gentle, child.*
> *Be, child.*

The gentleness opened a new place within. A place where my soul, cracked open by the week of writing, stepped outside of my known world, and entered the unknown.

The inner voice I feared for so long, the soft, quiet voice that preferred the secrecy of silence, was beginning to break through. As I drove the winding roads from Taos, through the forest, emerging onto a plateau filled with angel fire, my heart opened as big as the horizon. The density of the woods gave way to a magnificent sky that beckoned my still voice into an open space. I felt as though I could trust my inner voice. I felt as though I could trust my intuition, my spiritual hunch about what lay ahead.

But would I? I stopped at several points on the way home, pulling out my notebook and pen, writing for ten minutes here and ten minutes there. At one stop, I wrote this:

I know what's next... that's the new ache in my gut. I see the natural beauty of partners being together, of life beyond sexual hang-ups and other nonsense. I know what I must do. This morning I thought this will be my one and only year at Three Crosses, a natural break to have my sacrament, the celebration, a clean and clarifying break. Am I called to crack open a system that doesn't like to be cracked or even tapped? This isn't about a system. This is about me. Go...

I envisioned love with another man as not only possible, but real. I imagined a time when my life would be free of sexual struggles about identity and abuse. I knew I wanted to arrive in a spiritual landscape that was beyond, transcending the struggle between what is natural and what is not. I knew what I must do. In that moment, I knew that the direction of my life, in all its facets, would change forever. The wonderful high of being at Three Crosses Church would come to an end. The year there would serve as a sacrament, a sacred moment, for what would come.

I wondered aloud if I could stay in the United Methodist Church. If I stayed (which was remote) I would have to remain on the fringes. I didn't think I could crack the code of silence that so encased the issue of homosexuality and spirituality. I also realized that by staying in the system, I would further neglect my own soul. If someone were to ask me a year down the road, *Is it well with your soul?* I would admit that my soul was empty. By staying in, I would have to commit to a divided, secret life.

What would leaving the church I grew up in, the church I was ordained into, and the church I served for nearly twenty years, look like? Leaving on my own terms would be the best way to go. Be honest, open, authentic, and vulnerable. Write a letter. Since my colleagues had already received a letter about my voluntary leave of absence, sharing about my struggles naming brokenness and healing, another letter would clear the air. Driving through the desolate landscape from eastern New Mexico into Oklahoma, I pulled over into a safe space and wrote a draft:

My dear colleagues,

I am writing out of gratitude for our years together in this journey of ministry. From the earliest days of call, to the shaping moments and events of discernment, to the itinerant travels through these plains, I am grateful for your steadfast support and gracious care. You have created a space for me to discover and embrace who I am.

On the day I entered Southwestern College, I sat in my parents' car, basking in the memory and comfort of their love and terrified about what lay ahead, beyond the car and into an adventure of education. My mom gently nudged me from the back seat and said, "Joe, it's time to go." That was nearly twenty years ago.

Today, I find myself sitting in a familiar place: the warmth of a car that has seen its share of bending roads and long quiet highways. I'm alone this time, nudged only by the inner voice of love saying, "Joe, it's time to go." I do not feel alone. I feel surrounded by the many voices clamoring their great love for my voice, a new voice, to speak up and be heard.

And so I am speaking, because I must share my story for those who will receive it and for those who will ignore it. My story is simply this: I am a gay man, created in God's image, madly in love with my children and my life. I am celibate, but will not vow to remain so. I can only speak of the wonder within which I live, not of what will be. I can celebrate the mystery of what will be.

I will be leaving you and going onto a new path, full of
fear and risk. I pray for the day when we will recognize
what I know to be true: that our gay and lesbian brothers
and sisters are gifts from God, just as they are.

I would send the letter to the bishop, and let it go from
there. I would finish out my year at Three Crosses and go into
my new world. As I left the wilderness and arrived home, I
knew what I needed to do.

Queer (Joe)

Journal entry, January 29, 2001

Queer is such a queer word. The edge of life, a frontier in
fragments, different, strange, oblique, nuanced, fringe, outer
limits, cracking open what is not yet visible, ideal in a real
world. I love being queer. The more I love it, the more queer I
want to be. There's something extremely fun about being on
the edge and putting others on edge. This morning I walked in
the office at Three Crosses with my goatee and wild hair,
catching some stares along with the question, "Did you wake
up on the wrong side of the bed or just get out of bed?"

No, I just like it wild. "Earrings next?" the receptionist
asked. Maybe. I feel like pushing the limits, stretching people
beyond their comfort zone to a new sense of life, to help them
crack open their minds, like Humpty Dumpty. We always talk
about him being broken. He was not just broken, he was
cracked open! Falling was his gift to us.

God knows we need people who are queer, who keep us
guessing about life. We are the keepers and bearers of
mystery, every bend in the road a new chapter, the story never
ending, just more exciting and intriguing. Be odd, different,
walk a different step, dance out of step, in heart. Try and flip.

Don't do normal. Create moments that nudge others toward queer, that boot them to the edge of justice, beyond good or bad, to equality.

Queer is wild at heart, free to give expression to form, stepping through complexity to the simplicity of being. This is a remarkable gift, natural, different, abnormal. Oh, how queer. Oh, you're queer. Yes, I'm cracked. And I love it!

And what do the scriptures have to say? (Joe)

I was introduced to the Bible by my parents, in *The Bible in Pictures for Little Eyes*. The book is filled with full-color art pictures of biblical stories, along with a brief telling of those stories and questions for conversation.

This was one of my favorite books as a child, introducing me to many stories that are now woven into the story of my life. Sitting in my mom or dad's lap gave me a sense of security, and I loved looking at pictures of people who lived so long ago and had such incredible adventures. I remember the book being filled with stories that made me feel good and stories that made me feel sad. On an emotional level, it was good to know that people I was learning about had feelings too, especially people in the Bible.

My relationship with the Bible continued when in third grade, on Promotion Sunday in church, I received a red, faux-leatherbound Revised Standard Version of the scriptures. I loved that Bible. I loved carrying it to church, opening it to read stories in Sunday school, and learning to follow along with the pastor in worship. The cover became worn and it is now held together by a forty-year-old piece of gray duct tape.

As they introduced me to the Bible, Mom and Dad also introduced me to divine love. Both of them grew up in the Methodist tradition, and they wanted me to know early on that I was not only their child, but God's child. So they had me baptized, and in their telling, as I was able to understand, this also made me special. Love, human and divine. I was surrounded by Love. With them, I felt loved and I felt safe.

The United Methodist church I grew up in provided a strong foundation for my faith development. I continued learning about the Bible, sang a lot, memorized Bible verses, made a matchstick cross in vacation Bible school, had two long-serving pastors, and great Sunday school teachers, including my parents. Mom taught the junior high class and introduced me to the concept of exegesis, though I didn't know what that meant until college. We went deep into books of the Bible, looking at each verse, exploring their meaning, history, and context for the day. She drew a lot from her participation in a Bible study fellowship and the notes she kept.

Dad taught the high school class and loved to teach with modern parables. One of his favorite pastors was George Gardner. When Mom and Dad attended a Methodist church on the west side of Wichita where George was pastor, they attended a class on modern parables. Dad loved the scenarios they posed, the questions they raised, and the insight they brought to understanding the Bible and life. Dad loved to teach, to ask questions and to create conversation. I often marveled at the ease with which Dad talked, about anything. He can still spin a great yarn. Through his teaching, I learned that questions and dialogue are keys to learning, especially regarding the Bible.

I don't remember ever believing the Bible was literally true. I believed then, and believe now, that it conveys an ultimate truth called Love and that, through the wisdom and inspiration of God's spirit, it was given to people who lived well before I or anyone connected with me ever imagined me into being. I'm grateful for the Bible's presence in my life and, each time I open it, am inspired by some new sense of Love's calling in my life.

When I became a philosophy major in college, I began learning how to study the Bible from a variety of perspectives. I learned about historical context, who wrote what books and letters, and what types of literature are included in the Bible. Dr. Cecil Findley opened my mind in courses like "Understanding the Old Testament," "Understanding the New Testament," "Faith and Fiction" and "Liberation Theology."

Cecil also introduced me to biblical exegesis and the concept of exploring the meaning of scripture within the context of its time and culture and how to discern its meaning for today. My studies continued when I entered seminary at Perkins School of Theology and had the great occasion to learn from excellent biblical scholars.

One of the more practical courses I took during seminary was "Teaching the Bible to Adults and Youth" by Dick Murray. We learned countless methods of opening the scriptures in new ways that also opened my own sense of wisdom. Dick said, "It's one thing to know about the Bible. It's another thing to get involved with the Bible." This was the first time I'd considered inviting the Bible into relationship, as a companion for the journey.

Seminary threw open every door, window, and dusty closet of my mind, inviting me to think about my beliefs and my life in radical ways. From the moment I learned that the Red Sea Moses parted in Cecil B. DeMille's *Ten Commandments* was more like a Sea of Reeds, fairly easy to cross at certain points, my sense of approaching the scriptures as inspiration and metaphor clicked.

I carried my new understandings of scripture along with the theological tools gleaned from writing a Credo, including a tool called the Wesleyan Quadrilateral. John Wesley, who founded the Methodist movement, invited the preachers he trained to look to the scriptures as a primary source, with the wisdom of tradition, experience, and reason as secondary guides. Together they formed four quadrants of a balanced theological perspective.

Having never experienced a fundamentalist church, other than what I saw on television or heard horror stories about, I wasn't fully prepared for what I would experience in the dance of biblical interpretation and coming out as a gay man.

With my background in biblical studies and exegesis, I quickly realized that many people and churches were taking a minimum of six scripture texts and a maximum of nine texts, pulling them out of scriptural context, and saying to anyone who would listen, "This is what the Bible says about homosexuality. End of discussion."

Using the tools I've practiced through the years, I've reached some conclusions that leave me no ambivalence about being both a gay man and a Christian.

First, I am created in the image of God and when God created humankind, God said this is good.

Second, Jesus said nothing about homosexuality. He said a lot about loving God and loving our neighbors.

Third, for every verse that someone pulls out of scripture pointing the finger at the sin of homosexuality, I respond with an invitation to look at the verses through current biblical scholarship, historical perspective, cultural realities, and life experience. While I believe that God's love is revealed through scripture, I don't believe God's revelation is limited to scripture. Texts often pulled out of context and used to clobber and belittle persons who are gay and lesbian include Genesis 19:1-14 (the story of Sodom and Gomorrah, which is primarily a story of inhospitality, not homosexuality), Leviticus 18:22 and 20:13 (texts from the ancient Holiness Code, identifying a man lying with another man as an abomination), Romans 1:26-27 (where natural sexual acts are exchanged for unnatural), I Corinthians 6:9 (a reference to male prostitutes and sodomites), and I Timothy 1:10 (another reference to sodomites).

Fourth, same-gender love stories in the Bible include Ruth and Naomi in the book of Ruth, and Jonathan and David in I and II Samuel. These stories both exemplify committed, loving relationships. In the story of Ruth, Naomi and her two daughters-in-law (Orpah and Ruth) become widowed through the ravages of war. Because they are widows, and without protection because they are not bound to men through marriage or their fathers' households, Naomi urges them all to return to their homeland. Orpah returns, but Ruth refuses, offering instead to go with Naomi.

The vow Ruth makes to Naomi is often used in wedding ceremonies by heterosexual couples to state their love and commitment to each other: "Do not press me to leave you or to turn back from following you! Where you go, I will go; where you lodge, I will lodge; your people shall be my people, and your God my God. Where you die, I will die—there will I be buried. May the Lord do thus and so to me, and more as well, if even death parts me from you!"[18]

In the story of Jonathan and David, the intimacy of their language and vulnerability with each other indicates a relationship far deeper than good male friends. In their first meeting: "When David had finished speaking to Saul, the soul of Jonathan was bound to the soul of David, and Jonathan loved him as his own soul. Saul took him that day and would not let him return to his father's house. Then Jonathan made a covenant with David, because he loved him as his own soul. Jonathan stripped himself of the robe that he was wearing, and gave it to David, and his armour, and even his sword and his bow and his belt."[19] In a later verse, as Saul is trying to kill

David because of his own jealousy, "Jonathan made David swear again by his love for him; for he loved him as he loved his own life."[20]

A final compelling verse is found in II Samuel, when David learns that Jonathan has been killed in war. Lamenting the death of the one bound to his soul, David says, "Jonathan lies slain upon your high places. I am distressed for you, my brother Jonathan; greatly beloved were you to me; your love to me was wonderful, passing the love of women."[21]

A couple of additional stories that receive minimal reflection in this context include Jesus' affirmation of a gay couple in Matthew 8:5-13 (the story of a centurion and his beloved servant) and the unique life stories of eunuchs in Matthew 19:10-12 (where Jesus discusses eunuchs who are so by birth, and others by acts of violence) and Acts 8:26-40 (a more in-depth story of the role of eunuchs in ancient culture).

My intent here is not to explore the meaning of these passages, but instead to show that some exceptional scholarly work has been written through the years providing appropriate context for these scriptures while maintaining the authority and authenticity of scripture. Some excellent works include *What Does the Bible Really Say About Homosexuality?* by Daniel Helmeniak, *Jesus, the Bible and Homosexuality* by Jack Rogers, *The Children are Free* by Jeff Miner and John Tyler Connoley, and *Take Back the Word,* edited by Robert E. Goss and Mona West.

Each of these works offers thoughtful and faithful reviews of the scriptures and their context and meaning in today's world. My own encounters with these texts and writers have helped restore unity of my spirituality and sexuality, counter to the attempts of the church to tear them asunder.

I have learned and claim as my deepest spiritual practice the belief that I, along with my heterosexual and homosexual neighbors, am God's beloved. I am here to discover and learn with people I am in community with—loving each other through our differences into relationships shaped by the intimacy Jesus modeled in his life.

Jesus made love real. He listened. He touched. He challenged. He rebuked. He welcomed and he sat. He taught and he received. He held, blessed, broke and gave. His essence was and is Love. All the rules that preceded his arrival, that patriarchal systems are still trying desperately to cling to, he summarized into two: Love God. Love your neighbor. Period.

If there's a heart to any of scripture, this is it. For those, like me, who love the abstract beauty of scripture, this opens the door wide to all of the nuances of love we can imagine. For those who love concrete expression, the simplicity of scripture is profound: Love and love.

My parents got it: Love and love. This love shaped them before they knew me, and it shaped me from my birth.

I think this is why, in some strange way, I've never questioned the depth of love present in my life, but have always questioned the mind-numbing ways people try to shut down love in its most beautiful and natural expressions.

Mom and Dad never quoted scripture to me in a demeaning or demanding way during my coming-out process. They lived its wisdom. They loved me and love me still. And in the annals of parental love, Bill and Marilyn Cobb will be listed as extraordinary, and very nearly divine. We welcomed you in love, I hear them say. We shaped you in Love to become Love.

For five years I wrestled with it (Leigh Anne)

For five long years, I struggled intellectually, emotionally, and spiritually with homosexuality.

Before Joe's coming out, I did not spend a lot of time thinking about it. I was a music major in college and had been friends with a number of fellows whom I thought were gay, though I certainly never talked about it with any of them. I appreciated their music and hoped that their parents didn't reject them. After Joe's coming out, I read everything I could get my hands on, which wasn't a lot. I wanted to know what causes a person to be gay. Is a person genetically predisposed to homosexuality? Is it a choice? Did Joe have any choice? Is it caused by same-sex experimentation in adolescence? Is it caused by sexual abuse? Does everyone who is gay cross-dress? What about changing genders? Did I have to worry about that, too? I just about made myself sick with all my questions.

I got some answers from a book called *Is it a Choice?* by Eric Marcus and I felt some solidarity when I read Amity Pierce Buxton's *The Other Side of the Closet: The Coming-Out Crisis for Straight Spouses and Families.* But I still struggled.

I wondered about reparative therapy, like the kind that is advocated by Exodus, the Christian "ex-gay" ministry. After a lot of prayer and thought, I rejected the idea. Would any amount of counseling, prayer, or Bible study cause my body to re-wire the arousal patterns that took me completely by surprise when I was about 15 years old and continued throughout my adulthood? Did I have any conscious control over arousal then? Do I have any control over it now? I agree that I had and have control over my actions in response to arousal, but arousal itself is hardwired and completely out of my conscious control. If that is so for me, why would that not also be so for Joe, and for every other person, gay or straight?

As a straight person, I have always had the opportunity to express those attractions freely, within limits that were appropriate for me. What about my gay friends? If they were in consensual adult relationships, is that causing harm to anyone? If it is bringing the kind of peace and joy in relationship that I hope for myself in a heterosexual relationship, why should I have the privilege of enjoying that and deny my gay friends that privilege? Isn't that heterosexism? If my gay friends are born that way, why should they not be able to have relationships appropriate for them? Do I want to deny my gay friends appropriate relationships because I think same sex is weird or wrong or dirty? Is that a good enough reason? Do I want to deny my gay friends the opportunity to have appropriate same-sex relationships because I think it is sinful? As a sinner myself, I simply cannot judge.

Weary after five years of struggling and coming up short on answers, I finally surrendered the fight. I still have unanswered questions (such as why does homosexuality exist? And why one person and not another?) but I have decided that I can live with the mystery.

Over time, I have made peace spiritually with the whole matter. I am not a biblical scholar, I have not studied Hebrew or Greek, I have not read all of the scholars on both sides of the argument about whether homosexuality is a sin and whether self-avowed, practicing homosexuals should be ordained as clergy. But I have read, studied, and prayed enough to come to a sense of peace about it for myself. What I do know is this: I am a sinner. I believe all people are sinful. Gay and straight, clergy and lay people alike, we are all sinners. Twenty-first century American Christians are so obsessed with sexual sin that we have ruined generations of innocent people who have rejected the love of God because of our utter lack of integrity. Heterosexual Christians are prone to point fingers at what we do not understand in our gay brothers and sisters, so we can divert attention from our own sorry, sexual sin.

I believe that no one is in a position to blame or point fingers at anyone else. My deepest longing for the church, for all of God's people, is that we would be honest with ourselves about our own failure to honor the sacred worth of our own bodies, that we would admit our propensity to use others for our own pleasure, that we would confess our own sin before God, that we would come to the table of God's mercy to hear each other's stories with respect and honor, and that we would ask for and grant one another forgiveness. In that place of utter humility, we can wait together for God's kingdom to come, God's will to be done on earth as it is in heaven.

BECOMING

Love first (Leigh Anne)

"**H**ere, have a cold one!" my brother John said to me as he handed me some sort of mixed drink the moment I walked in the door. I had just arrived at the beach house that our extended family had rented for the week in June 2001. I had driven there from a meeting of the Mid-Atlantic Annual Conference of the United Methodist Church where I had, just a few days before, been ordained a deacon.

My parents had stood with me on the platform as the bishop laid his hands on me and made it so. As I received my first official deacon's stole, one of my colleagues said, "Congratulations, Rev. Taylor," and I wondered why she was addressing my grandfather. It took a while for the reality to sink in that I was the "Reverend" she was speaking to. When I arrived at the beach house, I didn't need a drink to make me happy—I was overjoyed that I had finally achieved my life-long goal of ordination. After some time, my brother noticed the untouched bottle on the table and said, "If you're not going to drink it, I'll drink it myself." It was "the drink" that got all of our attention that week at the beach.

Over the seven-plus decades of my dad's life, the frequency and amount of alcohol that he consumed gradually increased, to a degree that none of the children were aware of until we spent a week together in the same house for vacation. The reality slowly dawned on us that week that our dad was no longer a social drinker but was quite possibly dealing with addiction to alcohol. Concerned, my brothers and I began to talk about what we could do. Butch was the first to mention doing an intervention and we agreed that we'd investigate the possibility. We did our homework after we got home and found a great print resource called *Love First* published by the Hazeldon Institute. We contacted a counselor at our local hospital, who worked with us to arrange the intervention and a sixty-day stay at a rehab hospital for him. Six months later, we met and prayed and read our letters to Dad, asking him to get treatment. His response was immediate and positive. "I like to think that I've helped a number of people in my life. If the people that I love think I have a problem, then I'll get help." I am so proud to say that Dad has been working his twelve-step recovery program faithfully every day since then and has been clean and sober for more than a decade. He is an inspiration to our family, friends, and many in his AA groups.

A man with a secret (Leigh Anne)

I learned so much about myself and my family the year my dad began his recovery from alcoholism.

For one thing, I simply never realized that I was an adult child of an alcoholic; that I had grown up in an addictive family system. I did not know that there was such a thing, or that I had been formed and behaved in ways that are typical of children of alcoholics. I had no idea that there were ways to understand the behavior patterns of addicts and the co-dependents who love them and live with them. I had no idea that there were ways to create healthier relationships within family. It was amazing how healing came to our family in waves as we each faced the reality of our situation, learned and practiced new and healthy behaviors. I read *Co-Dependent No More* and every book I could find by Melodie Beatty, making her words my daily devotions. I wrote in my journal and prayed every day and worked with my therapist frequently.

This learning and understanding overlapped with the process of growing and healing after my divorce from Joe in a very significant way. I was desperate to understand how I could have been so gullible. How could I have fallen for a gay man? How could I have not known? Why didn't I see it and run? I was desperate to answer these questions because I was terrified that I would repeat myself. I wanted to be in a relationship with a man. I wanted a husband, a lover, a companion in life, but I had little confidence in my ability to choose an appropriate one. I was afraid I would repeat the same mistake.

Over time, I was able to see that my family of origin and my early life experiences had formed me just as Joe's had formed him. I came to understand that in my family of origin, my alpha male was a man with a secret, whom I dearly loved, in the words of my grandmother, "in spite of his idiosyncrasies." When I fell in love with Joe, I had, completely subconsciously, repeated a familiar pattern established at home. My new alpha male was a man with a secret, only his secret was not alcoholism. I had learned the behavior pattern of denial from my family and was comfortable carrying that into my relationship with Joe. In fact, at the time, it felt like home.

The giant leap in my own recovery came when I was able to forgive my father for his addiction and the suffering it had inflicted on his body and our family. He may have chosen to drink but he had not chosen to become an alcoholic. When he was confronted with the opportunity to be treated and released from his addiction, he said yes, and has been stubborn about staying sober every day since then. He deserves credit for that and has more than earned my forgiveness and admiration.

It wasn't a huge leap from forgiving my dad to forgiving Joe. In his emotional immaturity, he chose to keep secrets and to act out unfaithfully in our marriage, but he did not choose to be gay. Most people in his position would have done the same thing. He is human flesh. Humans are fallible. Once he told the truth, he was stubbornly devoted to telling the truth and doing the right thing. He likewise deserved credit for that and has more than earned my forgiveness and admiration.

Having worked through all of this, I had practiced enough truth-telling myself to know that I would recognize denial if I saw it, that I could ask the hard questions and make decisions based on what was good for *me* now. I no longer had to protect the feelings of an alpha male with a secret. There would be no more of that in my life.

My mother (Leigh Anne)

I cannot overstate how much my mother has done to help me during these painful passages.

The day I called to break my silence with my parents, Mom's first words were, "I'm heartbroken for you both." How I grieved that the troubles in my life caused my mother heartbreak. It hurt me so much to hurt her but I knew that I could not continue to survive if she didn't know, if she wasn't there to support me. I can't count the times I called to talk, to cry, to hear her reassuring words that everything would be all right, that she and Dad supported me, that they trusted me to make the best decisions for my life and for our kids. Mom and Dad came to Wichita to help me and the children pack, and Dad drove the big rented moving truck for three days halfway across the United States to bring me home. Mom and Dad welcomed Emma and Taylor and me into their home for six weeks when I was between jobs. That six weeks was a Sabbath rest. I was not able to do much but sleep, eat, and soak up their love for me. I was emotionally exhausted and had little to offer my children as a parent. My mother filled the gap for me and loved the children as much as she loved me. After we moved into our own home, the three of us would escape to their house often to rest and eat and get away. I could not have survived without my mother's love or without my parents' support.

The most valuable lesson that my mother taught me, she modeled for a lifetime. She never liked a gossip. Nothing made her angrier than someone gossiping in her presence. She did not tolerate it and did not participate in it. Whenever the conversation at our table turned to someone's bad behavior, she would turn the conversation toward trying to understand the person, his or her motivation, the brokenness or hurt that might have precipitated it. We never heard her judge anyone. She was a student of human behavior and she taught us not to judge a person by his or her behavior, but to separate the behavior from the person. I have thought many times that she could have had her own therapy practice. I suppose, in reality, she did, she was just never paid for it. Truth to tell, I suppose I was her primary client and I owe her my sanity.

After I processed my anger toward Joe, I was able, by my mother's example, to separate the behavior from the person, to look at his motivation and begin to understand what precipitated it. I was able to forgive him and accept him as he is, without judgment, because I had been shown how by my mother.

Last days (Joe)

After returning from Taos in January of 2001, I took time to discern what I would do next. I decided not to send the letter I had written to my colleagues. Instead, I wondered what I could do as an appointed pastor besides serving a church. I thought of Urban Ministry.

I approached the outgoing director, Rev. Cheryl Bell, and the incoming director, Rev. Deann Smith, about the possibility of creating a new position that would combine elements of volunteer coordination and fund development. They liked the idea and worked on a proposed job description. They presented it to the board and they affirmed the creation of the position. When we met to finalize the details, Deann asked me if I was certain I wanted this to be an appointed position, or if I would like to be hired outside of the appointive system of the church. This was her way of encouraging me to be true to myself. If I remained under the appointive system, I would still be accountable to the discipline of the church should something happen.

I decided to stay in the system. I made a trip to Salina, Kansas, to share the news with the incoming senior pastor at Three Crosses, Rev. Paul Wilke. Paul was sad to learn of my decision, but encouraged me to move forward. I shared the decision with the staff/parish relations committee at Three Crosses and then wrote a letter to the congregation.

They were sad to see me go, but excited that I would continue to work in the area.

I found a new home in Wichita, a newly-renovated duplex in the Riverside area, and moved in June.

On my last Sunday at Three Crosses, I left the celebration dinner and went home to relax.

That afternoon, I received a phone call from David. He told me that Sarah had gone to the senior pastor of their church, where I had served previously, and told him about David and me. David had decided to come out and leave his marriage and Sarah was angry.

The senior pastor and Sarah had written letters of complaint about me and sent them to the bishop. On Monday, the bishop called and said, "I have a serious matter to discuss with you." My heart sank.

A meeting was scheduled on Wednesday and I went, along with a friend who agreed to be my advocate. The bishop and district superintendent were in the room with us. They shared the letters of complaint and I read them in silence. The letters asserted that I had manipulated David into the homosexual lifestyle over the four years I had known him. The letters also spoke of my professional misconduct, breaking of boundaries, and unworthiness to serve as a clergy in the United Methodist Church.

I didn't know how to respond. I could attempt to answer each complaint and explain that there was no manipulation involved and that everything about our friendship had been out of a mutual desire to help each other through a painful time. I acknowledged that I had broken boundaries in regard to their relationship. I also expressed surprise that no one had talked with David.

We moved to a different room and discussed options. I could refute the complaints and seek to exonerate my name. Because of the nature of the complaints involving homosexuality, the resolution process would be difficult at best. I would likely face a trial.

The bishop suggested that I could voluntarily surrender my credentials, and receive a two-month severance package. I asked for some time to consider my options. He granted my request. He also notified me that I was not required to face my complainants unless I chose to do so. I decided to forgo that session and left the building to go home.

I went to my parents' home that night and told them what had happened. We all wept. I stayed with them that night and cried myself to sleep.

Liberation (Joe)

July 5, 2001

I drove to Topeka, sat down with the bishop of the Midwest Area United Methodist Church, and handed him my credentials as a United Methodist pastor.

In two short weeks, a dream had come apart. My anticipated ministry, my new home, and the energy of what I believed to be God's call unraveled. I thought back to the letter I'd written in early February, and I weighed the inner despair I felt knowing that my authentic self couldn't bear any more secrets, and couldn't bear putting any more of my soul through a public grinder.

I carefully laid out my framed ordination certificates, the first as a deacon in 1985, the second as an elder in 1991, on the table, face down. I found an X-Acto knife, and pierced the brown paper holding everything inside. I carefully cut along the edge of each wooden frame, wondering if I would ever use them again. I gently lifted the brown paper from the frames, and looked at the back of the certificates. Pieces of paper. A life of calling, dreams and ministry, removing and removed. This was like looking through a mirror dimly, now face to face.

The first certificate stuck a bit as I pried it from the mat. Hold on, are you sure you want to do this? I heard friends' voices urging me not to give up, or give in. Fight. Don't let the bastards get you down.

I heard my own voice saying, it's time to go. Lift this up, hold it, bless it, break it, share it: these certificates of ordination, this ministry, my life. I moved to the second frame and followed the same ritual. Once the certificates were free from their binding, I held them and gave thanks. Then I placed them in a folder for the journey ahead. I turned to the opened frames. They reminded me of bodies opened for autopsy, skin laid back, table underneath, everything open and empty. I picked them up and threw them away.

Sitting in the bishop's office, I gave him my written response to the complaints and we talked briefly about them. We talked about what steps might lead to a just resolution. We both agreed that the options were slim without referral to the investigative committee, which I had no interest in pursuing. After reviewing with him the sixty-day compensation (another gift of grace), I carefully handed him my ordination certificates and surrendered my credentials. He offered me kindness and prayer. "I know these are not offered lightly, without much prayer and consideration. I receive them with sadness."

I took a deep breath. We talked about the gifts I had shared with the Midwest Conference. He had just spoken with a colleague who commented on the fine hospitality provided through the conference. I remembered when George Gardner called me years earlier and asked if I would lead the new conference hospitality ministry. Now, it was my legacy.

The bishop ensured that I would receive after-care and transitional help for vocational counsel. I thanked him.

I didn't stay long; there was no need to linger. Through tears, I got back in the car and set out for home.

As I drove through the rolling flint hills, the horizon opened and, for a moment, all my fears dissipated, and I felt completely free.

Out (Joe)

When I got home, I called my friend, Larry, who had been a source of strength during the past two years of my journey. He came over and we went for a walk. "This is your day of liberation," he said. "We need to get you on the cover of OUT magazine!" I smiled and felt a spring in my step.

The South will set you free (Joe)

"Why would you move to the South to come out?" a friend asked as I pondered where to go next. With my world wide open, I knew more than anything I wanted to be closer to my children. Some close friends invited me to consider moving to Atlanta. I could stay with them until I found a place and I would be seven hours from Emma and Taylor. Plus, I would be in a city with an open spirit and a well-established gay community.

I packed a suitcase and drove to Atlanta. For the next month, it became my temporary home as I explored the eastern states.

Early on, I drove to Blacksburg to spend some time with the kids and get better acquainted with the area. While I was married to Leigh Anne, we would often travel back to this beautiful spot in the Blue Ridge mountains, and I would drive into Roanoke, exploring the downtown galleries and bookstore. The city had a small feel to it, easy enough to get around in, but it was never on my radar of future homes.

Because I was in a state of transition, I wanted to be able to spend time with the kids, but didn't want to intrude on Leigh Anne's space and their home. I knew I was welcome, but my trips were more frequent now and I thought about alternatives. In one of our conversations, Leigh Anne told me that one of her choir members, Caroline, heard I was coming for a visit and offered to let me stay in her Blacksburg home, as often as I needed to. I was deeply moved by her generosity and hospitality, and a bit stunned that the offer came from a member of Leigh Anne's choir.

Caroline's home became a safe space to relax, visit Emma and Taylor, and not feel rushed to make a decision. I decided to explore Roanoke more fully. I wanted to see what the city was like, meet some people, and especially learn more about the GLBT community.

I remember looking online to see if there was a Metropolitan Community Church in the city and was pleased to find one. I called and spoke with the pastor, Rev. Catherine Houchins. She gave me directions to the church and we set up a time to visit.

The next day I drove into the heart of downtown, and up a narrow street called Kirk Avenue. I parked and walked to the storefront church. I opened the glass door, with a bell on the handle, and as I walked in, Catherine emerged from her office. She welcomed me into sacred space and holy ground.

I shared my story as she listened. She understood my grief, my need for healing, and she gently reminded me to care for myself in this transition, to forgive myself, and to embrace this new stage of my journey. We talked about the tragic shootings a year earlier in Roanoke at the Backstreet Cafe, when a man with the last name Gay opened fire in the gay bar, killing one man and injuring six others.

The violent act put Roanoke on the map. The moment opened new dialogue in the city and region, and Catherine, along with her congregation, became courageous leaders and witnesses in a time of fear and risk. She told me about Roanoke and the GLBT community. And she invited me to try Roanoke on. September was Pride Month in Roanoke and there was a series of events coming up that would provide great opportunities to meet people and learn about their experiences.

One Saturday evening in the middle of the month, I dressed and went to the Pride Prom at the Unitarian Universalist Church in Roanoke. I was amazed at my courage. I went without a date, in a new city, into a room full of strangers, and began introducing myself and connecting with new friends. That night I met many kind and open people who welcomed me and encouraged me to check out Roanoke. Toward the end of the evening, a charming man, outgoing and exuberant, introduced himself as David Charles Campbell. He had recently moved to Roanoke as the new organist and choir master at St. John's Episcopal Church. We hit it off immediately, as he also was emerging from a difficult transition in his life.

David Charles invited me to come back the next weekend and join him for a Pride spaghetti dinner and auction. His kindness and invitation gave me a sense of connection and desire to return. I met him and his friend Barbara the next Saturday and we had a lovely conversation over pasta.

As the meal came to a close, we moved from the small dining hall into the sanctuary of the Unitarian church, which had been transformed into a Pride auction. The auctioneer, a man named Dale Weddle, welcomed everyone and made the evening fun with his easy-going manner.

I sat in the back against the wall, with a good view of the proceedings. The room was packed: men, women, all ages, children, families, different colors, and a vibrant energy.

Early in the evening, I looked over and noticed three handsome men walking into the room. I felt my heart leap and wondered who they were. I stayed put and watched. Over the next few minutes, one of them, a beautiful man with dark black hair, ivory skin, and piercing eyes, looked back at me. Our eyes met, we smiled, then looked away.

This glance dance went on throughout the evening. He bid on several things over the next hour, and at intermission went to purchase his items and stood next to the stage looking over at me. I knew this was an invitation for me to get up and go over to meet him, but I sat still.

As the evening came to a close and I kicked myself for not making a move, he came toward me and we met in the middle of the sanctuary. He introduced himself as James Matthews, a radiologist in town. I told him my name and a little about myself, including having been a minister. We talked and agreed to meet at Pride in the Park the next day to get better acquainted.

In case we didn't see each other in the sea of people the next day, we agreed to meet at a fountain near the entrance of Highland Park. He handed me a card with his name on the front, and his number on the back. This is good, I thought. I thanked him, and we both left.

Following the auction, I joined some new friends from Metropolitan Community Church of the Blue Ridge, Jeannie and Tom, at a candlelight memorial outside of Backstreet to remember the one who died and the six who were injured there. James was there too.

The next morning I went to church at St. John's and sang with the choir. We then made our way over to Pride in the Park, and as we arrived amidst other people just beginning to make their way to the park, I looked over and saw James laying out a blanket. We connected early and visited throughout the afternoon.

I wanted to give Roanoke a try. I wanted to be close to Emma and Taylor. I wanted to explore the possibilities of starting over in a place that was brand new.

I shared my thoughts with Leigh Anne and the kids. I asked her, "How close is too close?" I wanted to move here and be part of the children's lives while honoring the space she needed to thrive. We both agreed that Roanoke was ideal.

Threshold (Joe)

After two days and twenty hours of driving from Wichita, Kansas to Roanoke, Virginia, I pulled the large yellow Penske moving truck to a stop in front of 13 24th Street SW. I turned off the ignition and sat still, though my body was still bouncing from the vibration of the drive.

Stretching my legs and feet, I climbed down from the cab and went into my apartment. Once inside, I was determined to do only one thing: sleep. Everything I treasured in personal belongings was safely locked away in the truck. I would start unloading in the morning.

I went upstairs and began inflating my queen-sized mattress. I inserted the plug, tested the firmness of the mattress, made the bed with sheets and a blanket, then lay down, exhausted, and wide awake.

For the first time in months I didn't have anywhere else to go. My mind was racing down all the roads I had traveled since my day of liberation. And now, when I could finally rest, I couldn't sleep. I tossed and turned, trying to get comfortable. Some time later I disappeared into a dream.

I awakened in my Grandma's small house. I was standing on the threshold between the living room and the kitchen. The edges of the rooms were blurred. Peering into the kitchen, I could see a large mound, with curves and valleys, hidden under a large green carpet. I looked to see if there was a place I could lift the carpet and as I reached down, a dark figure, faceless, approached me from the right.

As I lifted the carpet, the figure disappeared. I threw back the green covering and watched in silence as a colony of termites carried on with their work. One, quite large, was carrying a can of soda in its tentacles. Others, of various sizes, were carrying smaller objects to and fro, their wandering a maze of unknown knowing.

Across and beyond the mounds I could see the door where Grandma had greeted me so many times; a door that transported me into comfort, security, warmth, and peace. I wondered if I could reach it.

Why were termites infesting a room that embodied physical nourishment? Why were their mounds in the middle of the room? How could I get from the threshold to the door across the kitchen?

I stayed on the threshold, standing still between the two rooms, the two planes of existence. I had been straddling for so long, it seemed only natural to pause and rest. The termites went on with their work and I went back to sleep.

Dating again (Leigh Anne)

After my divorce from Joe, it was about five years before I was ready to date again. I described those first five years as living in a bubble. I was not attracted to men. Men were not attracted to me. I'm sure I was too broken to seem like much of a date in those days. But after five years of dedicating myself to knitting my life together again, I was ready to open up my life to the possibility of being in a relationship with a man. I hated the idea of being a single woman in my early forties, with two young children, dating again. But at that point, sitting at home alone was a worse option.

I did not date a lot, but I did learn a lot from every man I spent time with. I'm thankful for every clarifying lesson that I learned and wish all of my teachers well. I discovered a number of traits that I did not want in a partner. I came to realize that a man with a comb-over (one date) is only fooling himself; a man who calls his ex-wife "bitch" (one date) is likely to call me that one day; a man who says he doesn't fart (one date) is a liar and who knows what else he'll lie about; a man who goes out of town to have his hair colored is not at peace with himself and will probably not be at peace with who I am. I came to know with absolute certainty that a man who wants to be with me but can't tolerate my children is not at all worthy of my time. I came to know with absolute certainty that a man who cannot accept the fact that the father of my children is gay and an active part of our family life is not at all worthy of my time. What an education!

I came to the point that I finally gave up looking. I had been complaining for some time to God about how lonely I was, about how I wanted God to send me a husband who matched the list of what I wanted in a man. My prayers were obviously not being answered. Sheepishly, I finally realized it was probably my prayers that needed modification. So I began to pray, "God, you know I would like to have a husband some day. You know I have a lot of love to give. Help me be the person that you want me to be. Help me to see the man that you have prepared for me to love. Open my heart to receive the love he has to give me. Help me to know him when I see him. In the meantime, bless him and keep him and help him to recognize me when he sees me."

And then I gave up trying. I enjoyed reading novels at home on my blue couch on weekend nights. I began to enjoy my own company. I began to enjoy my life.

Hugh (Leigh Anne)

The summer I met Hugh, I was teaching a seminar at a regional church music conference and so was he. We were assigned to teach in the same room in consecutive class periods. Hugh's class was first and when it was time to prepare the space for my first lesson, he was still visiting with his students and his papers and storyboards were littering the front of the classroom. I needed some time to set up for my class so my first words to him were a bit feisty: "Are you going to stand there and talk or are you going to tidy up so I can teach my class?" He gathered his papers quickly, sat down in the front row and attended my class each day. We spoke a few times that week and I learned that he had recently been divorced. I could tell the wounds from his divorce were fresh and I was not interested in dating him, though I did think I would like to get to know him better someday.

The following summer, Hugh was teaching at a national church music conference in San Francisco that I was attending. Our first meeting, by chance, in the café of the hotel conference center, was electric. I couldn't believe the emotional response I had when I saw him again. I decided that this time I would take his class and looked forward to getting to know him better. His mother became very ill and he had to leave the conference without saying goodbye.

A few months later, I got in contact with Hugh to continue the conversation that we started and to ask about his mother. I learned that she had died soon after he arrived home from San Francisco.

We began a long-distance friendship from Alabama to Virginia that came to mean more and more to both of us. In December, Hugh asked me, "Are you portable?" In a split second, I decided I was going to have to hang it all up and thank God for what had been, because I was sure that it would be over when I told him that I was not. I had a home of my own, a good job, my children were settled and I had promised myself that I would stay in one place until they graduated from high school. My parents were near, they were aging and I wanted to be near them to be a part of their lives for as long as possible. I was willing to give up a promising relationship with the kindest man I had ever known to be true to myself. "No, I'm not," I replied.

He shocked me with his reply. "I am."

Nine months later, he had sold his house in Alabama, I had sold mine, we bought a home together in Blacksburg and were married on the deck at dusk with one hundred surprised guests who thought they had come to our house for a housewarming party.

There are so many things that I love about Hugh. I love him for all the wonderful things that define him: his integrity, his spirituality, his love for his family, his gifts of intellect and character, his humor, and his wisdom. I love him because he understands me, which is no small feat since I'm an over-emotional mix of southern, mystic, musician, and dreamer, among other challenging traits. I love him because he accepts and loves me and my family just as we are. He never balked at the fact that my former spouse is gay. He appreciates the fact that Joe and I are in frequent contact when it comes to parenting our children. He is my number-one supporter, my rock, my harbor, my comfort, my shelter, my lover. I am so blessed to have him in my life. He is so much more than I ever dreamed was possible in a husband and I am thankful every day for him.

Do I make it sound like we have no challenges? We do. But we are both mature enough to be able to work through them and come out stronger on the other side.

Meeting James, remembering Grandma (Joe)

James and I began dating in September 2001, before I moved to Roanoke. I was surprised and delighted by our connection. First, he didn't run away when I told him I was former clergy (though he was tempted to). And second, he seemed genuinely interested in me. Plus he was a great listener at a time when I needed someone to listen.

I didn't want to put too much on him and did want to simply enjoy our dating, but I was also making some major life decisions, and the most important priority at the time was moving to Roanoke, finding a place to live, securing employment, and reconnecting with Emma and Taylor.

We began seeing each other a couple of times a week and we grew close very quickly. I threw myself into meeting people, volunteering and finding temporary work. I met Pearl Fu, a local festival organizer and community builder. She introduced me to Local Colors, an international festival held in downtown Roanoke, which helped me meet a lot of great people. I also volunteered at the Bradley Free Clinic, which provides free medical care and medications to the underserved in the community. I sent out resumés, met with a number of non-profit agencies, and eventually secured temporary work at a mortgage company in Daleville, a small town near Roanoke.

At the same time, back in Wichita, my grandma's health was declining and Dad told me she probably wouldn't live much longer. I traveled back in December to be with her and see my family and friends. By this time, Grandma was not responding to conversation. She would occasionally call out names and one evening, while listening to her, I wrote down everything she said. "Joe, please bring me some songs." Since it was Christmas time, I sang several carols: "Silent Night," "Away in a Manger," and "Joy to the World." Her words were sporadic, sometimes mumbled and other times very clear. She called out names of people I'd never heard of, and names of relatives who had already died, now on the other side of the threshold of heaven.

I stayed with her as long as I could. I knew I needed to step away and spend some time with my friends who wanted to offer their support.

We gathered one night for dinner and I was excited to tell them all about my new boyfriend, James. I pulled out a CD cover with his photo, from a recording he had made of his piano compositions. He was handsome, with his dark hair, olive skin, and black shirt, and I felt proud to carry his photo in my wallet. When I showed it to my best friend, Larry, he laughed and said, "Well, we need to just go on over to Borders so I can pick out a CD cover photo of my new boyfriend!"

During my visit to Wichita, we learned that my mom's brother, Uncle Herb, had died from his battle with cancer. Mom and Dad decided to drive to Arlington, Texas for the funeral and I agreed to stay with Grandma. I remembered the time I stayed with Grandma when Grandpa was dying. Grandpa had gone into a coma and we all took turns sitting with him at the hospital. On Sunday evening, when there seemed to be little change in his condition, Mom and Dad needed to get back for work and I offered to stay. Later that evening, while Grandma and I were sitting in the living room, the hospital called telling us we needed to come back. I touched Grandpa's feet, while Grandma stood next to him and held his hand. We watched as he took his last breath.

I wondered if this was Grandma's time.

My flight was scheduled to return to Roanoke on December 30. When I left Grandma, I knew she would not live much longer. The next day, around noon, Dad called and told me Grandma had died that morning. I felt a deep sadness that I wasn't with her when she died. I called James and he gently listened and comforted me.

Earlier that fall, James purchased his dream home in Roanoke, a stunning Roman Colonial house, built in 1913. He was the third owner and excited about his future there. On New Year's Eve, he threw a party to welcome friends who could see the house before his restorations. I met some great people that night, including some of his family, and after they all left, we spent a quiet, intimate evening in front of the fire. We danced to the song "What are You Doing New Year's Eve?"

As he held me that night, I sobbed, releasing much of what I had been carrying for so long, the grief of many losses and changes, and most recently the death of my grandma. He just held me.

The next day I made arrangements to fly back to Wichita for Grandma's funeral. Dad was preparing the obituary and asked me to create the service. He also wanted to list me as Rev. Joe Cobb. I reminded him that I had surrendered my credentials. He told me he was still listing me as Rev. Joe Cobb.

Before the service, I walked into the chapel to see Grandma. The last time I had seen her was in her bed, as she called out the names of people who were already beyond her, yet within her reach.

Her cheeks were drawn, and she hadn't worn her teeth for many years. Gray and white whiskers poked out from her chin.

I moved down the aisle. The last time I was here was when Grandpa died, twenty years ago.

I stood next to her casket. Her hair was fixed. Her face was full. Her cheeks were rosy red. She looked too young to be dead. Is this my grandma? My sister, Nancy, walked in and we stood arm in arm, looking. "Who does she look like?" I asked.

A pause. Nancy said, "Euvageneva Doubtfire."

"That's it!" I said. "You're right! Grandma is Mrs. Doubtfire!" The laughter was a respite to the sadness.

The service was a great remembrance of her life and faith, and in the spirit of Grandma's love for creating photo albums for all of her grandchildren, I shaped the service as a photo album of her life, recalling snapshots and moments that had shaped her and all of us. Everyone had an opportunity to share their special connections with her and the gift of her life was evident in the stories we told.

Courage (Joe)

I carried this good memory home with me to Roanoke and forged ahead with my new life. In February, I was invited to speak at New Life United Methodist Church in Atlanta where my friends Rev. Paul and Jennifer Morris attended. They had invited me the previous summer to officiate at their wedding near Seattle, on the shore of Lake Crescent. They had extended hospitality to me while I searched for a place to live.

As part of the church's Lenten study on transformations, I was invited to speak about my experience and understanding of spirituality and sexuality. I shared my story, and for the first time in a United Methodist Church, came out as a gay man. Paul and Jennifer's presence there gave me the courage to speak with authenticity and boldness.

James's presence in my life also gave me renewed courage. He had been out since he was nineteen and was comfortable in his skin. He introduced me to new ways of experiencing the connection between my spirit and my sexuality, and, one afternoon, invited me to lie down on the floor in the living room and listen to Rachmaninoff's second symphony. The moment was incredibly sensual.

Over the course of that year, we continued to date, but it became apparent that something was awry. While I desired more time with him, he was feeling confined. In November, a year after we met, he told me he needed a break.

I was devastated. I felt lost. I listened to what he tried to say and gradually accepted it. But not without effort. I didn't want to lose the depth of connection I felt with him as a friend and we talked about ways we could maintain our friendship while allowing some space. We agreed to have dinner often. On a few occasions, when I was feeling especially lonely, I asked if he would hold me, and he did.

He began dating someone else and I had a difficult time adjusting. In the back of my mind I'd wondered if my relationship with James would move as quickly as my relationship with Leigh Anne had. I was more tentative this time around, and tried not to focus all of my social energy on James. I was still meeting people and felt lonely and insecure.

We stayed in touch, through conversation and regular dinners. In the spring of 2003, I began looking for a home and when I found the one I wanted to buy, he helped me with the down payment. In June of that year, I purchased my first home and invited James, his boyfriend, and my new neighbors over to celebrate.

Pride (Joe)

Summer 2003

One Sunday morning, the kids and I went to a worship service at the Metropolitan Community Church and Emma noticed a poster in the church's window. The large print announced "Pride Idol," a musical competition as part of the annual Pride in the Park festivities in September. "Daddy, can I be in Pride Idol?" asked Em. "Sure," I answered.

I called the coordinator of the event for more information and learned that Emma would need to audition. We scheduled a time on Friday prior to the event and Emma's excitement grew.

We arrived for the audition, Emma sang a bit of her song for the coordinator, and he confirmed her participation. While Emma and Taylor were in another room, the coordinator pulled me aside and told me, in a compassionate way, that the competition would also include a professional entertainer who had experience performing at Walt Disney World.

Though he didn't say it directly, the implied message was that Emma probably wouldn't win.

On Saturday of Pride weekend, Taylor had a soccer game in Blacksburg. We all jumped into the car and made our way up Interstate 81. Driving time is always good talking time. And that particular morning, Taylor said, "Dad, I've been thinking about Boy Scouts. I've decided not to be in Boy Scouts anymore because of their stand against gay people."

His mom and I had talked to him two years earlier, simply saying that we were uncomfortable with the scouts' stance toward gay leaders, but that if he wanted to participate he was welcome to do so. Taylor actively participated for two years, but reached a different decision in his own time.

Sunday arrived and the day was beautiful. The theme for Pride was "We are Family." I was proud to have my children there, and proud to be part of a community of people open to new definitions and expressions of family.

The time for Pride Idol arrived and I escorted Emma to the wooden stage, set in front of the natural grass amphitheatre in Highland Park. The emcee welcomed everyone and announced the first contestant, Emma Cobb, and she walked confidently onto the stage. She took the microphone in her hand and sang "Castle on a Cloud" from the musical *Les Miserables*.

She sang a capella, from memory. Her voice soared. When she finished, the crowd broke into wild applause, many standing to cheer. As tears fell from my eyes, I smiled. Emma happily bounded off the stage and into my arms. I told her how proud I was and we made our way back to Taylor and our blanket in front of the stage for the remaining acts.

Many people from the church and the audience came to Emma and shared their congratulations and their pride in her beautiful gift.

She was the first of five performers. We were eager to hear the remaining acts and I was looking forward to the much-touted professional entertainer. The second performer was a young woman who played the guitar and sang a lovely country song. The third performer was the professional entertainer, a drag queen with lots of performance experience. As I watched her, several thoughts came to mind.

First, there I was sitting on a blanket with my eleven—and nine-year-old children, watching a drag queen lip sync and dance. What are the kids going to tell their mom when they get home? Second, Emma noticed that people were lining up to give the entertainer dollar bills. "Why didn't I get dollar bills, Daddy?" she asked. Attempting to be quick on my feet and in my mind, I told Emma that this was called "tipping" and people did this when they liked an entertainer. (The more I tried to explain, the more I thought, she isn't going to buy any of this.) So, I said, "Emma, you sang live, with your voice, and from your heart. She is lip syncing. Your talent is priceless." I don't know if she bought a word of it, but she kept watching and seemed content with the answer.

The fourth performer, another young woman, played the keyboard and sang. The final performer was another drag queen. My only recollection of the performance was that she rolled around on the stage and her wig flew off.

The emcee called all the performers to the stage and the crowd gave them all generous applause. He then announced that the crowd would determine the winner through their applause. Each contestant was called out in the order of their performance. Emma stepped forward and Taylor and I, along with lots of people around us, stood, clapped, whooped, hollered, and cheered wildly. Emma smiled from ear to ear.

The professional entertainer also garnered loud applause. The winner was clear to me, the unbiased father. However, the emcee asked both Emma and the professional entertainer to step forward for an "applause-off." I looked at the stage and there was my daughter, with her sweet, gap-toothed smile and short black hair, standing in the shadow of the great professional entertainer decked out in big hair, heavy makeup, gold lamé and heels.

The emcee put his hand over Emma's head and the crowd broke loose in applause. He then placed his hand above the queen. The winner was clear.

"The winner of the 2003 Pride Idol is Emma Cobb!" I ran over and gave her a big hug.

Moving on (Joe)

I learned to enjoy my solitude. I had a good job with the Roanoke Symphony as director of marketing and public relations. I owned my own home, and had a lot of good friends. I dated several great men and my longest relationship was with Kevin, a musician, for about fifteen months. Kevin was a handsome, gifted man, but struggled with addiction and our relationship never really clicked. In the summer of 2004, I was experiencing growing stress in my work and the reality that our relationship was going to end.

That fall, after resigning my position with the symphony, I took some time away in Santa Fe, New Mexico, to reflect on my life and direction. James called me that week and after we talked through what was going on in our lives, I remember him asking me a question. "If the occasion arose again, and we are both in a good place, would you consider dating me again?"

"Yes!"

I felt a peace about our friendship and doubted, at the time, that we would ever be together again as a couple. But I was willing to hope.

By the summer of 2005, I had broken up with Kevin. He was in a downward spiral and I couldn't rescue him anymore. James was struggling in his own relationship and had decided to end it.

One of my friends, Pam Meador, nominated me for Roanoke's Most Eligible, a weekly interview in *The Roanoke Times* of a person interested in meeting someone special. I met with the reporter from *The Roanoke Times* and one of her queries was, "Describe your perfect date."

"Taking a picnic into the Blue Ridge mountains, sitting by a fire, enjoying a bottle of wine, and watching the moon rise." The date I described was one of the early dates James and I shared the first time around. He owned a beautiful section of land in Botetourt County and had taken me there to show me the incredible view of the Blue Ridge.

When the article appeared in the newspaper, I was eager to see how many responses I would receive. The first person who wrote me was the first gay man who had been nominated for most eligible. The second was a wonderful man I'd been dating some that summer. But I realized that the one I really wanted to date again was James.

We decided to try again.

Original calling (Joe)

While James and I were renewing our relationship, I was also seriously exploring ordination through the Metropolitan Community Church.

During the five years I'd been in Roanoke, I had visited numerous churches. For a time, I became a member of St. John's Episcopal Church and helped start Intimate Path, a weekly conversation on spirituality and sexuality for gays and lesbians. The group was designed as a supportive network of spiritually-minded people who could talk about integrating these aspects of our lives that had long been disintegrated. I was pleased by the support of the St. John's clergy and congregation and grateful for the opportunity to facilitate the group using some of my gifts as a former clergy.

I watched closely as the Episcopal Church struggled with its stance on ordaining openly gay clergy. When Rev. Gene Robinson was elected and consecrated as the first openly gay bishop in New Hampshire, great anxiety arose in local parishes throughout the country and the world. Some churches opted to leave the denomination. Others opted to stay in and create meaningful conversations about the theological, pastoral and ethical dimensions of the decision.

St. John's invited me and another parishioner to offer our reflections on Robinson's election at an adult forum. I appreciated the opportunity to have conversation with him about our different perspectives. He was disappointed in the election and expressed concerns about the church's movement away from its core doctrines. I applauded the election and saw this as a broadening of the church's doctrine to be a fully inclusive church.

Writing my reflections for this event made me realize my growing passion for seeking ordination. I decided to meet with a couple of rectors in the Roanoke area to discern the possibilities for ordination in the Episcopal Church. While their comments were affirming of me as a person, they had concerns that because I had surrendered my credentials in the United Methodist Church, the path to ordination would likely be difficult.

I began attending the Metropolitan Community Church of the Blue Ridge on a regular basis, singing in the choir, participating in worship. When the choir director left the church, I was asked to serve as the interim choir director and did so for eighteen months. My love for the church and its passion for social justice inspired me and formed my decision to make it my church home.

In the summer of 2004, I began conversations with the Metropolitan Community Church regarding their ordination process. I was informed that my situation was not unique. Many clergy in my position had also surrendered their credentials, for a variety of reasons. The Metropolitan

Community Church had made great efforts to strengthen their ordination process and they were thorough in vetting potential candidates. They were also clear that if a candidate had any history of misconduct with minors they would not be considered.

I approached Rev. Catherine Houchins about seeking ordination. She guided me through the process, and when I was ready to move forward, the board of directors voted to sponsor my candidacy.

I was received as a transfer clergy in the process, meaning that my credentials from the United Methodist Church would be honored. Over the course of the year, I completed a course in MCC polity and went to Scottsdale, Arizona in the summer of 2006 to participate in a clergy candidate intensive course and ordination interviews.

My interview was prayerful, challenging, and intense. We talked about my previous experience in the United Methodist Church, about my reasons for leaving the church, my desire to be ordained in MCC, and what I had learned through the complaint and resolution process. When the interview was completed, the chair of the three-person interview team thanked me and I went out into the hotel lobby to wait.

After about fifteen minutes, the team invited me back in and told me they were recommending me for ordination. They gathered around me and sang a beautiful song written by John Bell, "Take, O Take Me As I Am."

Tears poured down my face as their voices surrounded me with blessing and their hands rested on my shoulders and back.

Following my interview I called James, who was with me that week, and then Catherine. I called Leigh Anne and the kids. I called my parents. After the wilderness of the last five years I felt a new path opening toward a land of promise.

The next step was to plan my ordination service. When I was ordained in the United Methodist Church, first as a deacon in 1985, and then as an elder in 1991, the services took place during our annual conference. In the Metropolitan Community Church, I could pick the date, the location, and the people I wanted to be involved. I could also design the service.

In conversation with Catherine, I picked the date of October 8, 2006, the anniversary of the founding of MCC. I began working on the service and was eager to create an experience that was ecumenical, musical, and joyful. I invited several area clergy to participate, invited all of my family, and invited Emma and Taylor to sing. I also invited Leigh Anne to play for them. I also asked friends from the congregation and the community to form a choir and sing John Rutter's "For the Beauty of the Earth."

When I sent out the invitations, the outpouring of support was amazing. Rev. Paul and Jennifer Morris, who were so supportive in my initial coming out, flew from Atlanta to participate. One of my former colleagues in Kansas, who had also recently come out as gay, came to the service with his partner. Clergy from a number of congregations in the Roanoke Valley came to participate. Members of MCC of the Blue Ridge helped in a variety of ways, from serving as ushers, to assisting with communion, to singing in the choir, to running the sound board and hosting a reception following the service. My parents and my sister, Nancy, also attended. I asked Catherine to preside.

During the preparations, I was approached by Pam Podger, a reporter for *The Roanoke Times* religion section, who was interested in writing a story about my ordination. I agreed and we met several times to talk about the journey that led to this moment. Pam interviewed Leigh Anne and also attended the service.

The day arrived and we gathered in the sanctuary. I was deeply moved by those present—the faces represented the diverse, loving community that had welcomed me to Roanoke and this new direction in my life. When Emma and Taylor rose to go the microphone, Leigh Anne went to the piano to accompany them. Their voices soared on an arrangement of Charles Wesley's "O For a Thousand Tongues to Sing" and they set the tone for the rest of the service.

When it came time for my ordination, the various clergy came from the pews and gathered around me as I knelt on a prayer bench borrowed from Christ Episcopal Church for the occasion. As Catherine ordained me, I sang "Take, O Take Me as I Am." When the ordination was complete, the congregation broke into applause and I took time to embrace each of the clergy who had come to offer their support.

Following the ordination, we celebrated holy communion, a central part of MCC worship. That day, we had six serving stations around the sanctuary, with clergy and laity serving. Near the end of communion, at the station where I was serving, my parents, Nancy, James, Emma, Taylor, and Leigh Anne came forward. I gave each of them a piece of bread, dipped in the silver chalice that Betty had given me years before, and offered a prayer of thanksgiving. During the prayer, I felt my heart open and I felt God's presence fill me with healing and reconciliation. This circle of family blessed me beyond anything I could have imagined.

Following the service, I noticed Pam interviewing several people about the service. When her article appeared in *The Roanoke Times* the following Sunday, it included a large photograph of my ordination on the front of the Extra section. The photo resembled a contemporary image of DaVinci's last supper. The article recounted my path to ordination and included comments from Leigh Anne and Nancy about my gifts for ministry. When asked what this ordination meant to her, Nancy said, "this ordination is an affirmation of Joe's original calling."

Daddy, again? (Joe)

On the heels of my ordination, a dream come true for me, James and I began talking about one of his dreams: having a child of his own.

Early in his adult life, James set out a number of dreams he wanted to fulfill: becoming a radiologist, completing a CD of his piano compositions, and renovating a number of homes. Now he was ready to explore the idea of being a daddy. Emma and Taylor were in their early teens and I wasn't sure about being responsible for a baby again.

After my ordination, I wanted to get back into pastoral ministry and pursued a call to be the pastor of MCC Winston-Salem. I wanted to support James in his dream. I also wanted to become a pastor again. We had many heated discussions about being new parents and weren't ultimately sure how the decision would impact our relationship. James decided to move forward with the surrogacy process and I with being a pastor. We agreed to love and support each other.

Beginning in March 2007, we lived apart for half of each week. I split my time between Winston-Salem and Roanoke. Sometimes he would come to Winston-Salem and many weekends I would drive to Roanoke, leaving early on Sunday to begin my work week.

The same month I started in Winston-Salem, we learned that the surrogate we contracted with was pregnant, and we would become parents in November. There is nothing like a pregnancy test to bring everything into perspective.

As we began to tell family, friends, and the church about our pregnancy, we received incredible support. Leigh Anne, Hugh, Emma, and Taylor were thrilled.

Most people assumed we were adopting, but through an ongoing process of information and education, we told them about the process of visiting and choosing among surrogacy agencies in California, identifying an anonymous egg donor and a surrogate. We chose California because of its friendly laws toward gay parents.

James flew to California to meet our surrogate, Dana. He also made his sperm donation and once the donor eggs were available, was present in the clinic where the eggs were implanted in Dana. In a couple of weeks we received word that Dana was pregnant.

When we initially received word of the pregnancy we were told there were twins, so, for about a week we prepared ourselves for this surprise. The following week, we learned there was just one fetus, and we settled into this new reality. We then learned that we were going to have a daughter and made arrangements to be in California in early November for the delivery.

We flew to Los Angeles in late October, and then spent our last few "pre-child" days in Palm Springs. We drove into San Diego and I met our surrogate, Dana, for the first time. She was scheduled to go into the hospital on November 6. We arrived early and went into her room. She thanked us for coming and told us that she wanted to be alone during labor and she would have a nurse come get us for the delivery. We both appreciated Dana's honesty and disappeared to the waiting area.

While the day dragged on, I remembered the births of my first two children. Emma was born in the Rice County District Hospital in Lyons, Kansas. After spending a long night in labor, walking the halls, Leigh Anne and I went back to the room to rest. The next morning our doctor came by, checked Leigh Anne's dilation and told us that Emma was stuck. We would proceed with a caesarean section.

Emma was born in the early afternoon, and when she emerged in the doctor's hands, he sang "Happy Birthday" as we smiled and cried. We held her for a while and then a nurse took her to the nursery. She had a full head of black hair, so much so that a baby stocking cap wasn't necessary to keep her head warm. She was the talk of the hospital.

Because our room was next door to the nursery, we could hear all of the comments from visitors: "Look at all that hair!" We listened and smiled.

Taylor was born in the large Wesley Medical Center in Wichita, Kansas. We were living in Medicine Lodge at the time, and the hospital there no longer delivered babies. We left early the morning of February 3 and drove to Wichita. Once we arrived and got settled, they induced labor. Leigh Anne worked hard all day, and by early evening we were faced with a similar situation. The baby seemed to be stuck. So the doctor talked with us about another caesarean section. Leigh Anne had really wanted to deliver naturally and cried from exhaustion. After talking about it, we agreed to go ahead with a caesarean section.

Around 10:00 pm that night, a nurse took us to the delivery room, and as the doctor began prep for the caesarean section, she checked Leigh Anne's dilation. She was fully dilated, so the doctor said, "Push!" Leigh Anne did, and Taylor was born!

As James and I struggled to find the best way to rest on uncomfortable couches in the waiting room, one of the nurses came to get us and take us back to Dana's delivery room. I stood by her left leg, and James by her right leg.

We both participated in the support team for the delivery. In about 30 minutes, Virginia Jane Alexandra Matthews entered the world at a whopping ten pounds and one ounce. Dana rested and we watched the nurses prep Ginny and wrap her for the nursery.

The staff was excellent in their hospitality toward us as Ginny's two dads, and in their care for Ginny. After twenty-four hours in the hospital, the doctor released Ginny to us and we drove to Venice, California, where we stayed for a week with our dear friend, Michael Downs, a long-time friend from high school. My sister, Nancy, came for most of the week and we had some great experiences walking into Venice—three men, a woman and a baby!

Ginny changed our lives and deepened our love for each other. Within a year of her birth, I knew I wanted to be back with James and Ginny full-time, so I completed my pastoral ministry in Winston-Salem and moved back to Roanoke in January 2009. I moved into our home and for the first time in our relationship, we began living together and parenting together.

A series of events at the table, Part 3: Joe's Ordination (Leigh Anne)

I was reluctant to go. I was only going because the children had asked me to accompany them on a song they were singing for the service at the Metropolitan Community Church in Roanoke. I raced off after my duties at church that morning, dressed in my red Pentecost suit. I wear it when I really need to call on the power of the Holy Spirit to help me and I was sure that I needed Her help on this day. I had been at both of Joe's previous ordinations. I had stood with him, a starry-eyed fiancée at his first ordination as a deacon at the church that we would eventually serve. I had stood with him at his second ordination, as an elder. He had stood with me at my consecration as a diaconal minister. These were the highest moments in our personal and professional journeys and ones that we had shared intimately as a couple.

Being there for this ordination brought up too many images and memories of the past, of loss, of what had been. I was not sure what my emotional response would be, and if it was intense, I was not sure that I would be able to bear it with dignity in such a public and solemn setting as this. On the one hand, I wanted to go to this church that had welcomed my children so warmly; I wanted to meet the people they talked about so fondly. But on the other hand, I didn't want to get near what I called, in my mind that day, "that freak church." What would a whole church of gay, lesbian, and transgendered folks look like anyway? I confessed my reluctance to God as I drove to the service that afternoon.

I was a total stranger to each person that I met at the door, in the sanctuary, in the hallways at that church that day, and I have never been greeted more warmly at any church, anywhere, in all my lifelong professional experience in churches. I discovered that a church full of gay, lesbian and transgendered folks looks like any other congregation you might walk into: young, old, dark, fair, casual, formal, folks alone, in pairs, in family groups, just folks. And I was made to feel welcomed, very welcomed, that day.

I accompanied, I sang, I worshipped, I sat in the front pew with my children and my former in-laws, surrounded by a congregation of friends who supported Joe in his ordination as a minister in the Metropolitan Community Church. Eventually, I was invited to receive communion at the Lord's Table.

That is where it happened. That is where heaven broke in. I didn't want to go, didn't want to be in that "freak church." I didn't want to walk into the pain of my past, of my losses.

But the Holy Spirit had another thing in mind. I had not worn that Pentecost suit for nothing, because I was wrapped in the powerful and loving embrace of God's Holy Spirit at the Lord's Table that day.

We were invited to come to the front of the sanctuary in a small group to receive communion. When it was our turn, our group included Joe, Emma, Joe's parents Bill and Marilyn, Joe's sister Nancy, and me. We held hands or wrapped our arms around each other as Joe prayed. We each received the bread and the cup, the gift of Christ's body and blood, broken and poured out for our forgiveness, for our welcome at Christ's table. I sobbed during Joe's prayer, not dignified sniffling, but full-throated, shoulder-racking sobs. As he prayed, I literally felt as if a river of reconciliation coursed through my entire being. If there was any unfinished business left anywhere in my spirit, it was totally washed clean that day.

After each one of us received the Lord's Supper from Joe, I embraced him for the first time in years, offered him the kiss of peace on each cheek and asked God to bless him. I do not feel that I bore the intense emotional response to Joe's ordination with dignity, but I did bear it with honesty.

After the service, two men approached me to tell me how much my presence had meant to them in that service. I suppose it is not a very common experience for a straight ex-spouse to show up in church with a blessing to offer. I was glad that they could be encouraged by my presence. I did not confess to them how hard it had been for me to attend. Likewise, after the service, James approached me to offer me kindness that I will never forget: "You are the classiest person I have ever met. If I could have one tenth of the class you have, I'd be lucky." It may have looked like class that day, but I am sure it was more like grace.

Living into new vows (Joe)

Living into the vow Leigh Anne and I made on the day of our divorce, I imagined what "speaking and acting in loving ways toward and with each other for the sake of our children and our health and wholeness" would look and sound like.

Language became important to us in new ways. So did presence. So did listening. Every moment would provide an occasion to shape and be shaped in love.

I began thinking about the role of gender. Though I identify as a male, and my children identify as female and male, I don't want to be bound by traditional gender roles. Also aware of my transgender friends, I want to keep my perspective and appreciation for the whole spectrum of human experience and expression as open as possible.

As an adolescent, I was keenly aware of the feminine and masculine natures in my body. My skin was smooth and I took a long time (what seemed like eternity) to sprout any hair, anywhere. I wasn't muscular or hairy, yet longed for both.

I remember being startled when a single hair, long and squiggly, popped up near my penis. For a while it was the lone "who-hair" in "Whoville." I pulled Dad into my room one night and asked him to explain this strange phenomenon on my otherwise smooth skin. "It's a hair," he said. "This happens as you grow."

The only anatomy lessons I received growing up came through observation. In elementary school, fifth or sixth grade, we saw an old reel-to-reel film about how boys develop physically and sexually. The girls had to leave the room for that one. I was curious about both genders, mostly because I wanted to see the differences. In fact, it would have made sense for all of us to watch both, together, and begin talking then about what makes us unique and the same. It seems to me this would expand the conversations about healthy bodies and healthy sexual behaviors and remove some of the secrecy and stigma about our "privates."

As Emma and Taylor began to move through childhood into adolescence, I wanted to approach my conversations with them regarding physical and sexual development in healthy and meaningful ways. I also wanted to keep our conversations gender-neutral, especially when it came to whom they might fall in love with.

When Emma and Taylor were in elementary school, the school sent a note home saying that they would be participating in a learning unit called "Family Life." Leigh Anne responded to the note with a visit to the school, asking the principal to see the curriculum. When the principal asked the nature of her concerns, she responded, "Our children have a unique family, with a straight mother and a gay father, and I want to make sure the curriculum reflects a variety of expressions of family."

The principal showed her the curriculum and it was neutral in its approach of family.

Leigh Anne knocked it out of the park then and there. She was living the new vow.

As Emma and Taylor began expressing interest in boyfriends and girlfriends, I decided not to ask the question I was often asked as a young man: So, Joe, do you have any girlfriends? Yes, I had girlfriends and boyfriends and just friends.

Tell me about your friends, I would say. Anyone in your life you're really attracted to? These questions always generated lively conversation. Now, because they are teenagers, and dating frequently, my new question is, who are you falling in love with? Tell me about who you love.

When Taylor and Emma fall in love, I want them to fall in love with the heart, soul, wisdom, and passion of the other person, which, for me, moves beyond the narrow confines of gender.

I was led to believe that I had to fall in love with a woman, the opposite gender, to live a meaningful and fruitful life. And I did. I wouldn't trade meeting Leigh Anne, falling in love with her, being sexually intimate with her, having children with her, and loving her soul, for anything in the world. Yet, I also know that I fell in love with Leigh Anne's heart, soul and wisdom, which transcends gender. The problems became real when we both acknowledged the need for a mate who was compatible physically and sexually. For her, this was and is a heterosexual male. For me, it is a homosexual male.

I realized I had hurt Leigh Anne by attempting to live with my inner torment and sexual struggle without communicating directly and honestly with her. At a subconscious level I wanted her to be able to understand my homosexual longings and somehow connect with them through her heterosexuality. She couldn't, and this was unfair of me to consider. The irony of this was the discovery that what was physically and sexually natural for each of us became, at a core level, unnatural and harmful.

I don't want the same struggle for our children. While I know I can't and don't want to control their own struggles, I do want to create an environment in which they can grow and mature in ways that are unique for each of them. In my studies and practice of hospitality through the years, this seems to me one of the most valuable gifts a parent can give a child.

Henri Nouwen, in *Reaching Out*, writes, "Hospitality means primarily the creation of a free space where the stranger can enter and become a friend instead of an enemy. Hospitality is not to change people, but to offer them space where change can take place."[22] This transforming wisdom shapes the way I interact with everyone I meet, especially my children and family.

Prior to Ginny's birth, James and I talked about how we wanted to welcome her and raise her. When some friends offered to host a baby shower, we requested a wide variety of toys and colors of clothes. Branch out, we said. Try colors other than pink.

Her room is a neutral color, but her books, toys, clothes, and spirit add an abundance of color and energy. She loves jeans and dresses and her favorite outfit is tie-dyed. She's into alphabet puzzles, Legos, and a bunny with fairy wings and a green tutu.

Much like any practice taken seriously, the vow we made on a day in 1999 has become my daily spiritual practice. The wisdom of this act, and the power of the vow, has changed the way I live and love.

Gene pool (Joe)

July 2005

On a hot summer day in July, our family gathered in Branson, Missouri to celebrate Mom and Dad's fiftieth anniversary. While the grandkids splashed around in the water and my siblings talked poolside, I waded over to Mom and asked how she was doing. We talked for a while, and then she told me about an article she'd read about gay orientation/identity being a matter of genes, not choice. Something she believed and wanted me to know. Mom found moments like this to share her own searching and confirm for me the gift of her love and support in my searching.

A drive-by blessing (Joe)

August 2008

On a beautiful summer day, James and I were returning home from a stroll into downtown Roanoke to visit the market. Ginny loves to stroll. She pulls herself up, grasping the tray, looking around at everything she can possibly see.

As we crossed the major intersection of Elm Avenue and Franklin Road, and arrived just on the other side, a white car pulled up next to the curb, the passenger window down. The driver, Keith, a friend from the Intimate Path group I formed years earlier, leaned over and said, "I never thought I'd live to see this." He was celebrating the vision of two dads out for a stroll with their daughter.

We asked if "never" meant anywhere, or just Roanoke, and he said, "anywhere."

Unclenched fist (Leigh Anne)

My mom and dad and I were sitting at their dining room table, talking after dinner. Our conversation centered around the struggles that dear friends of ours were having adjusting to family life in the wake of a wife/mother/daughter-in-law's coming out. We were talking about the strong love of the grandparents, who chose to extend love and acceptance to the mother of their grandchildren. Dad turned to me and asked, "When are you going to get that book finished? There are folks out there who need it."

With both hands in front of him on the table, he clenched his fists tight and shaking, and said, "I used to be like this about Joe."

Relaxing his fist and turning his palms upward, he said, "and now I'm like this."

Healing, at last, for my dad.

Cross to bear, Part 2 (Leigh Anne)

July 2009

Joe's homosexuality is your cross to bear.

The first time I heard these words, they were spoken by Lance, our marriage therapist, the year Joe was searching to discover his true sexual identity. Lance's commitment to marriage was so total that his advice to us was to stay married, no matter what Joe's final decision about his sexual orientation might be. From Lance's perspective, Joe's challenge was to refrain from acting on his same-gender sexual impulses for the rest of our lives and my challenge was to accept Joe's homosexuality (and therefore, this skewed version of marriage) as my "cross to bear."

In the years that Joe was suffering in the loneliness of his secret, we both suffered from serious depression. Now that he was finally able to admit the truth to himself and to me, we were both gradually healing from depression. Continuing to live together as husband and wife, knowing that each of us could never be the spouse that the other needed to be whole, seemed like an equally deceptive arrangement.

It seemed absurd that this therapist, a licensed mental health professional, valued the institution of marriage more than he valued our individual mental health. It seemed impossible to me that we could ever be happy or healthy as a couple if we were not mentally healthy as individuals. Living a lie would have been slow death for both of us and would have infected all of our relationships, primarily our relationships with our children. When I considered our future as leaders in the church, the implications of living this lie were so far out of integrity that I could not even imagine it. While some gay/straight couples may find this arrangement acceptable, I knew that I would never be able to accept staying in a marriage where my husband's homosexuality was my "cross to bear."

245

A decade later, in the summer of 2009, I took a five-day individual spiritual retreat at Richmond Hill Retreat Center in Richmond, Virginia. At the end of the week, I spoke at length with my spiritual director Kristen, telling her the story of my former marriage and my decision to write about it with my former spouse. I was struggling at that time with a strong sense of being called by God to tell this story and my reluctance to make myself so vulnerable by being public about our private lives.

After listening quietly for some time, Kristen repeated the words that our marriage counselor had spoken a decade earlier, "Joe's homosexuality *is* your cross to bear."

This time the words did not feel like a death sentence. I began to understand that bearing the cross of Joe's homosexuality could be understood as a call to sacrifice my privacy for the sake of others who are suffering in similar situations. I began to understand that if I was courageous enough to tell the story of how God had worked in our lives, other gay/straight couples and their families might be encouraged to trust God to work the miracle of forgiveness in their lives and find healing in love for themselves and their families.

The cross is a symbol of the power of God's love to overcome death. Joe and I experienced death both individually and as a couple. Because of our commitment to love, death did not have the final word. Our lives have been renewed, individually and as extended family, because we have been guided by truth, love, and forgiveness.

The cross can also be an intersection where darkness meets light. At the time of crisis in our lives, we stood at the intersection where secrets met truth, deception met compassion, and mistakes met forgiveness. Because of our commitment to love, light broke through the darkness and now we enjoy relationships that we could never have hoped for when we were in the middle of our trials.

I have come to understand that it is a privilege to bear this cross, to tell the story of how the power of God's love has enabled us to have a new life. If Joe's homosexuality is my cross to bear, then I accept the task and lift it high enough to light the way for all who are struggling in the dark.

My brief history in drag (Joe)

The aging photo shows a boy in a brunette wig and hat, with a hint of rouge on his cheeks, lipstick, wearing a pantsuit. A purse is on his left arm. A woman stands behind him, smiling.

My mother introduced me to drag. I'm sure she thought nothing of it at the time, but years later she led me to believe she knew something was up with her oldest child. I was off to a Halloween party and Mom helped make my transformation possible.

My next gig was years later, in college, when as a student pastor I donned a flowered swim cap and joined three ladies in an on-land Esther Williams routine in the church's social hall.

The beauty bug was beginning to bite, right along with the insecurity bug that was already imbedded pretty deeply.

During my last year in college, for another Halloween party at the same church, I sought help from the college president's wife. Though we never talked about sexuality, I think she instinctively knew about my orientation and encouraged me to dwell in possibility. I picked out a simple dress, we found a brunette wig, and she helped apply my makeup. We decided to test my appearance on some good friends, and when we arrived at their house, my voice pitched higher than normal, they were baffled. They didn't know who I was. But of course, in college, *I* didn't know who I was. These incognito moments were bits of freedom I longed to experience in life.

As my college experience came to a close and seminary was about to begin, I wondered secretly if the path of drag would be a good match with the path of clergy.

During seminary and my first appointment in the United Methodist Church, I sufficiently buried the need to "dress."

At my second stop, the Peace United Methodist Church, in the beautiful Gyp Hills and ranch country of southern Kansas, a friend talked me into recreating Dana Carvey's infamous church lady skit from "Saturday Night Live" for a church talent show.

We had such fun picking out a gray polyester jacket and skirt, an ivory polyester blouse, a gray wig, knee-high hose, and sturdy black shoes. Accompanying accessories included horn-rimmed glasses, a practical black purse, and a Bible. I practiced—and nailed—the church lady's famous phrases: "Well, isn't that special!" and "Perhaps...*Satan?*"

When we moved to our next stop, Crown United Methodist Church in Wichita, I reprised the role countless times: for a church conference, a singles' book chat, an administrative council retreat, a twentieth-fifth wedding anniversary for the pastor and his spouse, and several jurisdictional singles' retreats. The church lady became my soul sister. I found in her a way to be someone I didn't have the courage to be on my own. Through her I could say, and get away with saying, things I couldn't say in my own skin.

My favorite rendition of the church lady came after I'd given her the affectionate name "Polly Esther." During a singles' jurisdictional retreat, Polly did an interpretive dance: the transformation from being wrapped in a quilt, forming a cocoon, to writhing on the floor, wiggling and emerging from the cocoon to reveal the rainbow fan design of the quilt as my wings.

The skit came just prior to the moment I entered my own cocoon and hibernation, dying to what was and forming into what would be. I put Polly Esther away, in a brown paper bag, in a closet. The thought of pretending to be someone I wasn't didn't feel good anymore. I was tired of "putting on" and being funny to entertain others.

Polly Esther led me away from the church and my calling as a pastor into an exploration of my vulnerability. It wasn't until five years later, on Sunday, June 24, 2001, that I re-entered the realm of drag. Working with a friend and a committee planning a farewell celebration for the senior pastor of the church I was serving, I emerged as a southern female evangelist, with long, flowing red hair, stunning makeup, a blouse and a skirt. I attempted to teach the senior pastor, bound for television ministry, the fine art of appropriate makeup, color schemes, and sermon delivery to the televised masses. We had a great time.

That Sunday was my last as a United Methodist clergy. I don't know how many other clergy can say it, but I went out in drag. And it was good.

+ + + + +

That moment was a catalyst. During the year, I'd struggled with being out to my friends and family while keeping my sexual orientation a secret to the congregation and the United Methodist system. I wasn't happy about this, but it was the reality. I know that a few people in the congregation had inquired about whether I was gay, but no one ever asked me directly. I hated the stress and suppression of secrecy. I kept things a secret to protect myself, but also because I knew the church as a system encouraged secrets. There was no healthy way to discuss questions of orientation, because in a climate of complaints and charges, it was hard to know whom I could trust.

I continued to feel authentically called and gifted to be a pastor, but the writing was on the wall. In order to live out this call in the United Methodist Church, I would have to fit the good boy, heterosexual-male model and live with the risk of always walking too thin a line between caution and inhibition.

Within two weeks, I surrendered my credentials and moved on with my life. The night I told my parents, my mom asked me not to do drag anymore. I said okay, but thought, "okay, I won't do drag in front of you anymore." This was a promise we both could live with.

Through the darkness of those days, I focused on claiming what was beautiful inside and on how I could let it shine on the outside.

When I moved to Roanoke and began attending the Metropolitan Community Church, I felt the veil of secrecy begin to lift. Catherine invited me to preach. To celebrate the occasion, I invited three female friends to dinner—Karin (an Episcopal priest), Kathy (a local television executive), and Judy (a local artist)—and they helped me add glitter to a pair of ruby red slippers.

I carried the ruby reds with me to the church the next morning and used them in the sermon as a symbol of my new life. The experience was so affirming that I began to think of other ways I could honor this new stage of my life. I called my friend Greg, a neighbor from Wichita with whom I had recently re-connected. Greg lived in Atlanta and I talked with him about having a coming out party. Greg said, "Joe, you're in the south. You need to have a debutante ball!"

So, in honor of my forty-second birthday, I created a debutante ball in the home of my dear friends, Chris and Sarah

Muse. Chris and Sarah, along with some other neighbors on Day Avenue, Jim, Anne and John, had welcomed me into their Monday night dinner group. When Chris and Sarah heard that I was going to throw a debutante ball, they immediately offered their home, called the Lewis Reserve, which had a grand staircase and was an ideal home for a party. I sought the help of a friend, Russ, a former Miss Gay Roanoke, and we created a fun, sleek black gown with Dalmatian fur neckline and wrist pieces. I went to his house the afternoon of the party and sat while he applied makeup. When he was finished he added a brunette wig and invited me to look in the mirror.

"Oh my God, Russ! I'm beautiful!"

The night was filled with fun, laughter, and song. I celebrated with friends, old and new, and my best friend from seminary, Tom, introduced me to the crowd as "Cruella Divine."

The debutante ball was so much fun and such a release for my creativity and theatrical nature that I decided to continue the tradition and hold an annual ball in celebration of my birthday and life in the middle of winter.

In 2005, I became the Snow Queen, donning a fabulous white wedding gown, covered initially with a black and silver cape and hood, looking something like Cher on tour. My hair was black and very tall, but the tiara and wig were securely anchored with bobby pins.

In 2006, for the Black, White and Pink Ball, inspired in part by Truman Capote's famous black and white balls, I had two gowns designed and handmade by local designer Patsy Bessolo. The gown I wore for the opening musical set was flowing black with a large black and pink bow in the back and a portion of the pink lining visible just under the hem of the dress in front. The second gown was a pink cocktail dress. This ball took place in James's house, with its grand entry hall, dual staircases converging on a landing and a large central staircase. A champagne fountain and a special toast completed the evening.

2007 was the year of the Coronation Ball. The idea for the ball came from a comment Catherine Houchins made during my ordination the previous fall. During the service, with all of the clergy in their flowing robes, she said, "This ordination seems a lot like a coronation!" My sister Nancy, who had been Miss Kansas in the Miss America pageant, would be present to crown me.

I asked Patsy to design a royal gown, and she created a deep blue gown, complete with train and a Victorian flair in the neckline and wrists. This was the first year my kids attended the ball and I made sure they knew it was optional. I didn't want either of them to feel forced into doing something they were in any way uncomfortable with, but I also wanted them to know the whole of my life, not just parts.

They were both eager to join in the celebration. Emma sang a duet with Nancy, and Taylor even came up with a great introduction, announced with an exquisite British accent: "Ladies and gentlemen, my father, the Queen!"

In 2008, we decided on a rainbow theme, and my friend William, who was also a previous Miss Gay Roanoke, did masterful makeup work on my face and also provided my gown. I affectionately called it the "gobstopper gown," because it had beads of assorted colors hand-sewn all over it to complement the rainbow-tooled train. I had the odd feeling throughout the night that guests wanted to suck my gown.

In 2009, I envisioned a theme of feathers and fans and William came through again, this time producing an amazing feathered neckpiece to accompany a brown velvet gown with gold-lined sleeves. For the first time in my drag history, I wore a blond wig. I was stunning.

Toward the end of the musical set, I announced the theme for the 2010 winter ball: Ruby Red—A Musical Tribute to Judy Garland. Inspired by the 70th anniversary of the release of *The Wizard of Oz* and the timeless voice of Judy, it seemed a great way to celebrate the seventh anniversary of the ball.

When Greg suggested having a debutante ball to celebrate my coming out, I never imagined what it would open in me— reviving a new sense of creativity reclaiming the delight of dressing up, and celebrating the joy of being me. All of this contributed to my health and outlook on life. I wonder how much healthier clergy would be if we all had debutante balls?

That will be dangerous (when you mean "exciting") (Joe)

These words were spoken by me at age three. They are recorded on page 42 of my baby book under the heading "Your Bright Doings and Sayings." It is a special book to me because my mom, Marilyn, prepared it, and because it is about love and truth.

The title page makes it clear: "All About You: An Adopted Child's Memory Book."

Mom and Dad grew up in small towns in central Kansas. They met in chemistry class at Southwestern College in Winfield, Kansas.

They were married in June 1955, and were both teachers in Marion, Kansas. In the early years of their marriage they discovered they could not have biological children and made the decision to begin the adoption process. They worked with the Jackson County, Missouri court system, completed the adoption paperwork and home study, and received word in early 1962 that they were approved to be adoptive parents.

After receiving the call that a child was waiting for them, they drove to Kansas City with a handwritten description of the child. They were expecting a brown-haired, brown-eyed boy. They received a red-haired, blue-eyed boy.

My parents always shared with me, from my earliest recollection, their joy in welcoming me as their child. They had such a good experience, that they decided to adopt three more children over the course of six years.

Adoption was never a secret, but an honor. I always felt special, because they made me feel special. When people would look at pictures of our family, many would comment on how much my sister, Nancy, and I looked like Mom, and my younger siblings, Alan and Peggy, looked like Dad. We would listen, then smile and tell them we were adopted.

Mom recalled the time they brought me to Lyons to see her parents and grandmother. Her grandmother was very set in her ways and had grave concerns about adoption. After holding me for a while, she looked at Mom and said, "Well, if this doesn't work out you can always take him back!"

When I was old enough to understand more about adoption, Dad and Mom told me that if I wanted to search for my birth parents, they would be fully supportive. For years, I never considered the idea of a search. But when I began my coming out journey, the yearning to know my origins intensified.

My first inquiry was a letter sent to the Jackson County court in 1996 asking about the process of doing a search. Rosemary Smith, who had been with the adoption office for decades, told me about the opportunity to receive my social history, which was a composite of information shared in an initial interview with my birth mother, but with no identifying information.

As with much in my life at the time, I set the letter aside and turned inward, giving myself to coming out. In 1999, after talking with my sisters Nancy and Peggy, who had both searched for and met their birth parents, I signed up with the

International Soundex Reunion Registry, in hopes that my birth mother had also registered and we might connect.

In the fall of 2001, after moving to Roanoke and opening the whole of my life, I shared my adoption story with James. When we sat next to each other, opening gifts for Christmas, I opened an envelope containing a check for $50 and a note: "Please use this to get your social history."

I wrote the Jackson County court immediately, and within ten days, received another letter from Rosemary Smith, along with my social history. Holding these pages in my hands was like holding my original birth certificate, unveiling some of the mystery of my origins.

I tucked the social history into my baby book, and often wondered: what did my birth mother look like? Did my birth father know I existed? After I was born, who held me? What was I called? What did I eat? Who rocked me and sang to me? Who helped shape me during those eight weeks?

In January 2008, I attended a workshop at Metropolitan Community Church in Winston-Salem: "Mapping Our Dreams," led by Ana Tampanna, a member of the church. Ana guided us through a process of imagining what we would like to have come true in our lives. Then we selected photos and words from magazines and books, cutting and pasting them into a collage on poster board.

The photos I selected focused on the inner journey I was making, including a man in the center of the page holding a paintbrush, waiting to paint the next scene, and an open door, leading into unknown waters. I cut out the word "origins" and then cut apart each letter, gluing the letters one by one across the center of the page. It became clear, through the guidance of my heart and hands, that the time to reach beyond my social history and learn more about my origins was beginning.

I wrote Rosemary again and inquired about next steps. I also did some online research about the Willows Hospital where I was born, and signed up on an adoption registry through a link on the Willows site. Much to my surprise, I received a quick email response from a woman who was also born at the Willows and had great success in locating and learning about her birth parents. She recommended the name of a search agent, Mary, and encouraged me to contact her.

When I contacted Mary, I asked her about the search process and she told me I needed to get a signed consent from my adoptive parents, mail it to the court in Jackson County, and then contact her. This process began in late August, and within a month, Mary signed on as my search agent, received the court documents regarding my case, and began the search.

Two weeks passed and I grew more eager each day. I emailed Mary to ask if she'd discovered anything and she called me. There was a slight hesitation in her voice as she told me that my birth mother had died at the age of 40. She had located a brief obituary, with very little additional information. I was filled with questions that all seemed pointless.

She was disappointed that she couldn't offer more, and said she would attempt to locate my birth father, though she didn't hold high hopes. After another two weeks, we talked again and she said she wasn't getting anywhere. The last step she could take would be reviewing voting records. I agreed and she brought in a colleague who began the search. It was then they discovered that the alleged birth father's last name had been misspelled by the caseworker. By changing one letter, they did a new search and located the correct name of my birth father. In November she placed a call to him.

When I spoke with Mary following the call, she said that he was shocked to learn of my existence and needed some time to think about it. He would call her in a few days. He did call and said he couldn't imagine keeping my origins from me. He wrote a letter and sent it to her, and she then sent it on to me.

The letter opened with "Dear Son" and was filled with detailed information about his family, his health, his hobbies, and his spirit. He told me that this was the first letter he'd written in forty-plus years and would likely be the only one I'd get, but that he enjoyed talking on the phone. At this point he was the only one who knew and he wanted some time to tell his wife.

He called me on December 19, 2008, and I sat in silent awe as I heard the voice of a man I thought I'd never know. We talked several more times, and then made arrangements to meet in San Francisco in mid-January. James, Ginny, and I were traveling there for a vacation and it made sense to meet.

On January 19, 2009, on a grassy knoll above the San Francisco Bay, I met my birth father and his wife. We began sharing our stories, looking at photos, and filling in the gaps of many years of unknowing. During our meeting, I shared my adoption book with him and his wife. They both commented on what a treasure it is. My birth father shared with me a thumbnail photo of my birth mother from their high school yearbook. It was the only photo he could find.

When I looked into her face, and into his, I felt peace. The many pieces of the puzzle now came into focus, fitting together and knitting together answers to my many questions. Combined with research I'd completed on the Willows in Kansas City, I began writing the story.

Birth (Joe)

I was born on January 30, 1962, at the Willows Sanitarium for Unwed Mothers in Kansas City, Missouri, a safe place for the unfortunates of society. My birth mother became pregnant when she was 17 years old. She had just graduated from high school and discovered that she was two months pregnant. She decided to have the child and made arrangements, with her parents' help, to find a place, away, far away, where she could have the baby in solitude and go on with her life. She made the trip to Missouri in October 1961 to enter The Willows.

The sanitarium was nationally known for its care of mothers and their newborns. Maps in the hospital's brochures showed train routes from every corner of the map converging in Kansas City's Union Station, just three blocks away.

When I was born, my birth mother named me Steve Larsen. I was known as "Baby Steve" and was cared for by the staff at the Willows for eight weeks, before being adopted by Bill and Marilyn Cobb.

New family (Joe)

I went back to my baby book, filled with details of the day my parents brought me home: what I was wearing, who greeted me when I arrived with my new parents. Words, photos, names, and events fill the pages. They all took on added meaning now.

Page eight: "Dear Joe, You are the most wonderful thing that ever blessed our home. One needs children to love and care for. Only God could make it possible for us to find each other. Love, Mother."

When Mom and Dad arrived at the Willows on March 27, 1962, and received me into their arms, they gave me a new name, Joseph Leslie. Joseph, because they liked it. Leslie, because it was my grandpa's first name and my dad's middle name.

Mom changed me into an outfit she brought and wrapped me tightly in blankets. Dad drove us all home.

When I began the search for my birth parents, it was out of curiosity and gratitude. The search took me to the depths of my origins and my life and confirmed the truth my parents embraced me with in 1962: You are a beloved child. I embrace the love and truth of my birth mother making the courageous choice to carry me full-term and then share me with another family. I embrace the love and truth of my birth father, who, though he never knew of the pregnancy, couldn't imagine denying me the opportunity to meet my biological family.

I embrace the love and truth of my adoptive parents who received me in love and raised me in truth.

I embrace the love and truth of my adoptive parents whose love didn't waver when I spoke my truth and came out to them as a gay man ten years ago. Truth is dangerous, but when spoken in love, reveals the deepest beauty of who we are: beloved.

Poured out 2 (Joe)

August 22, 2009

Driving Dad's burgundy Dodge Tundra out of Wichita into western Kansas, I made my way to Dodge City to have coffee with my friend, Nancy, with whom I had worked at Crown United Methodist Church. I hadn't seen her since June 2001.

When I had surrendered my credentials that summer, I left a lot behind, including my friendship with Nancy. I often wondered about her, and thought about reaching out, but kept the thought inside. Her name came to me often, helping me remember the gifts of our friendship, and the connection we experienced as friends.

Through the wonders of virtual grace, I signed onto Facebook one day and noticed that one of my clergy friends from Kansas sent me a friend request. It read: "Nancy is new to Facebook. A friend thinks you may know Nancy and want to connect with her as a friend. Send request. Ignore."

Much like the broken chalice, first broken and strewn on the floor, then behind the curtain, I let the request sit there for a few days.

I decided to take the risk and clicked "send request." Within a few days, I received a message: Nancy has confirmed your friend request. I smiled and felt grace doing its work.

When I read that she was preparing to retire I sent her a message of encouragement. We wrote each other about our current journeys, the challenges of caring for aging parents, and the possibility of reconnecting and reconciling.

I noticed on Facebook that Nancy was going to be in Dodge City visiting her dad, so I wrote and asked if she'd like to have coffee. She said yes.

I made my way into Dodge City, and found her dad's house. I parked and sat still for a moment. Is this what reconciliation feels like? A mix of awkwardness and delight? I got out of the truck and walked toward the glass front door, and could see Nancy in the large living room. I rang the bell. She opened the door, smiled, and said, "Does this feel as weird to you as it does to me?" "No," I said. "This feels good."

We talked for hours, pouring out coffee and stories, woven with pain, grief, goodness, and joy. We remembered what those days in 2001 were like, how each of us had wondered what the other was thinking. How each of us had lived in our own torment over the complaints filed against me. How our parting of ways was left unresolved and felt like a death.

As I prepared to leave, Nancy told me that when our friendship seemed dead, she asked Jim, a colleague and friend, to keep the chalice I had given her. He received it in grace, and never asked why. I had also given her a heart stone, carried back from Bolivia for her garden. She told me that the stone became a grave marker in her garden, symbolizing the death of what had been. She also thought, often saying to the stone, "only God can raise the dead."

"When I brought it out of the rock pile, I put it near my water garden, made of Kansas limestone rock, now by the fountain of life." She smiled and told me it was time to move the stone and place it in her new garden as a symbol of resurrection. "By golly, God did raise the dead."

My "coming out" had opened the way for reconciliation, acknowledging that everyone involved had experienced some brokenness and how, through reconciliation, everyone could experience new life. What Nancy and I had been through needed to be redeemed and we both believed that God could do that through us.

Christmas blessing (Joe)

As we drove along the wet, black pavement of Interstate 81, rain falling and snow blanketing the mountains, Taylor asked if I'd like to come into his grandparents' house for a while once we arrived.

Nice idea, I thought, feeling my body tighten with anxiety. The last time I was in my former in-laws' home was Christmas 1997. When I moved to Roanoke, I prayed and hoped that some day we could all experience some form of reconciliation. I also knew that the most important thing I could do was to continue being a good dad, and celebrate the love of Leigh Anne's parents as they were bringing love and healing to her and the kids.

The rain was a light sprinkle as we exited the interstate and took the ramp to Dixie Caverns on Route 11. Since moving to Roanoke in 2001, Dixie Caverns had become our meeting place, about halfway between Roanoke and Blacksburg. This was the place of exchange, about ten miles from Clarence and Ora's home.

I remember the first time Leigh Anne asked if I could bring the kids to Shawsville. I was reluctant, but agreed to meet at the convenience store, just down the road from their house. Another year later, she invited me to bring the kids to their house. I remember the first time I turned onto the lane leading up to their house. I felt tense and nervous, afraid of getting too close. I helped the kids out of the car with their luggage and Leigh Anne came to the car to greet them and thank me.

Each visit brought us closer, but the space had to open in its own time.

When Leigh Anne's parents and I were in the same space, we were present for Emma and Taylor at a school concert or theater production. We were constant with our presence, and I'm certain the kids understood the challenges of this, but most importantly, treasured the support of their family. For years, our interactions were very distant, often cold. I especially felt this with Clarence who would rarely acknowledge me. I understood this, though it hurt. I had to acknowledge that the peacemaker role I grew up nurturing didn't work in every situation.

Our encounters shifted from distant nods, to calling one another by name, to being able to sit within a couple seats or rows of each other. One summer afternoon in 2007, James and I were walking in downtown Blacksburg, heading to the Lyric Theatre to see Emma and Taylor in a community production of *High School Musical*. I noticed Clarence and Ora crossing the street ahead of us and told James. I wondered what would happen.

When we arrived at the theater and made our way inside, we found ourselves standing right behind them. Clarence turned and extended his hand. I reached out, we shook, and he said, "Hi, Joe." We all exchanged greetings and commented on looking forward to another Emma and Taylor production.

I was touched. James smiled. We sat in the balcony (it was a full house) and I later went down to talk with Leigh Anne at intermission. I told her about her dad's handshake and she smiled. After that, the dimensions of space changed and the spirit of our gatherings with the kids began to open more conversation, albeit casual.

The tension that filled our earliest meetings began to dissolve. In the summer of 2009, on the occasion of Ora's eightieth birthday, Leigh Anne invited us to attend a party in her honor. I was happily stunned. I told her we'd be honored to come, as long as her mom and her siblings were comfortable with our presence there.

I had seen Leigh Anne's older brothers Mike and Butch on brief occasions, but had not seen John for at least thirteen years. I wanted to ensure that the space would be welcoming for everyone. Leigh Anne knew this in asking us and had confirmation from her mom: "I'll be glad to see whomever you invite."

James, Ginny, and I went to her party and had a lovely time. James knelt next to Clarence, and while they talked doctor, I went around greeting family and friends I hadn't seen in years. Several of the grandchildren, including Emma, sang for Ora and Clarence and we all cried.

Throughout the afternoon, I was filled with gratitude for Leigh Anne's vision, her intentional practice of our new vow, and her parents' generosity in opening their lives to healing and reconciliation.

The memory of that day came to mind as we turned off Route 11 and onto the lane leading to their house. I pulled into the driveway, and as we both climbed out of the car. The sliding glass door opened and Emma and Leigh Anne poked their heads out and said, waving with eagerness, "Come on in here out of the cold!"

My body tensed again as I helped Taylor get his suitcase from the trunk. The driveway was my threshold. I'd grown comfortable with calling out a greeting and waving from a distance.

I followed Taylor to the door, paused, and stepped inside. Warmth surrounded me as I hugged Emma. Clarence was standing inside. He pointed to Emma's feet, laughing at her purple toenails, and describing some kind of shoes she wore in the rain. He said, Merry Christmas, Joe. We embraced. He was happy. There was lightness in his being.

My London Fog coat was buttoned up, my scarf wrapped around my neck. I'd made it past another threshold and felt stuck. What should I do now?

Reconciliation is strangely like meeting someone for the first time, that awkward moment of walking into the unknown, but somehow knowing that the unknown is safe.

Ora walked into the room, greeted me with a Merry Christmas, and stood behind Clarence. The moment seemed a bit awkward for her, too, as we all continued to stand, huddled, by the door. Sit down, she said, sit down.

I slowly took off my coat, folded it and placed it on the chair near the door. I sat down on the ottoman, in front of the Queen Anne chair. Hugh walked in, filling the room with his height and smile, fidgeting with his phone. I told them about Mom and Dad, and then Emma suggested we move into the front living room so Taylor could open his gifts.

Emma and Taylor have always made a way. Perhaps our own practice taught them. Somewhere along the way, they observed, listened, and started creating space, in their own way, for family, once estranged, to become friends again.

I remember how their images of healing took shape through the years. During our separation and divorce, and the early years following their move to Virginia, their vision of happiness was to have Mommy and Daddy together. Eventually, the vision shifted to wanting each of us to be happy in our own lives. Assured of our love for them, they began to work their love on us. Whenever I was sad, and that seemed to be most of the time, Taylor would look at me and say, "Daddy, why are you so serious all the time? You need to smile more!" I'd listen, smile briefly, then go back to being serious and sad. His words stayed with me and became my new mantra. Smile. Smile. Laugh more.

Leigh Anne and I agreed that whenever a decision or a change in our individual lives affected the children, we would share this with each other. This became very important when we began dating. After James and I began dating, I told her about preparing to introduce the kids to him. When she started dating someone seriously, she told me.

This was important for the kids to see and hear, and it was a way for us to be supportive of each other in our quests for meaningful relationships. This also opened the door for interactions with people we were dating and a chance to observe how the kids responded to these new people in their lives.

I remember being invited to their house on Broce Drive to meet a man Leigh Anne was pretty serious about. The kids seemed to like him, and it was both strange and wonderful to share a meal with them, and be able to give, if requested, an opinion on "the date."

I also remember a time when I was dating Kevin, in between my first and current relationship with James. Leigh Anne had left her car at my house in Roanoke, while she and her mom drove to the United Methodist annual conference in Hampton Roads. On the evening they returned to get her car, I stepped outside to wave and watched as Leigh Anne pulled too closely to the sharp concrete curve and punctured the back tire. They got out of the car and I worked with Leigh Anne to find the spare donut tire and the jack. I went inside and got Kevin, who came out to help.

This was another first. My former mother-in-law and former wife and I visited on the sidewalk while Kevin changed the tire. In her consistent kindness, Ora thanked him and us. They got back in their cars and headed home.

These memories flashed by as I walked through the den into the kitchen, glancing around to see what looked familiar and what had changed. As I arrived in the living room, I noticed a small, decorated tree on the cushions of the bay window, with gifts for children and grandchildren yet to arrive. Taylor sat down and surrounded himself with gifts. Leigh Anne sat across from him, and his grandparents and Emma sat on the couch watching him. I sat a little further down.

Tearing open the presents, Taylor pulled out shirts, sweaters, a Harry Potter DVD, a box of trucks, screws, and a skate tool for his skateboard. One box remained, and when "Bamma Ora" returned from a quick trip to the kitchen, he opened a new skateboard.

I glanced toward Emma, who smiled and asked if it was time to go. I nodded and we stood up to get our coats. As I passed by the kitchen counter, Ora approached me and handed me a plate of homemade fudge. Twelve years of distance evaporated. I thanked her and wished them both a happy new year.

We bundled up and made our way to the sliding glass door and the threshold of a new heaven and earth. Dashing from the warmth of their home into the cold sprinkles of rain, we climbed into the car. "Thank you for inviting me in, Emma. That was nice."

"You're welcome, Daddy."

"It's been a long time, you know."

"I know, Daddy. It was time."

Table talks (Joe)

May 12, 2008

James, Ginny, and I climbed into the car and made our way to Blacksburg. We drove to the Blacksburg Middle School and followed the labyrinth of hallways to a classroom in one of the teaching pods. When we arrived, we sat around a group of four tables pushed together in the center. Seated around the table were Taylor, our fourteen-year-old, his teaching team, Leigh Anne, Hugh, myself, James, and Ginny, in her stroller.

We were present as Taylor's family, his "team" of parents, to offer, along with his teachers, support and encouragement in his school experience. We were building on our belief that any challenges and celebrations the children face, we want them to know that all of us are there for them. The loving relationship that created them, though broken early in their lives, never wavered in love for Taylor and Emma. Through our presence and our visible, spoken support, we sat with Taylor that morning to let him know we are with him in all of life.

Taylor spoke about his challenges in certain classes, and the teachers offered their perspectives and how he could strengthen his grades in each class. We each offered our support and together we created a way, through communication and follow through, to support Taylor and strengthen his own sense of personhood and growth as a student and young man.

The table that day was filled with conversation, questions, challenges, and, dwelling beneath it all, love.

Emma's sixteenth birthday dinner (Leigh Anne)
May 12, 2008

That same day, two hours later, we were all at our house to celebrate Emma's birthday. More than anything I wanted her to be surrounded by the people who loved her most as she celebrated her birthday. One of the many reasons I love my husband Hugh so much is his total openness toward and acceptance of my family, including my former spouse, his partner, and his family. He is totally committed to creating a loving home and that includes giving a welcome at our table to all the various people in my life. He knows that he can count on me to give a similar welcome to the folks in his family and life. It wasn't hard for either of us to invite Joe, James, and Ginny to come to our house to help us celebrate Emma's birthday, especially since we had been welcomed at the table in their home. We cooked hamburgers on the grill, ate together around our table, sang "Happy Birthday" as Emma blew out the candles on the birthday cake and opened gifts.

We ate cake and ice cream and strawberries and enjoyed the sweetness of being family for a while. During dinner, between bites of baked beans and hamburgers, the birthday girl said, satisfied, "This is what family is supposed to be like." *Yes!* my soul shouted as my eyes filled with tears and my throat tightened. Her heart knows it too.

By forgiving each other for the hurts of the past, by taking responsibility for ourselves and our own emotional, psychological, and spiritual healing, by committing ourselves to speak and act in loving ways, we had given the greatest gift we could possibly give to our children and to ourselves—the gift of love. The recognition of the healing power of love was sweet on the tongue and in the heart that day.

Baby shower (Joe)

April 17, 2010

Within a year after Ginny was born, James and I began talking about having a second child. We both wondered if we were plum crazy for even thinking such a thing, yet we knew that a sibling would be great for Ginny. James also wanted to try to have a boy.

We contacted Dana and the egg donor and they both agreed to try the process again. After two attempts and one brief pregnancy, our hopes began to fade. James went to California and donated a fresh batch of sperm and the egg donor donated new eggs. The clinic went through the procedure of fertilizing the eggs, implanted them in Dana, and within a few weeks, she called and told us she was pregnant.

The pregnancy went well and we made plans to leave for California in the last week of April to allow two weeks before the baby would be born on May 7.

A new friend, Chelsea, wanted to host a baby shower for us, so we created the guest list and she created the party. On a Saturday in April, we gathered in Chelsea's living room for the shower. Several of our neighbors were there, along with good friends from the church and community. Leigh Anne and Emma also came. As I sat looking at the group of guests, I smiled at the idea that my former spouse and our daughter were present at a baby shower for my current partner and our new baby.

One of our friends, Margaret, pulled Leigh Anne aside later, commending her for the book we were writing and the incredible support we were offering each other. She said, "You all are making the best lemonade on the planet!"

That night James and I went to dinner and when we arrived home, around 10 pm, his phone rang. It was Dana. Her water had broken and she was on the way to the hospital.

Our flights weren't scheduled for another ten days. James spent the entire night keeping tabs on Dana, re-arranging his flights, and packing his bags. Early the next morning we took him to the airport.

When he arrived in Orange County, he checked his messages and our baby boy had just been born. He raced to the hospital and was there within the hour. We named him James Joseph David Matthews. James stayed with him for four days and then brought him home to us.

In the year following J.J.'s birth, we talked about having both of the children baptized. James had asked an old friend to be Ginny's godfather, and his sister, Jackie, to be her godmother. As we talked about godparents for J.J., we decided on his brother Fletcher to be the godfather. When James asked me whom I thought would make a good godmother, I paused for a while and said, "Leigh Anne." "Do you think she'd even consider it?" he asked.

"I think we should ask her."

James called Leigh Anne and asked her to think about it. After a few days, Leigh Anne called back and said, "Yes, I'd be honored to be J.J.'s godmother.

The game of life (Joe)

July 11, 2011

Ginny was sitting at the kitchen table laying out the pieces to The Game of Life. She asked me to place the buildings and houses on the game board. We placed the five cars—red, green, blue, orange and white.

I took a handful of the pink and blue people and laid them on the board. After a few minutes, I noticed that one of the cars was full.

"Ginny, tell me who is in the car."

"Papa, Daddy, Taylor, Emma, Connor [Emma's boyfriend] and Leigh Anne."

"Wow, that's great. Where are J.J. and Hugh?"

"They're in this car."

Within a few more minutes, J.J. and Hugh were joined by a carful. With her imagination opened wide, the remaining cars were filled and off for another family outing.

Notes

1. Eliot, T.S. *The Four Quartets, Burnt Norton.* Harcourt, 1943, 1971, p. 15.
2. Manning, Brennan. *The Ragamuffin Gospel.* Multnomah Books, 1990, p. 62.
3. Nouwen, Henri. "Moving From Solitude to Community to Ministry." (*Leadership,* Spring 1995).
4. Benson, Robert. *Between the Dreaming and the Coming True.* Harper San Francisco, 1996, p. 144.
5. Johnson, Thomas H, ed. *The Complete Poems of Emily Dickinson.* Little, Brown and Company, 1960, p. 116.
6. Mayers, Gregory. *Listen to the Desert.* Liguori/Triumph, 1996, p. 9.
7. Nouwen, Henri. *The Way of the Heart.* Seabury Press, 1981, p. 15.
8. Benson, Robert. *Living Prayer.* Jeremy P. Tarcher/Putnam, 1998, p. 24.
9. Glaser, Chris. *Coming Out to God.* Westminster John Knox Press, 1991, p. 16.
10. Nouwen, Henri. *Reaching Out.* Doubleday, 1966, p. 59.
11. Ibid, p. 30.
12. Whitcomb, Holly, *Practicing Your Path,* pp. 71-73. Copyright © 2002 Holly W. Whitcomb. Reproduced by permission of Augsburg Fortress Publishers.
13. Munsch, Robert. *Love You Forever.* Firefly Books, 1986.

14. *The Book of Discipline of The United Methodist Church 2000.* The United Methodist Publishing House, 2000, p. 101.

15. Ibid, p. 101.

16. Ibid, p. 185.

17. Ibid, p. 185.

18. *New Revised Standard Version of the Bible.* The Division of Christian Education of the National Council of the Churches of Christ in the U.S.A., 1989. Ruth 1:16-17.

19. *Ibid.* I Samuel 18:1-4.

20. *Ibid.* I Samuel 20:17.

21. *Ibid.* II Samuel 1:25b-26.

22. Nouwen, Henri. *Reaching Out.* Doubleday, 1966, p. 71.

Our Family Outing

A memoir of coming out and coming through.

JOE COBB & LEIGH ANNE TAYLOR

JOE COBB

Joe Cobb lives in Roanoke, Virginia where he serves as a clergy with the Metropolitan Community Churches. A native of Kansas, Joe earned a BA in Philosophy from Southwestern College in his home state and a Master of Divinity from Perkins School of Theology at Southern Methodist University in Dallas, Texas. Raised in the United Methodist Church, Joe was called into ministry in 1981, and was ordained as a deacon in 1985, an elder in 1991 and served for 20 years in parish ministry. Five years after coming out, Joe was ordained in the Metropolitan Community Church where he currently serves a growing community in SW Virginia. A creative spirit, Joe also enjoys writing and singing. Alongside his two young adult children, Emma and Taylor, he and his partner, James Matthews, have two young children, Ginny and JJ.

LEIGH ANNE TAYLOR

Leigh Anne Taylor resides in the Blue Ridge Mountains of SW Virginia where her family has lived for generations. Ordained in the United Methodist Church, she has worked as a church musician and musical director in Texas, Kansas and Virginia. Leigh Anne is a graduate of James Madison University and Southern Methodist University but feels her most advanced degrees have been earned from the "school of life." She enjoys a lifelong interest in music, worship, spirituality and the symbolic language of dreams. She is married to Hugh Ballou and has two young adult children, Emma and Taylor.